Praise for *Dreaming Against the Current*

"A significant contribution to the literature chronicling the inner lives of the bravest, boundary-breaking Jewish spiritual seekers." — Rabbi Vanessa Ochs, Ph.D, author of *The Jewish Dream Book: The Key to Opening the Inner Meaning of Your Dreams*

"Reverend Rabbi Dr. Haviva Ner David blesses us with her third and most powerful memoir yet. Her journey from a healing woman of Judaism to a healing woman of all of humanity brings with it stunning insights, aching moments of clarity, and a glimpse of what it means to live a life of freedom. Haviva is one of the most honest, compassionate, and caring writers, and demonstrates what it means to live with authenticity and loyalty to oneself and the universal spirit. The story, threaded between lofty dreams and the mundane of everyday existence, is a wonderful teaching about life." — Elana Sztokman, Ph.D, author of *Conversations With My Body: Essays on my life as a Jewish Woman*

"What happens to a groundbreaker when the ground keeps on breaking? In this memoir, Rabbi Rev. Haviva Ner-David powerfully chronicles her struggle to be accepted as a rabbi and scholar within the Orthodox movement, and her eventual discovery that Orthodox Judaism doesn't fit her any longer. Along the way, she shares the love story of her marriage, her struggle with chronic illness, her path as an interfaith minister, and her pain over the Israeli-Palestinian conflict. Throughout the fabric of the book, Ner-David weaves in the bright thread of her dreamwork practice, showing how, over time, her dreams tell her the truth of her life and reveal her path forward. A must-read for anyone who has changed more than they expected—or anyone who wants to learn how dreams can open the door to a new life." — Rabbi Jill Hammer, Ph.D, author of *Undertorah: An Earth-Based Kabbalah of Dreams*

"How did a nice Jewish girl from the Orthodox New York suburbs become a post-denominational interspiritual rabbi minister? By following her heart step-by-fascinating-step through the difficult work of being human. In *Dreaming Against the Current*, Haviva Ner-David invites readers to gently brush away the excuses and justifications that keep them from living fully. Throughout the pages, she models how to gaze lovingly at our disappointments, missteps, and lingering heartbreaks to seek the healing lessons these outcast moments can offer. Weaving together religion, spirituality, and personal introspection, Ner-David creates a glorious tapestry that inspires each of us to become the artisan of a meaningful and sacred life." — Rev. Sarah Bowen, author of *Spiritual Rebel: A Positively Addictive Guide to Finding Deeper Perspective and Higher Purpose*

"Haviva's beautifully-written *Dreaming Against the Current* is a glorious interplay of daily living, dreams, and powerful spiritual realizations. As such, it has called me to a deeper level of trust, surrender, and authenticity in my own life and spiritual practice. In learning more about Rabbi Reverend Ner-David's devout practices and the depth of being they have developed in her, I am inspired. I suspect this book will extend such a gift to all its readers."
— Rev. AnnE O'Neil, author of *If You Want the Rainbow, Welcome the Rain*

Other Books by Haviva Ner-David

Hope Valley: a novel

Life on the Fringes: A Feminist Journey Towards Traditional Rabbinic Ordination

Chanah's Voice: A rabbi westles with the women's rituals of baking, bathing and brightening

Dreaming Against the Current

Dreaming Against the Current

A RABBI'S SOUL JOURNEY

Haviva Ner-David

 *Bink Books*
Bedazzled Ink Publishing Company • Fairfield, California

978-1-949290-75-2 paperback

Cover Art
by
Meira Ner-David

Cover Design
by

Bink Books
a division of
Bedazzled Ink Publishing Company
Fairfield, California
http://www.bedazzledink.com

DEDICATION

A dream:

I am falling down a treacherously steep pull-down attic ladder. Tumbling from rung to rung, wanting my fall to end, yet dreading the impact when I hit bottom. I am about to hit the hard wooden floor, and just as I see the panels before my eyes, someone, blurred by shadows, catches me, scoops me up, and carries me to safety.

I am at the bottom of an impossibly steep staircase in the New York City subway system. There is no elevator at this stop. I look up. I long to reach the sunlight and fresh air at the top of the steps, but I know I cannot make it alone. Someone, obscured by the almost blinding rays, reaches out a hand to help me. Together, we ascend the staircase and enter, hand in hand, a tunnel of beaming halos of light.

In this case, Jacob, I am the dreamer seeing the ladder, and Jacob, you are the angels ascending and descending, catching me when I fall, and helping me reach the light when I just can't do it alone.

INTRODUCTION

I am in my freshwater naturally filtered lap pool, the smell of algae in my nostrils and the feel of cool wetness on my skin. The kids are off to school, and I am blessed to be starting my day with a swim.

The sun is still low, skimming the water with its warm morning kiss. Seeing the world through foggy goggles, I glide slowly but rhythmically back and forth, back and forth, length after length, lap after lap, my face in the water, dreaming while awake, as my body melts through its boundaries and remembers how to just be.

I swim every day. I live with a genetic degenerative muscular disorder called FSHD (fascioscapular humeral muscular dystrophy) which makes many forms of movement on dry land difficult and painful. It is only in water that I move freely and without the heavy soreness and stiffness that has become part of inhabiting my God-given body.

Like the amphibian I was in a former evolution, I return to this element to be quenched, supported, held, and embraced—by Divine Spirit, back in God's watery womb.

For my last round of laps, the final quarter of my two-kilometer ritual swim, I remove my goggles. I float on my back and put my face to the sun, which is rising higher in the cloud-spotted sapphire sky, relaxing my muscles, my mind, my whole being. My swim almost behind me, I greet the morning and bless with my breath whatever is to come in the day that lies ahead.

The hours spread out spacious before me. A rare day with nothing planned but to write. My computer, this book, is beckoning, but I will not cut my swim short. I savor this time in my element, even if I feel chilled with the sun now hidden behind a puffy white cloud.

Then I see Spider. She has been working steadily and determinedly for days now. I have watched her spinning up and down, twirling and swinging on her threads, focused on her task. The work at hand. The work of her hands. Or should I call them legs? I have been mesmerized by this creature who has not granted me a glance, she's been so busy.

But today she is still. Resting, it seems, from her days of labor. I float past her, supine, watching, curious if she will make a move. But she doesn't. She is the epitome of patience. Waiting to see what will come from her creation.

Then, just as I pass beneath her, the sun begins to emerge, and I see it—a most magnificent web, a round and intricate weave of delicate threads glistening in the sunlight. A mandala. A prayer. An exquisite piece of art coming out into the light. And I know the work of my hands, this book, too, will come out into the light when the time is right.

"Said Rabbi Hisda: A dream unexplored is like a letter not read."
— Babylonian Talmud, Tractate Brakhot 55b

"You must give birth to your images. They are the future waiting to be born. Fear not the strangeness you feel. The future must enter you long before it happens. Just wait for the birth, for the hour of the new clarity."
— Rainer Maria Rilke, from his poem "Fear Not the Strangeness" in *Letters to a Young Poet*

"Is appearance no more than the reflections thrown back and forth by a set of mirrors?" asked Reb Ephraim. *"You are no doubt alluding to the soul, Reb Alphandery, in which we see ourselves mirrored. But the body is the place of the soul, just as the mountain is the bed of the brook. The body has broken the mirror."*

"The brook," continued Reb Alphandery, *"sleeps on the summit. The brook's dream is of water, as is the brook. It flows for us. Our dreams extend us. Do you not remember this phrase of Reb Alsem's: 'We live out the dream of creation, which is God's dream. In the evening our own dreams snuggle down into it like sparrows in their nests.'*

"And did not Reb Hames write: 'Birds of night, my dreams explore the immense dream of the sleeping Universe.'"
— Edmond Jabes, from "Mirror and Scarf" in the *Book of Yukel/Return to the Book*, translation by Rosmarie Waldrop

KAVANAH

SACRED INTENTION

The following book chronicles my journey into interspirituality and dreamwork during my four-year course of study at the One Spirit Interfaith-Interspiritual Seminary in New York City. Although I grew up in New York, I live in Israel, so when I studied at One Spirit, I did so as a distance learner, over Zoom, which has since (because of the COVID-19 pandemic) become a popular way of interacting and studying with others across long and even short distances. Although then, it was just beginning to become an option.

Those four years helped prepare me for the pandemic in more ways than familiarizing me with Zoom. The inner work I did while at One Spirit helped me connect with my innermost self, with what she truly wants and needs, and at the same time helped me connect with the Spirit of the Universe that Unites All. Through touching my core and accepting the destiny only I can live out, while also recognizing its humble place in the larger universal whole and flow of life, I became better able to face the uncertainty and suffering that has become the "new normal."

This book is about learning to let go into my destiny, be true to myself, stop fighting my own inevitable suffering and have compassion for others as they do the same. It is not my intention to tell others to follow my specific path of self-discovery, but rather to suggest that it is only through treating our own most wounded places—rather than looking for answers and seeking spiritual paths outside ourselves—that we can heal the world, one soul at a time.

In this book, I have written about conflicts with people close to me—not to hold a grudge or point a finger, but to show how by addressing where we most hurt, we can begin to heal and even flourish.

One major lesson about relationships I have learned in my humbling years as a daughter, parent, and spouse is that it is from healing our sacred wounds—even those we cause one another—that we grow. In fact, perhaps that is why some of us were brought together in this life.

We parent not only to support our children and help them see their wholeness, but also to make "mistakes" that help our children develop into who they were meant to be. Like in marriage, decisions that cannot please everyone are inevitable, as different souls rub up against each other in the dark. It's from them we learn to stretch ourselves outside of our comfort zones and discover we, like in our dreamscapes, are more flexible than we imagined we could be.

Thank you to all who have been in my life and continue to be, as we stumble along together in the dark, looking towards the cracks of brokenness that let in the light.

And thank you, readers, for honoring my process with your time and attention. Please check out my website at rabbihaviva.com to read more about my work. Or contact me at rabbihaviva@gmail.com.

Rabbi Rev. Dr. Haviva Ner-David
Kibbutz Hannaton
September 2021

PROLOGUE

CALL IT SLEEP

MY SON NACHUM is having a third bar mitzvah, and like at all my seven kids' bar and bat mitzvah ceremonies, I am planning to speak.

The problem is, I cannot find the notebook in which I wrote the speech. To make matters worse, I am not even sure I know which notebook that is. Still, I look everywhere—on all my bookshelves, in my study, in my desk drawers, on my bedside shelves, in all my various backpacks and bags—but I cannot find it.

I try to remember what I wrote, but my eyelids feel so heavy I can't keep them open long enough to think or even keep looking. I try to fight sleep, try to keep my eyelids open, but I begin nodding off.

Defeated, I think I will have to pass on giving the speech altogether, or just wing it. All I want to do, really, is sleep.

I open my eyes and look at my computer screen into the wise and kindly face of Judith (Jude) Schafman, my dreamwork teacher. She lives in Upstate New York, while I live in northern Israel. I met her when she was teaching a seminar at the One Spirit Interfaith-Interspiritual Seminary in New York City, where I was a distance learner in their Interspiritual Counseling (ISC) program. One year earlier, I had been ordained at One Spirit as an interfaith-interspiritual minister, after having been the first woman to publicly receive Orthodox rabbinic ordination only ten years earlier.

And still, I am seeking.

"Okay," Jude says. "That's a powerful dream. Are you ready to work it?"

Through a window behind Jude, I see a buttercup sun rising, while behind me, I know she is seeing a flaming sun setting. I think of the biblical Jacob drifting off to sleep after sunset, dreaming of angels, and then waking and exclaiming, "Surely God is in this place, and I did not know it. How awesome is this place! This is none other than the house of God, a porthole to the divine."

"Yes," I say. I am ready to enter the porthole.

"I want you to be your son, Nachum. Let me speak to Nachum . . ."

Studying dreamwork with my teacher for several months has accustomed me to Jude's method of dream analysis. Each element of the dream is another aspect of the dreamer's unconscious, while the dreamer's character in the dream is usually the ego, the least wise of all the elements in the dream.

To understand the dream's message, or meaning, the dreamer must speak from the dream elements (for example: a character in the dream other than the "dreamer," an animal, an inanimate object, a natural element), or sometimes even from a feeling in the dream, the weather or a word or phrase someone says. Every element in our dreams is a piece of our unconscious. I am not surprised Jude is asking me to speak as my son.

I lean in. "I am Nachum," I say. "I am about to have a third bar mitzvah."

"How did it feel to have a first bar mitzvah?" Jude asks.

I lower my head and cover my eyes with my hands to help me focus. One symptom of the genetic neuromuscular disease with which I live is that I cannot close my eyes completely. "It felt good. It felt right for when I had it," I answer. "It marked that stage in my life, but I still have growing left to do."

"And so that is why you had the second?"

My actual son, Nachum, had only one bar mitzvah, but when Jude asks me this question, I am the Nachum in my dream, and I know how it feels to go through two major life transitions and be on the cusp of a third. The Nachum in my dream merges with me, the dreamer, who has written two memoirs about the first two stages of her spiritual journey. But the journey does not feel complete.

The answer flows, without my having to think. "That one too felt right at the time. Marking another stage. A more advanced stage. I felt done then, after the second. As I did after the first. But like with the first, I now know that was premature."

"Is that why you are having a third?"

"I guess. But I am not sure what it will be like."

"Great. Now I want you to be the eyelids in the dream. How do you feel, eyelids?"

"I feel heavy," I answer. "I want to close, but the dreamer is not letting me close. I want to rest, but there is a force inside me blocking me, preventing me from closing."

"Can you feel into that part of you that is trying to stay open? How does *it* feel?"

I feel into that sensation of trying to keep my eyes open, of trying to stay awake in my own dream. "I think it is afraid. Afraid of losing control. Afraid of what may happen when the dreamer is sleeping."

"And why do you want to rest?"

"I'm tired. Life is exhausting. I want to stop fighting and just rest. Just trust in the process and hope everything will be okay when I'm sleeping, when my guard is down. But there's that force trying to keep me open. Trying to prevent the dreamer from sleeping."

"Thank you, eyelids. That was very helpful. I'd like to speak to sleep now. Describe yourself, sleep."

"I am sleep," I begin. "I am a state of completely letting go. When the dreamer is sleeping, she rests, which brings what is hidden to the surface. When I, sleep, am present, the dreamer can dream; she can access a deeper part of herself, her essential core. She can access her unconscious. Her soul."

"Why are you so important to the dreamer now?" Jude asks.

"The dreamer needs to sleep more before she can find the notebook and what's written in it. The speech is not ready yet, because she still has sleeping to do."

"To be able to find the notebook?"

"Yes. But not only. The dreamer needs to learn to let go into me. She needs to learn to trust in me."

"Trust in you? In sleep?"

"Yes. But not only in me. She needs to learn to trust in general."

And so, this next stage in my spiritual journey begins. As strange as it may sound, I might as well call it sleep.

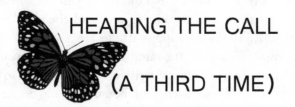

HEARING THE CALL

(A THIRD TIME)

THE FIRST TIME in my life when I heard "the call," I answered and began a journey towards becoming a rabbi. I was twenty-four, a new mother of a one-year-old daughter and right out of an MFA program in creative writing.

I had been working part-time running a *mikveh*, a Jewish ritual immersion pool, in which I officiated full-body water immersion ceremonies, some innovative and some traditional. Without knowing it back then, I had been part of spearheading a movement to reclaim and reframe this ancient ritual, and I loved the work. I felt drawn to a spiritual vocation in addition to my writing. Having grown up an Orthodox Jew, becoming an Orthodox rabbi could have seemed logical—had I been a man.

As a woman, becoming an Orthodox rabbi was not only illogical; it was unheard of. No woman had publicly received Orthodox rabbinic ordination (although two had done so in secret, I later discovered). If I was going to become a rabbi, I would only do so openly. There was no significant argument in the classic rabbinic sources against a woman becoming a rabbi. I knew the reasons were sociological and felt the time had come for women to be ordained in the Orthodox Jewish world. If no women demanded this, it would not happen. I felt up to the challenge.

I applied to a mainstream all-men's modern Orthodox seminary, the most liberal at the time in the U.S. Orthodox world, and the place where my own father had earned his undergraduate degree. My application was never recognized. The dean of the school told the press the admissions office had never received it—which I do not believe is true—but had they, he added, they would not have felt a need to send a reply, since a woman rabbi is an oxymoron.

Disappointed but not surprised, I ultimately studied in various liberal Orthodox frameworks, some co-ed and some only for women, but none were programs that would grant me ordination at the end of my studies. I could gain the credentials but not the title.

I never felt accepted in any of these frameworks. I was seen by many as the troublemaker who wanted to be an Orthodox woman rabbi. In some places I was even shunned. Many questioned why I didn't study in one of the liberal Jewish movements, where women were being ordained already. Why was I bothering the Orthodox? They were happy with the status quo.

Looking back now, I ask myself the same question. My life would have been easier had I chosen the path of least resistance. But I wanted to fix (as I saw it) the system in which I was raised, push boundaries and create change from within. I owed that to myself and other women. I had seen the light and wanted to spread that light to others.

Through my own studies (both religious and secular), I had discovered that women did not have to play a second-class supporting role in ritual life. There was room in the classic rabbinic sources for progress. Jewish religious praxis and even law had always developed over time. But it required a push from the masses. Change would not come from the male rabbis, especially not if it meant granting women equality. Why would men agree to give up their power? Women would have to fight for change.

Even if I knew I did not quite fit in, even if my theology was not mainstream Orthodox and my attitude audacious, I was a woman with a mission, and I was stubborn. I had a vision, a goal, and it felt within reach. Despite the ridicule and scorning I received from many establishment and non-establishment Orthodox Jews, some who even called themselves feminists, I would not back down.

My life partner, Jacob, and I moved to Jerusalem with our then-two children after I studied for a few years in New York. Three more children later, I was ordained thirteen years after sending in my rabbinical school application. With no institutional backing, after studying with me for ten years, Rabbi Aryeh Strikovsky granted me his personal ordination and permission to announce so publicly.

I framed and hung the ordination certificate on my wall, next to my doctoral certificate. While studying for rabbinic ordination, I had worked towards my Ph.D at Bar Ilan University on the Philosophy of Jewish Religious Law. I wrote about the changing interpretations and applications of *mikveh* and the menstrual purity laws from the Bible to the present—reaching conclusions that only proved to me more how vital reinterpretation and change are to keep Judaism relevant and effective.

Finally, after years of intense study and public shaming, I had stuck to my goal and was the first woman to announce to the world she had received Orthodox rabbinic ordination. It was disconcerting, therefore, when I heard "the call" for a second time—an inner voice telling me to leave Orthodoxy. Wasn't it for the title *Orthodox* rabbi I had been fighting all those years?

Yes. But there was no denying it. Inside, I was no longer Orthodox. Throughout those years of struggle and study, I had evolved. My ideas were becoming more radical, less traditional. I no longer felt bound by classic religious Jewish law that delineates to the last detail how one should live their life, based on the ongoing interpretation, by men only, of the words of ancient texts all written by men.

I knew this reality was changing, and that I was part of a movement empowering women to study and interpret these texts as well. But change was happening too slowly for my spiritual needs and moral conscience. My intuition told me that religion should be at the fore of the struggle for human rights—as I understood Judaism had in its origin been—not holding it back.

Religion may be conservative in some respects, assuring change happens organically and not drastically, but it should not compromise compassion in the name of caution. I made a conscious decision to place my values before what these texts prescribed and proscribed.

I could no longer condone prayer services that were not fully egalitarian, even if I was part of a movement successfully pushing for more (but not equal) women's participation in the synagogue. Nor could I be a rabbi in a denomination that did not recognize gay marriages, even if I was a voice for more acceptance of LGBTQ+s (although back then not all these categories were included) in the Orthodox world.

Moreover, I could no longer buy into a system—no matter how ancient and wise—that had been created by straight men alone, where female and queer voices had been silenced completely.

My previous decision to remain inside the Orthodox world and try to change the system from within, which at the time felt like the perfect way to honor both the wisdom of my faith tradition and the moral high ground of full equality for all, seemed disingenuous for me now. I no longer felt compelled to work within that system or contort myself to play by its rules. Like a coat I had outgrown, it felt too constricting. I needed to breathe. The coat no longer fit.

With my evolved theology and ideology, I could no longer claim to represent even the most liberal stream of the Orthodox movement, nor did I want to be confined by that label. I wanted to be free to say what I felt, to remain true to myself. Most importantly, I wanted to keep exploring, to continue the journey of life wherever it led me. Orthodoxy did not allow for this approach.

An open-ended spiritual journey is antithetical to Orthodoxy, which is about following the rules and fitting in. There are clear boundaries as to what is acceptable. There is some room to stretch those boundaries; and I did. But I then realized there was not enough wiggle room for me. More importantly, I did not want to watch my step. I wanted to spread my wings and fly free.

I listened to my inner voice, a notion that is also against what Orthodox Judaism is about. Authority lies outside of oneself, in the rabbis, because if left to our own devices, we will stray from the proper path. Instincts are not meant to be followed, but rather, to be curbed. Yet, I followed my heart and gave up what I had spent the past thirteen years achieving. My integrity was more important to me than the cause of Orthodox women's ordination.

When pressed to choose a title, I found I did not identify with any one denomination of Judaism, or even believe in religious denominations at all at that point. I saw them as part of the patriarchal system I had rejected. I did not want to be contained by any one box. I wanted to move, and think, outside all boxes. I decided to call myself a post-denominational rabbi, and the name fit, like a coat tailored just for me.

When I admitted to myself who I truly was at that juncture, I felt a heavy weight lifted from my shoulders. It was a physical sensation of lightening and expanding. I did not have to wear a coat at all. I did not even have to cover my hair or shoulders to prove my piety and modesty.

I let my hair feel the breeze for the first time in years, and I exposed my shoulders and neck bone to the world. In fact, I discovered those are my most attractive features. I mourned those years I had kept them hidden. If a man could not appreciate my beauty without being aroused, I would no longer accept the blame.

I was nervous what people would say about my decision to leave the Orthodox Jewish fold—especially my parents, who had raised me Orthodox and still had strong feelings about passing on that heritage and lifestyle. I felt guilty about letting down all of those who had been rooting for me— especially the young women who wanted to follow in my footsteps.

This was a significant decision, and not a simple one. By leaving Orthodoxy, would I be proving right those who ridiculed me and my struggle? In some sense, I would, but it felt impossible to continue this path.

When I began my studies, there had been no one else willing to take that step, but it heartened me to know there were others now speaking publicly about Orthodox women's ordination. I may have been abandoning the cause, but there were others to fight that fight. Which was good, because I no longer felt I could.

I was no longer Orthodox. I did not believe in rabbinic authority as the sole interpreters of God's word. I did not agree conforming to strict communal norms in all aspects of life was the best thing for humanity, or at least not the best thing for me. Especially when in relation to matters of the spirit.

I would be a fraud if I accepted the title Orthodox rabbi. I would only do harm to the cause, unless I decided to play the part without speaking my mind. But I did not want to be an actor. I wanted to be a rabbi. Better to let those young women continue the struggle.

I had another path to follow, another current pulling me in a new direction. Since running a *mikveh* years before, I had a vision of creating a pluralist educational and ritual *mikveh* in Israel.

I founded *Shmaya: A Mikveh for Mind, Body and Soul*, on Kibbutz Hannaton—the only *mikveh* in Israel not monopolized by the Orthodox Rabbinate. Every other *mikveh* in Israel is controlled by them and open only to those who comply with their myriad regulations.

Women who immerse must be Orthodox Jews (or willing to toe the Orthodox line) who are married (to men), and their immersions are circumscribed with rules and regulations that can be an invasion of privacy and feel intrusive and violating. Their bodies are checked for loose scabs or hairs, they are asked a series of personal questions, and if they do not pass this verbal and physical examination, they are not allowed to immerse.

Men are not required to immerse at all, so when they do, it is for spiritual reasons and without regulations. But the men's facilities for immersion are without privacy and often unsanitary.

Shmaya, on the contrary, is a non-gendered space and is open to all humans to immerse in the manner they choose. It is the only *mikveh* in Israel with this stated mission. We run by appointment only, and with the choice whether to be accompanied by an attendant or not. Each person immersing has a private and clean space and full agency over their own immersion experience.

At *Shmaya*, which means "sky" in Aramaic, we invite people to do a wide variety of immersion ceremonies, not only at the traditional times usually associated with *mikveh* immersion (such as conversion, after uterine bleeding, before *Shabbat* or the High Holidays, and before one's wedding). *Shmaya* is also an educational *mikveh*. I meet with groups of all ages, genders and faith identifications, teaching about *mikveh* and its deeper spiritual meaning, and doing experiential workshops.

When I moved, with Jacob and our then-six children (number six we adopted soon after I was ordained as a rabbi, and our seventh was born four years later), to Kibbutz Hannaton—a community made up of a spectrum of religiously liberal Jews—and opened *Shmaya*, I felt I had finally found my life's purpose.

Water is my element. It is where I feel most at home. Water gives me both physical and emotional relief. It is where I can let my mind wander and my ideas and dreams form.

I am drawn to ritual and ceremony, although I do not like performing in front of large groups. I prefer intimate spaces. The opportunity to provide the immersion experience to all and accompany people in such transformative moments in their lives, fit my personality and played to my strengths. And opening this *mikveh* was filling a need. It was holy service.

Because I felt fulfilled in my new calling, it was unsettling when I heard "the call" yet a third time.

It was the summer of 2014. Come March, my oldest son, Adin, was to be drafted into the Israel Defense Forces—to my great dismay, they had placed him in a combat unit—and Israel and the Hamas-ruled Gaza Strip were unofficially at war. Officially, we were involved in a military operation called Operation Protective Edge. But to someone like me who was born in the U.S. in 1969, moved to Israel in 1996 and knows little about military nuances, it sure felt like a war.

Israeli soldiers were fighting and dying, missiles were flying overhead, some landing in cities like Tel Aviv and Haifa, and hundreds of Palestinians in Gaza were being killed and wounded by Israeli bombs.

To make matters worse, racism within Israel was running rampant. Palestinians hated Israelis, and Israelis hated Palestinians. And Palestinians with Israeli citizenship were caught in the middle of this contentious atmosphere, suffering abuse from Jewish Israelis for being Palestinian and from Palestinians for being Israeli.

Hate crimes—kidnappings, stabbings, lynches—were becoming a regular occurrence, as were increasing numbers of victims of Israeli bombings in Gaza, victims of Hamas rockets in Israel and photographs on the front page of the newspaper of young men—many Adin's age—who were no longer with the living.

As a mother, I feared for my son's life and moral fiber. As a rabbi, I felt the foundations of my faith in religion as a positive force in the world uprooted yet again, but this time not because of gender inequity. With people killing in the name of God, how could religion be a good thing? Yet, something told me it still was, or could be—only perhaps in a different container than I was used to experiencing and pondering.

That summer, the only time I felt any comfort or hope, the only place I felt at home and at peace, was when I participated in fringe interfaith and inter-cultural gatherings, where Jews, Christians, and Muslims (the three Abrahamic religions) came together to sing songs of peace and love. I was experiencing a religious crisis, and I intuited that the answer lay in finding what can connect in religion rather than separate.

Towards the end of that summer, when I was on a book tour with my second memoir, a woman approached me after one of my Manhattan talks to tell me about One Spirit Interfaith-Interspiritual Seminary. The institution's two-year ministry program weaves intense inner work with studies of the world's major religious faiths and culminates in interfaith-interspiritual ordination. If I took this path, I would become an interfaith-interspiritual-post-denominational rabbi. What would that mean, exactly?

I was familiar with interfaith, but I had never heard of interspirituality. One Spirit's approach is not about dialogue among people of different religions with each religious practitioner maintaining the ultimate Truth of their religious tradition. It is not about tolerance or simply getting along. The idea behind interspirituality is that all faiths are equally valid paths to the summit.

A person can choose to stick to a specific faith tradition—whether it is their faith of origin or not. Or, alternatively, they can incorporate practices from a variety of faith traditions into their spiritual life. What is essential, however, is the belief that all paths are sacred. The approach is universalist and at the same time about supporting individuals in their own unique spiritual journeys.

Even liberal Jews, as far as I knew, considered Judaism to be the Truth, and Jews to be the "chosen nation," or a "light unto the nations." Or, at the very least, they considered one's exclusively Jewish identity to be sacred. One Spirit's approach intrigued me, felt right, but I did not know enough about other faith traditions to judge its veracity or know how much these other religions had in common with mine. How could all religions be true? And how could other religions fill a spiritual need for me, a Jew?

When I spoke to people at the seminary, they were excited to have a rabbi in the program. They encouraged me to enroll. I decided to take a leap of faith that this was the next right step for me. The coat I had chosen for myself was, again, growing too small. But what would it mean to expand even further than post-denominational rabbi? How much more could I stretch the title rabbi? How much more could I stretch myself without becoming so thin, so translucent, I would disappear?

The first two times I heard the call, I had the courage to listen to my inner voice and follow where it was leading me; but this time felt harder. I feared it was asking me to go too far, both for myself and for others in my life who cared about me and who would be affected by my life's course.

I kept hearing my father's voice in my head, trying to convince me I was making a huge mistake: "You're so open-minded your brains will fall out!" Yet, enrolling in interfaith-interspiritual seminary was not a choice made from the brain. It was made from the heart.

Still, would I, like the biblical Abraham, have the courage to go wherever "the call" sent me, even if it meant leaving all that was comfortable and familiar? I was not sure.

I GREW UP in suburban New York, in a tight-knit modern Orthodox Jewish community. The "modern" meant we were not like the "black-hatters," the ultra-Orthodox, who were so insular they dressed in a uniform that showed no skin except on their faces and hands and came in any color from black to gray. Those men wore black hats, and the married women covered their natural hair with wigs.

We were not like them, we knew. We considered ourselves enlightened and cultured. We went to the opera and the ballet and dressed in fashionable clothing. If women did cover their hair, they wore attractive hats and scarves, not wigs.

We studied in Jewish religious day schools, but we went on to study in secular universities. (My father's undergraduate degree was from a Jewish university, but his degree from Yale Law School was what he was most proud of, and he felt strongly about his children having a similar formative experience.)

But we integrated into society only to a point. The idea was to take part but be separate, different. Practicing and passing on our Jewish religious heritage was of supreme importance. It was a tightrope walk the adults in our community knew was risky, which was why people like my parents enforced so strictly the level of practice they had chosen.

We ate only kosher food, even when we went to restaurants. We kept a strict Sabbath, with no electricity, no driving, no writing or cooking, and we spent the entire morning on Saturday in synagogue. My mother immersed in a *mikveh* every month after she menstruated, and my father prayed every morning with a *tallit* (prayer shawl) and *tefillin* (phylacteries). These were considered ritual practices that kept us apart, in a good way. They made us special. After all, we had been chosen by God.

Socially, we modern Orthodox Jews kept mostly to ourselves. I went to Orthodox Jewish school and sleepaway camp. And my parents' friends were mostly from the synagogue—except those from their work, whom we did meet from time to time, but it was clear they were not like us. Being members of this community, playing the part, being accepted, was more important than what one felt on the inside.

In fact, the unspoken message I heard was that we were better. And not only better than the non-Jews, but also better than the non-Orthodox Jews. Being Orthodox was the only way to pass on an authentic Judaism that would last for generations to come.

My parents were more open than many others in the modern Orthodox Jewish world in which I was raised. I say "world" and not community, because it is not just the immediate community of my synagogue to which I refer, but rather the modern Orthodox community of the entire New York Tri-State area. It was a network, with each smaller community having its own character.

Where I grew up, in the suburbs north of Manhattan, we were considered (by ourselves and others) liberal and intellectual. Relatively speaking, of course. In comparison, the community where Jacob grew up, on Long Island, had a reputation for new money, white collar crime and a narrower, more conservative, approach to Jewish observance (and American and Israeli politics). New Jersey had its own reputation, the Upper West Side of Manhattan its own, very different, of course, from the Upper East Side of Manhattan or Brooklyn. And so on.

It was clear to me what I was meant to become: a modern Orthodox Jewish woman, married with kids, with a career like teaching, social work, or physical or occupational therapy (my mother's profession) that would not compete too much with my commitments at home.

My parents would have been disappointed had I not pursued a career after their investment in my Ivy League education. But a high-powered executive would have been too demanding a career path to be sensible. If I had become a doctor or a lawyer, or even a journalist or professor, they would have been proud—if I could afford live-in help, that is.

There was also a socio-economic layer to this life we led. Jewish Day School was almost as expensive as private college tuition. Jewish sleepaway camp was, per day, even more expensive than that. And with the biblical imperative to "be fruitful and multiply," this was a huge financial commitment for parents. The pressure must have been enormous. Add to that the space needed to house these children comfortably, the money to clothe them respectably, and the afterschool activities to enrich their free time.

All of this was a given in this community. Public school was not an option; nor was secondhand clothing or an apartment or small house on the "wrong side of the tracks." Communities were built around the synagogue in upscale areas of the suburbs; and being within walking distance of the synagogue was imperative, since driving on the Sabbath was forbidden.

It is important to note that these messages did not come only from my parents. In fact, the messages from my parents were more nuanced. Much of my extended family is not Orthodox, and my parents accepted their ways— for them, of course, not us. My parents invited these family members to Sabbath and holiday meals at our home, even if it meant my relatives would have to drive on the Sabbath.

We also attended my cousins' bar and bat mitzvah ceremonies in their non-Orthodox synagogues—where I assume I must have seen some women in prayer shawls (although even in non-Orthodox synagogues it was not common back then) and was exposed to a world different than mine— even if the message was clear that our way was better, that there would be consequences if I chose a different way.

Much of the pressure to conform came from the general modern Orthodox world of which I was a part. This was fine for some, I know. In fact, many of my childhood friends (although interestingly, none of my three siblings, perhaps because my parents' messages were not black-and-white) remained modern Orthodox, married, settled in the suburbs. But this was not to be my path. I knew that from an early age. This was for me the cause of great anxiety.

Even with my parents' relative openness, they are opinionated people by nature. My perception growing up was that I was meant to mirror their way, which they presented to us as the best way. The idea of following your heart wherever it leads you did not seem to me to be on their radar.

So, when I began to doubt Orthodoxy, I hid this from my parents. I locked my bedroom door on Friday nights when I wanted to read by my night light or write in my bed. I snuck out to eat pizza in a non-kosher pizza parlor.

It was not just Orthodoxy that was important to my parents and their friends. Proper behavior, proper dress: it was all part of the package. When I started to dress in bohemian clothing, my mother told me I looked like a homeless person. So, I learned to put my clothing in my school bag and change after I left the house.

When I went to my boyfriend's empty Manhattan apartment (his parents both had full-time office jobs) after school to make out, I told them I was going to a female friend instead. (The idea that I could be lesbian would never have occurred to them, although about ten years later, my older brother came out as gay, and while it took them years, they came to accept this.) When they found out where I had really been going, they told me they assumed the rumors they were hearing were incorrect, since they knew I would never do anything for which I'd be sorry later.

In the latter half of high school, I was diagnosed with FSHD, a form of muscular dystrophy that starts with certain muscle groups and spreads to others, causing increased disability and eventual death, as it progresses to the respiratory and heart muscles—although the expression and rate of deterioration is radically varied, so often people die of other causes before the FSHD kills them. Back then, I had weakness only in my face, shoulders and arms.

I started decreasing my food intake seriously and lost a lot of weight. I did not end up in the hospital. I was still able to function. But I did not eat enough to maintain a normal, healthy weight. My bones stuck out; my clothing hung on me; I had fainting spells; a light fuzz was beginning to grow on my skin to replace the fat that should have been keeping me warm. Yet I was unable to eat more. My subconscious was calling out for help.

My low weight and sparse diet drove my parents crazy with worry and frustration. That was the point, of course. Or at least one of the points. I was calling out to my parents and the world around me to see me as the free spirit I felt I was inside. This conformist environment stifled me, controlling me with its many rules and regulations, hampered by the lack of options open to me for expression and fulfillment.

I was an artist and a poet, things my parents encouraged in me, but as hobbies, not as professions or vocations. The question of "But how will you make a good enough living?"—meaning, how will you make enough money to live as a modern Orthodox Jew in the suburbs?—loomed over me and my siblings.

My soul was also calling out for attention. Ironically, with a life so circumscribed by religion, I felt spiritually starved. Being Jewish may have had inherent meaning for so many around me, but for me, it was not enough. Being Jewish was not a reason to be alive.

Being Jewish would not allay my anxiety around death, nor would it pacify my anger at God for giving me a disease that would make me increasingly disabled. I wanted answers and deeper meaning. If my parents, the society around me, and God were going to starve me spiritually, I would starve myself physically.

When I was in my senior year of high school, I was enrolled for the following year in an all-women's *yeshiva* in Jerusalem, where I would be immersed in an intense experience of Jewish religious text and practice. That is what all the good Orthodox Jewish girls did before going to secular college—to instill in them a strong religious foundation before they ventured into the "outside world."

But I did not want to go. I did not believe that was where I would find the meaning or answers I was seeking. My soul could not imagine spending a year in that kind of dogmatic and controlled environment. But I told my parents I did want to go, so as not to disappoint them. I was eating shrimp, making out with my boyfriend, turning on lights on the Sabbath, all while knowing what awaited me only months into the future.

When my weight was down to seventy-five pounds at five feet, and my period had stopped, it was clear to both me and my parents I would not be going to Israel unless I gained some weight. They could not send me thousands of miles away in such a condition. Little did they know that was what I wanted, at least subconsciously—to not be able to go.

When I finally got up the courage to reveal to them I did not want to go to *yeshiva* in Jerusalem for the year, they were disappointed, as I had expected, but they were also relieved. "You don't have to go if it's making you sick," they told me. "We just want you to get well. That's what matters to us most now."

Of course, that was what mattered most to them. And of course, it still is. Despite their clear messages as to how they most wanted me to turn out, I also knew they would love me no matter what, and that my emotional health was more important to them than my religious observance. They only wanted me to be happy, they said.

But I also knew they still believed being modern Orthodox was what would make me happy; they could not believe a Jew could truly be happy any other way.

By the fall, I returned to a normal weight, started menstruating again, and was able to nourish myself sufficiently. I began college prepared to spread my wings. I went to night clubs on Friday nights instead of to *Shabbat* services; I ate non-kosher food in public without shame; I smoked pot and took classes deconstructing social constructs like religion and patriarchy.

But I felt empty. The meaning I had been seeking was not in this kind of unencumbered, free life, either. Something was missing, and I assumed it was the religion I had cast off. Without my religious Jewish identity, what was I? With no rules or structure, life felt frighteningly more meaningless than it had before. I asked myself, *Was it worth giving up my parents' blessing and acceptance in the world in which I was raised, for this?*

After experimenting with liberal Judaism for a while, I came back to Orthodox Judaism, the only place I knew to look for meaning. But I returned on my own terms. I found a cause that helped give my life purpose but was still considered within the realm of acceptable to my parents and the community in which I had been raised. I became an Orthodox feminist, struggling for women's rights in the Orthodox community from within.

This approach satisfied my two strong and seemingly opposed spiritual needs—the need for meaning and the need for freedom. I was choosing freedom within boundaries. I could reap the benefits of religious structure without losing my sense of self.

Moreover, I could gain my parents' approval while still feeling in control of my own life. I found a way to please those I loved, remain "inside" in the eyes of those whose sanction I craved, while also expressing my dissenting voice.

But by the time I was ordained as a rabbi, this solution no longer worked for me. I had told myself covering my hair and wearing shapeless baggy clothing liberated me from the male gaze. I told myself different roles and seating in the synagogue for men and women was separate but equal. But now I could not help but see these practices as oppressive.

I thought I could live with these compromises of my liberal progressive values for the sake of community and belonging and the primal need to feel celebrated by my parents. But I managed to convince myself for only so long. My free spirit needed more space.

When I finally had the inner strength to leave the Orthodox world, despite all the prices I would pay for that decision, I understood that by adopting the Orthodox feminist cause, I had only been buying more time. Trying to fix the structures I opposed was not enough to set me free.

I had gotten my anorexia under control, but I had not cured myself of my longing for freedom from boxes with labels, nor from the need to force myself into coats that didn't fit. I wanted meaning but knew only to look in the familiar places—those of setting boundaries and following clear rules said to be divinely ordained.

Yet, my spiritual pain and longing did not disappear even with my decision to call myself a post-denominational rabbi, because I was still, on some level, buying into this same system. I was still restricting myself to only the tools for meaning making that had been presented to me in my youth, even when those tools were no longer working for me. And I was still trying to remain "inside," still seeking affirmation from a place outside myself.

I would have to look elsewhere for the inner peace and deeper meaning I craved. Jewish religious ritual was not going to be enough. In some cases, rather than try to fit into these Jewish structures that had always been an integral part of my life, or even mold them to my needs, I would have to let go of them entirely.

But as I had discovered through my college experience, freedom from rules does not necessarily equal inner peace. Letting go is not just a physical act. It is an existential one that requires difficult inner work and can take a lifetime to master—if you are lucky to even do that. For me, that knowledge would only come later and was gained through painful experience, which is the best way to learn.

LET ME GO

I AM SELLING our nine-seater van, the one Jacob and I bought to fit our whole clan. I find a buyer. We plan the exchange. He will pay me, and I will give it to him.

I pull up at the location where we had planned to meet. I roll down the windows. The theme song from the film Boyhood *is blasting from the car. "Let me go. I don't wanna be your Hero . . ."*

The buyer shows up. He is the father from the film Captain Fantastic. *He says he can't pay me now. His wife committed suicide. He has six children. He needs the van to save her from burial, to cremate her as she wished and spread her ashes over the ocean. He will pay me later. He promises. He is crying.*

I am torn. I don't know if I can trust this guy. In the film, he is an ideologue, but also a scammer and an anarchist. Maybe he just wants to take the van and chop it into pieces, sell its parts. It may never be whole again.

I DID NOT tell my parents about my interfaith-interspiritual ministry studies. This was an especially sensitive time in our family. My daughter, Michal, our oldest child, was in a serious romantic relationship with a Muslim-raised Palestinian-Israeli man from Jaffa. They had been living together in Haifa for a few years already, and they had just announced their intention to marry.

"This is your fault," my mother is telling me now over the phone. She is upset about Michal and Ahmad's engagement. I am standing in the kitchen of my kibbutz house, looking out my window at the Palestinian-Israeli village across the valley. It is a predominantly Muslim village, with few Christians, if there are any at all.

"You should have stopped it from the beginning. Instead, you encouraged it. You and your foolish ideas about everyone getting along. They"—by this she means Palestinians—"want to get along until they stab you in the back. Literally!"

It is true that when Michal called to tell me she had met this cute guy named Ahmad, I did not discourage her from pursuing the relationship. It is also true that had I discouraged her, she probably would have listened to my advice. She consults with me as both a rabbi and her mother. But I speak only for myself and would never tell anyone what they should do. Not even my daughter. I am a good listener, a supportive mother, and a rabbi who herself is on a journey. Who am I to tell others what to do?

I saw no legitimate reason to tell my daughter not to pursue the relationship. She had not been having success dating Jewish men, and from the way Michal described him, Ahmad seemed a stable, responsible adult with aspirations and a kind heart. An atheist, but not hostile to her own religious expressions. Love is a gamble. But Ahmad sounded like a promising prospect.

I do not see life the way my mother does. She is not an optimist or an idealist. She is not a dreamer. My mother is practical. And from my vantage point, she sees the world as divided between "us" (religious Jews) and "them" (everyone else). Only religious Jews will succeed in passing on Jewish tradition to future generations, and Jewish tradition must be passed on at almost all costs. This attitude is not atypical of her generation, many of whom are children of Holocaust survivors or survivors themselves.

Jewish tradition is a priceless heirloom, a superior way of life that must be preserved. It was almost obliterated by the Nazis, but we prevailed. Throwing it away so carelessly would be a travesty. For my mother and other Orthodox Jews, Judaism holds the key to a proper life for all born into this line, and for the select number who prove themselves worthy of being Jews by Choice. Not even non-Orthodox Jews, let alone intermarried Jews, have a good chance of passing on this tradition to their descendants.

Michal believes she has a strong enough Jewish identity to pass it on to her children, even if they do not have a Jewish father. She is also happy to participate in Muslim traditions with Ahmad's family. Like me, she does not believe Judaism is the only possible source of meaning. I do not intend to belittle or squander this precious heirloom my parents so lovingly passed on to me. It is, indeed, full of much wisdom and meaning. It is also full of things I find problematic. Like all faith traditions are.

What is most important to me is for the earth to be inhabited by emotionally and spiritually healthy people who support one another in their individuality. This is the only way to achieve true peace among humans. Whatever way we as humanity can reach this point is fair game. In my worldview, it is a spiritual imperative for people to express themselves fully and fulfill their God-given purpose in this world, in whatever way they can. Assuming they do not harm others in the process.

If Judaism helps my children feel fulfilled and contribute to the world in a positive way, as well as navigate the challenges of living as humans on this earth, wonderful. If something else helps them do this, that is also good. But I cannot say this to my mother. This outlook would sound like nonsense to her. In fact, I imagine it would sound like nonsense to many of my family members and friends.

I look out my window again, at the Palestinian village across the valley. Another traditional and closed society with clear societal norms. For those who choose that way of life, for whom that way of life suits their temperaments, that is fine. But for those for whom it doesn't, they should feel free to live differently.

Are we really that different? Ishmael and Isaac. Sons of Abraham. "*B'nei dodim*," cousins, as people here refer to Jews, Christians, and Muslims. Yet, we don't seem able to get along. And intermarriage is not practiced by the mainstream. In cities like Haifa where Michal and Ahmad live, it is more accepted, but not in a village like the one I see now, where even Christians and Muslims rarely intermarry. My parents are not the only ones who consider marrying out of the faith unacceptable.

I think back to when Michal originally told my parents about her relationship with Ahmad. "First you sacrifice your children on the altar of your ideology by sending them to that school. And now this!" my mother yelled at me on the phone after their conversation with Michal.

She was referring to when we registered our younger kids at the Galilee Hand-in-Hand School—a bilingual elementary school for Arabic and Hebrew speakers. Back then, my parents sent me an email comparing me to Abraham who was willing to sacrifice his son. We did not speak for over a month.

"You encourage your daughter to be with a Muslim man to satisfy your own political agenda," my mother continued to scold me when my parents first heard about her relationship with Ahmad. "You'll be sorry when it's too late."

My parents did not wait for me to feel sorry, however. They offered to pay for Michal to live and study at a New York university, where they could keep an eye on her. Rent and college tuition covered. It was a hard offer for Michal to refuse, but she did. Because it came with a condition: she would have to cut off all ties with Ahmad.

I was upset at my parents. It was bad enough they were interfering with my child's life, but Michal was an adult and could make her own decisions. What upset me most was that they were sending my children that same message of unconditional love but conditional acceptance that had scarred me: *We will love you no matter what, but we will only be proud of you if you do as we expect.* It was not an unreasonable approach, but it left me feeling guilty and confused. Should I try to please my parents or follow my heart?

It was their prerogative to send this message. Emotional support cannot be forced. But that approach came with a cost to them not only to me: I did not feel safe to share with my parents my full self. Perhaps they did not even want me to, as it would hurt them too much. Which is why I did not tell them about my studies at One Spirit. In fact, I shared with them as little as possible about myself, so as not to upset them.

But living with secrets takes a toll, and close relationships without transparency are missing a significant part of the point.

I say nothing now, either, as I again look out the window and hear the *muezzin* calling my Muslim neighbors to prayer. Then I hang up the phone on my own mother.

THE FIRST YEAR of my interfaith ministry studies was an introduction to the major world religions. We read from their sacred texts, studied their history and beliefs, and took on ritual practices from those religions. Speakers presented on each religion in day-long seminars. The idea was not to become experts in any one religion, but rather, to become familiar with and create a personal connection to (or dialogue with) each. Those who wanted to delve deeper into a specific religion could do so later.

I grew up in a strict religious environment that focused on social norms rather than on spiritual seeking, was more about dogma and rules than struggling with the meaning of life and human existence on this planet. In this program, we did tackle these existential issues, but through the lens of several world religions, not just one. I discovered at the core of all religions—despite their different dogmas and beliefs—the aspiration to live a life aligned with the force that flows through and connects all, and thus, to be at peace with being human.

Religion, I discovered, did not have to be about following rules and conforming to the group. It did not have to be about exclusion and superiority. Religion could be a human connector, a commonality among humans. Religion at its core is the human aspiration to connect with a uniting force and higher power, to live a life in line with one's individual purpose and with our collective human purpose to create a life good (physically and emotionally) for as many people, plants and animals on this planet as possible.

Different people in different times and places expressed these aspirations in different ways, thus the variety of faith traditions and denominations in the world. No way is objectively better than any other. Some people may decide to follow one path because it is the path their ancestors followed. Or they may decide to follow one path because it is the path that speaks to their soul, irrespective of, or even despite, their ancestral history.

Others may choose a more universal spiritual approach that gleans wisdom from the lessons and wisdom of humanity throughout the ages but is not limited to one specific religious tradition.

I had yet to figure out what my path would be. But the mere knowledge I could look anywhere for the answers to my spiritual questions, that we are all simply doing our best to find inner peace wherever and however we can, felt so right for me it was like coming home to myself.

WHEN WE LEARNED about Judaism in the interfaith ministry program, I was blessed with the opportunity to see my own faith tradition anew. Those presenting on Judaism emphasized concepts like *tikkun olam* (the repairing of the world through social action) and the One Unified God. I was also reminded of the talmudic value of asking questions and honoring and recording various points of view (even if the Code of Jewish Law ends up honing them down to a strict manual).

With each religion, we were invited to choose a ritual to perform for one month. For my Buddhist practice, I had chosen walking meditation. For my Muslim practice, I had taken on a full-body prostration pose while reciting, "*Allah hu akbar!*" God is the greatest! As my Christian practice, I had chanted with a beaded string. When Jewish month came, I had to choose a Jewish practice as well.

Many a morning during that period, I took out my *tefillin*—leather straps tied to leather boxes filled with parchment on which are scribed verses from the sacred biblical *Sh'ma* prayer—from their worn velvet bag and held them in my hands. I wondered if I'd feel inspired to take back this ritual, once a central spiritual practice in my life, but practically abandoned at that point. I wrapped them, even prayed with them a few times. But the magic was gone.

I had started wrapping *tefillin* during my morning prayers when I was twenty-two years old and thinking about having a child. I felt drawn to these ritual objects, even though in the community where I had been raised, only men wore them. A woman doing so would have been considered transgressive.

At my older brother's bar mitzvah, he received a shiny and stiff new pair of *tefillin* he was expected to wrap every morning for the rest of his life, so one day it would look as worn as my father's. I received no ritual tool or garment from my parents at my bat mitzvah. Not only that, but I was sent to the back of the synagogue, to sit with my mother behind the partition separating the women from the men, who led the service.

This was the accepted way of treating a bat mitzvah girl in that community. Becoming a bat mitzvah meant becoming a Jewish woman, which meant taking a back seat (and sometimes even making yourself invisible) while the men ran the show, especially in the public sphere, but also, to some degree, in the home.

I had seen my father pray with *tefillin*—except on the Sabbath, when *tefillin* are not worn—while wrapped in a prayer shawl called a *tallit* every morning of my childhood, no matter what the circumstances. This was his regular morning practice, as we all went about our business around him.

My mother would serve us breakfast while we heard my father's off-key rote singsong from his study. *Ashrei yoshvei beitechah, od yehaleluchah selah.* Praiseworthy are those who sit in Your dwelling place; they will continue to praise You forever. *Sh'ma Yisrael, Adonai Eloheinu, Adonai Echad.* Hear oh Israel, *Adonai* is our God, *Adonai* is One. And various such chants.

These are such vital messages to start the day, yet they lost their intense spiritual meaning because I heard them in this routine tone each morning. Although, looking back, I think that routine and structure were so important for my father, as well as the connection to generations of men before him who had performed this same ritual every day.

My father was cynical and critical of fundamentalist religion, but he was also attached to his modern Orthodox lifestyle of incorporating tradition into an enlightened view of the world. Praying with *tallit* and *tefillin* before heading out to his job as a corporate litigator in midtown Manhattan was a significant part of that.

My mother, like the mothers of all of my friends, did not pray with *tefillin*. Nor did she wear a *tallit*. As far as I knew, women were forbidden from wearing a *tallit* and *tefillin*. I had assumed that the biblical commandment to attach fringes to one's four-cornered garments and place a sign on one's arm and between one's eyes, applied only to men—even though it does not say as much in the verses themselves.

When I studied feminist theory in college and became empowered to open the rabbinic texts on my own, I discovered, much to my shock, that according to the rabbinic interpretation of the biblical text, women were not forbidden to wear a *tallit* and *tefillin*; rather, we were just not obligated to do so.

Moreover, according to the Ashkenazi interpretation of the law—my family is Ashkenazi, coming from Eastern Europe—the biblical commandment does apply to women; we are simply exempt from performing the ritual act. Therefore, if a woman does choose to pray with a *tallit* and *tefillin*, she recites the blessing which evokes that commandment.

This was a huge revelation for me. An act that had been taboo for me as a girl and young woman suddenly became an option. Although my older brother resented having to pray with *tefillin* every morning, I felt drawn to those sacred, mysterious black leather straps with their parchment-filled boxes and holy writing. Suddenly, they became within my reach. As did their accompanying prayer shawl with fringes, or *tallit*, in which to wrap myself while talking to God.

I decided to take on this ritual, and to do so before having a child, so that my children would not grow up with gendered associations around these ritual objects.

Jacob had old *tefillin* and a *tallit* that had belonged to his late uncle, and one morning, while he was wrapping his *tefillin*, he taught me how. With trembling hands, I placed the parchment-filled boxes on my forehead and arm. The leather felt cold and firm against the skin of my left bicep.

I wrapped the leather straps seven times around my forearm and fingers (forming *Shadai*, a divine name), while reciting, as per the tradition, these verses from Hosea: "I betroth you to me forever. I betroth you to me in righteousness, justice, lovingkindness, and mercy. I betroth you to me in faith. And you shall know *Adonai*."

I was not prepared for how powerful it would feel to have these straps wound around my arm and fingers, like a wedding ring with God, a pact to do my best to bring those important virtues from the verses in Hosea into the Universe.

These words my father had recited while performing this same ritual throughout my childhood, spoke to my heart. As did the traditional psalm about being sheltered in God's wings recited when putting on a *tallit*, which is also worn during the morning prayers: "How precious is your lovingkindness, *Elohim*! Humanity rests in the shelter of your wings." Now these words were also mine.

I began praying with *tallit* and *tefillin* daily. What I most appreciated about the ritual was its embodied quality. Like immersing in a *mikveh*, this ritual was a way for me to acknowledge regularly the sanctity of my body, even with all its imperfections and limitations. A time set aside for gratitude for what does work, and compassion for what doesn't: an especially important intention for someone with physical disabilities.

And feeling sheltered in divine wings, embraced and supported by God, was a spiritual necessity for me given the unorthodox Orthodox path I had chosen for myself.

I even purchased my own off-white woolen *tallit* with gray stripes. It looked enough but not too much like the traditional, black-striped *tallit* my father wore each morning and thus, it suited my need back then to be inside yet not conform, to play the game but by my own rules. Or what I felt was enough "my own rules" at the time.

For almost two decades I continued to pray each morning with a *tallit* and *tefillin*. I bought myself a new pair of *tefillin*, and over the years I made for myself a series of different prayer shawls as my needs and tastes changed. I had broken through a social taboo for my own spiritual expression and to pave the way for other women to do the same. And I had managed to get Jacob, and even my parents, on board. My mother even made me a needlepoint *atarah* collar piece for my *tallit*. I was rebelling, but within the boundaries of what was considered acceptable.

In the months prior to the ministry program, I had been wrapping *tefillin* less frequently. Binding leather *tefillin* straps to my arms became less and less appealing to my more freed spirit (although praying with a *tallit* still felt right, and *mikveh* immersion had become my major rabbinic focus). The straps felt confining and distracting when I prayed, especially as my physical condition was worsening.

With little muscle to wrap the *tefillin* or hold them on, they tended to slide off. I had even started using a small, light *tallit* which I loosely wore around my neck instead of a big, heavy one wrapped around my shoulders, for the same reason. The ritual objects had become cumbersome, pulling me down both physically and emotionally.

The less complicated, heavy paraphernalia to worry about the better, at this stage in the developments of my disease. These ritual objects that had made me feel embraced by God were making me feel the weight of my morbidity instead of the protection of Divine Spirit. I felt abandoned not supported. Was God keeping God's side of our wedding vows?

By the time I started the ministry program, I was hardly wrapping *tefillin* at all. Experimenting with walking and outdoor prayer made prayer paraphernalia especially impractical. I had a rational excuse to abandon my *tefillin*.

But there was a deeper reason involved. Part of me began to realize that although I was no longer obsessively controlling my food intake, I was still looking for meaning through control, restriction and rules. I was still trying to fill what was empty, give boundaries to the endless, and build structure where there was chaos.

These two sides of my psyche were still battling inside me: the side that wants freedom and the side that wants meaning. Can there by meaning without control? Can there be freedom and meaning at the same time? Can freedom itself be meaningful? That notion was frightening, yet my soul was pushing me in the direction of taking the risk of trying to find out.

At the end of the month devoted to Judaism, one of the speakers was a lesbian Jewish therapist and spiritual counselor who had grown up in an ultra-Orthodox Hassidic community in New York. She was married off (to a man) at age seventeen and described how she cried under the wedding canopy and for years afterwards, through the births of her children.

Finally, she gained the courage to leave. Without even a high school diploma, and with no help or support from her parents or ex-husband, she studied, worked and raised her children.

As part of her lecture on Judaism, she performed for the class her daily ritual of laying *tefillin*. She sang a beautiful Hassidic *niggun* to the line from Hosea about betrothing oneself to God, as she wrapped the leather straps around her arm and fingers.

Tears streamed down my cheeks. I was crying tears of joy at this woman's ownership of the *tefillin* ritual. I was in awe of how she had made peace with her childhood and found meaning in its rituals and traditions, despite the pain growing up in the Hassidic world had caused her. And I was remembering how powerful it had been for me to own this ritual myself when that is what I had needed to do.

I was also crying tears of loss. This ritual was no longer mine. It was not working for me in the way it once had.

This woman had made peace with her childhood, and with God—something I had yet to do. It would take more than wrapping leather straps around my arm and reciting verses and prayers—no matter how resonant or poignant—for me to forgive God for making me sick. I had been using religious ritual to bypass the inner work I had yet to do to make peace with life.

That day, I said goodbye to *tefillin* as part of my own regular spiritual practice. I did not want my relationship with Spirit to be about binding or restricting. I aspired to a more flowing and open relationship now. One of uplifting and embracing, not tying and attaching. Which is why *tallit* (at least in the lighter and smaller adapted form I had adopted) still worked for me. Because that was about being wrapped in God's wings—hopefully to be lifted, to fly!

Just as important as it had been for me to start laying *tefillin* when I did, it was equally as important for me to stop laying *tefillin* as a regular spiritual practice at this juncture in my life. This did not mean the ritual was off-limits to me, but rather, I did not feel obligated to perform it any more than I felt obligated to perform any religious ritual. The whole notion of obligation in the context of religious ritual fell away for me.

Obligation meant being forced to do something from a human-made (even if divinely inspired, or spiritually focused) system outside myself. Was it for my own good, really? Or was it for a greater communal good that sometimes sacrificed me as a fully expressed individual? Why *obligate* me to perform a ritual that was meant to enhance my spiritual life? If the spirit moved me to wrap *tefillin*, I would do so on my own. If not, not.

I was aware of the argument for daily ritual, both to ensure its regularity and therefore its efficacy, and to ensure it would not be lost for future generations. But this religious approach no longer spoke to me. I had enough of that in my childhood.

I had convinced myself that it was just the misogynist, homophobic nature of traditional Judaism that bothered me. If I could perform all the rituals, like a man, then I would be okay with this rule-focused religion meant to control every aspect of my life.

But now I realized my issues with Judaism went deeper. My soul was seeking freedom, even if I kept insisting on giving it rules. The part of me that craves control was trying to control the part that craves freedom. And I was caught in the middle.

Time was short. My life was short. I was impatient with rituals that were not helping me cope nor addressing my personal spiritual angst. Rituals that were feeling more a burden than a means to inner peace.

I let go of my commitment to *tefillin* as a regular spiritual practice. This step meant letting go of the guilt connected to that step along my journey. If I was going to ask others to "let me go," I had to let myself go first.

But letting myself go would require more than letting go of *tefillin*. It would require more than letting go of guilt. It would mean letting go of a need for *tefillin* or any other ritual to take its place.

With no religious Jewish identity, what was I? Like the nine-seater van I am selling to Captain Fantastic in my dream, what would become of me?

Would I fall apart, be broken down beyond recognition? What would I be after deconstructing myself?

Beneath all those layers that were applied on my essence like strips of *papier-maché* over a balloon, what was at the core? Was the balloon still there, or did it pop from the pressure of those layers? Disintegrate from lack of exposure?

Letting go would require relinquishing a need for control. It would require being able to sit in that empty place of unknowing. It would require surrender.

WHEN JACOB AND I met, I was nineteen years old and had just started college a semester before.

At age sixteen, I had been diagnosed with FSHD. This diagnosis, as much if not more than my desire for freedom from my restrictive childhood, threw me into a losing battle for a sense of control over my body and my life.

I met Jacob in the hallway of my Columbia College dormitory, when I returned one Friday night from a night club in the East Village. He was living further uptown, in Harlem, studying at City College. He had been at Orthodox Friday night services on the Columbia campus with a mutual friend he was visiting for the weekend who lived across the hall from me, in the Columbia dorms.

Jacob, too, had grown up modern Orthodox; he, too, had rebelled against this upbringing; and he, too, had felt an emptiness in the lifestyle of bars and nightclubs. He had recently begun to return to religious tradition, on his own terms—the step I was contemplating taking in my own life when we met.

Jacob was independent minded as well as financially independent from his parents, although he, too, was only nineteen and in college. He was on full scholarship and working to pay rent and buy food. He lived simply and minimally and modeled maintaining individuality and self-reliance within the conformist and materialistic world in which we both had been raised. And he was an idealist and an activist, trying to make the world a better place.

We quickly fell in love. There was a deep soul connection, as well as mutual appreciation and celebration. Jacob saw me in ways no one else in my life had. The way his face lit up when he spotted me lit up my whole being. He held me inside him, and I held him inside me.

The intensity of our relationship was on some level frightening. I had never felt connected to a person in my life in this visceral overwhelming way. But it also brought me deep comfort and a sense of existential security. His commitment to me and our love lent stability in a world and life that felt cruel, uncertain and senseless. My hunger for meaning was being satiated, finally. Our love itself gave life meaning.

I felt safe with Jacob to be the rebel I was. He was attracted to that side of me. And his appreciation did not feel conditional the way that of my parents did. He also grounded me. And my parents were thrilled with my choice of a partner for that very reason.

We returned to Orthodoxy together, influencing each other's choices of how to do so. I pushed him on feminist issues. He called me on my knee-jerk criticism and impatience with the religious system and community. We were both people not afraid to shake the status quo, yet we felt committed to Jewish tradition. Our *Shabbat* table discussions were known for their serious yet iconoclastic nature. We were considered eccentric renegades in our circle of friends.

Over the course of our first year together, our love matured and blossomed into a shared life. When we decided to marry, Jacob wanted to buy me a diamond engagement ring. I did not want a diamond ring, I did not want a symbol that I was "taken," and I did not think he should be spending what minimal money he had on such an extravagance.

But buying me an engagement ring meant a lot to him. We compromised on a vintage diamond ring we found at an antique jeweler on 47th Street. But it was too large for my tiny, bony fingers, so we left it at the shop to be cut.

When the ring was ready, the store called Jacob and he picked it up without telling me. He showed up at my dormitory room—on roller skates, his usual mode of transportation at the time—with the ring in a box. He was being romantic, wanting to surprise me.

I did not like surprises; they made me feel out of control. I was no longer starving myself, but that did not mean I had let go of my desire to feel in control. How could he, who knew me so well, not know this important fact about me?

I felt myself slipping away, being swallowed up by this partnership we had created. Jacob was offering me his eternal love, and I was perceiving it as a desire to control me—my worst nightmare, a repeat of my childhood. I felt trapped. I was twenty years old. I wanted to travel the world, become a journalist or maybe an author and close myself up in a beach house and write novels.

I cried. I told him to take the ring back. I was not looking for a life partner. But there he was. He cried. And I broke. I did not want to hurt him. I loved him. And despite my desire for freedom, I had an even deeper desire to be loved, seen and chosen. And perhaps even controlled on some level—setting boundaries for myself in my love life as well as my spiritual life. Again, those two sides of myself—that seeking freedom and that seeking control—battling inside me.

And Jacob still wanted me despite all my baggage, all the hurt I was causing him and would inevitably continue to cause him because of my own disquiet.

I pushed him, tested his love, as I would do again and again in years to come, and he passed with honors. He came back at me with that unconditional celebration I was seeking and knew I would never receive from my parents.

He knew I was a complicated choice of life partner, yet he took the risk. And so, I did too. I risked losing myself in his love. We married a little over a year later.

Yet, still afraid of losing control—even if I never had it, anyway—I resisted having children (although the fear of not being able to have children had been one main motivation to get my anorexia under control). Imagining the unequal parenting roles of my parents' generation, I told him children would sap my time and energy. But he convinced me. He said not to worry, he'd be an equal parenting partner, which put me enough at ease to agree. And once I agreed, I became an enthusiastic and devoted parent.

But still, I kept up my guard. With him, with the birth of each biological child. Six in all. With the adoption of another child. I protected myself, my space, my individual freedom, within all that love. Knowing subconsciously all along that one day, love, life, death—they would all win the battle.

The unrest would only settle once I addressed its origin: the assumption to which I still clung that life should be fair.

"YOU JUST DON'T feel it anymore, do you?" Jacob asks me.

We are sitting at our kitchen island over tea, after a kibbutz meeting about how we can help fight the Israeli government's decision to deport to Rwanda thousands of asylum seekers from Sudan who snuck over the border into Israel. Jacob, like me, is against the decision. In fact, we are discussing whether to take a few refugees into our home to hide them from the authorities. We both see the deportation as immoral, but for me, it's discriminatory, not just inhumane.

If those asylum seekers were Jewish, they would get automatic Israeli citizenship. Because they are not, they are considered alien and a threat. Plus, the fact that they are African with dark skin is another strike against them. And some are Muslim, too, no less.

In a Jewish country with a large minority Palestinian population, most of whom are Muslim and are seen as a threat to the country's Jewish character and security (because of the ongoing conflict between Israel and its neighboring countries, especially Hamas-ruled Gaza), this is a third strike. And we all know what three strikes mean.

"No, I don't. I do not feel more kinship with someone who has a Jewish label than someone who doesn't. It makes my stomach turn to think that this country rolls out the red carpet for Jewish immigrants, while we will go so far as to deport non-Jewish asylum seekers and even pay Rwanda to take them in!" My heart is racing now. "It smacks of racism and xenophobia if you ask me. It's perpetuating tribalism and the victim look-out-for-your-own mentality."

"But that's the basis of this country. It's a Jewish country. A homeland for Jews. A refuge for Jews." Jacob looks at me with exasperation. "That's who we are. That's why we came here."

"I know it's why we came here. And when we did, I felt the way you do. But I just don't anymore. I can't make myself feel that automatic kinship if I don't."

"So why are you here?" Jacob asks me, his voice frustrated, his expression angry.

I contemplate this. "This place has become our home and the home of our children. And I agree anti-Semitism makes it necessary to have a refuge for Jews. But my vision, my hope, is for this to be a liberal democracy that is a haven not just for Jews, but rather, for anyone who seeks asylum."

Jacob looks like I punched him in the stomach. "Are you saying you want to do away with Israel as a Jewish country?"

"Yes, I am. Once we've gotten over our trauma, both Jews and Palestinians, I'd like to see this country be a place we can share, and open to anyone who dreams of living in peace and non-violence. I figure, if we can do it here, it can be done anywhere. That is what keeps me here. The hope that one day we can all live in peace, with no one nation ruling over the other, and that I can be part of making that happen."

I look up from the kitchen table and see our wedding photo hanging on the wall. Even then I was pushing boundaries: wearing off-white instead of white (after all, Jacob and I were sexually active, so why pretend we were not?); demanding a relatively understated (for New York Jewish suburbia) vegetarian double-ring wedding and writing my own more egalitarian religious marriage documents.

But I gave Jacob his ring after the ceremony in private, because the officiating rabbi would not hear of a double-ring ceremony; and my parents served a lavish (even if vegetarian) *smorgasbord* while I was at my pre-*chuppah* (the traditional Jewish marriage canopy where the ceremony takes place) gathering in a separate room where I could not see it.

And while I did write my own egalitarian documents, those were not the official documents of the wedding. I read them aloud at the reception, but not beneath the *chuppah*. And while I knew my dress was cream, not white, it looked like a virginal wedding dress to everyone else, I am sure.

I was known as different, rebellious, even while playing the traditional bridal role. Jacob's friends mocked his wedding ring and our decision to create a new name out of our family names. His parents were not happy about that, either. Nor were they happy about when we took the photos.

Since the wedding was on a Thursday evening, Jacob and I saw each other before the ceremony, for photos to be taken, so as not to make our guests wait. This decision upset Jacob's mother. None of her friends' children did this at their weddings. We explained it was not Jewish religious law, just common practice in her community, to not take photos before the *chuppah* ceremony. That did not appease her. She would not speak to us at the wedding, is frowning in the photos, and it took several weeks before she cooled down enough to speak to us again. Even among adults, peer pressure is so intense in that world.

In the wedding photo hanging on our wall, Jacob and I are being danced around on raised chairs, and we are each holding one end of a blue-and-white Israeli flag. Both raised in Orthodox Jewish New York, members of a minority population in the United States, we felt passionately about moving to Israel and raising our children in a more idealistic society, where our lives would have meaning and purpose, and where we could live holistic, full Jewish lives. We wanted to be part of building a Jewish country, bringing our liberal values to Israel along with our commitment and idealism.

I close my eyes now and try to feel what it was like to be the twenty-one-year-old in the photograph. I try to find who I am today in that young woman in the photo. But as much as I try, I cannot feel what I felt back then: that feeling of belonging, or commitment to a righteous cause, of filling my life with purpose and meaning through Zionism and Judaism. I am still that soul in search of meaning, but I am no longer looking for it in "isms."

For many reasons, I am proud to be Jewish, but for others I am not. My Jewish identity is not stronger than my human identity. That message of superiority and separation that felt so distasteful to me growing up, was feeling even more so now, as it meant choosing one life over another based on national and religious identity.

I do not feel more connected to someone just because they are Jewish. My personal feelings of connection are not that easily delineated or narrowed down. My feelings of kinship are not automatic; they form over time and are based on feeling of connection, experience, and a shared worldview.

These feelings cross religious and ethnic boundaries, which, I think, is a healthy way for society in general to be. This way, I believe, the world will not only function and survive, but also thrive. The potential for deep human connection lies among all humans, irrespective of the identities we carry.

My feelings as a parent are different. Responsibility for a helpless soul can accelerate the connection process. I did feel an automatic connection to my biological children the moment they were born, but I also felt one to my adopted son the minute he was placed in our care. And he was not Jewish then. We converted him later as was required by the State in order to be able to adopt him. But I did not feel a need to convert him to be his mother. I did not feel a need for my son to be Jewish.

I honor every human's right to convert. I respect that decision. I even officiate scores of *mikveh* conversion ceremonies every year and consider this a privilege and significant aspect of my work. Accompanying others on their spiritual path, supporting their unique spiritual journey, holding space for them in non-judgment and celebrating their choices—this is all part of the work I do at the *mikveh* and as a spiritual companion in general.

But that does not mean I, personally, feel more connected to them after they immerse and emerge from the *mikveh* Jewish. I feel connected to them on a human level, especially as someone who has also made life choices that had spiritual benefits but social and familial consequences. I feel just as connected to someone who converts out of Judaism as to someone who converts in.

I know that for many, ancestral history is integral to their sense of who they are. It is for me, too, but I do not feel attached to that history. It informs me without defining or restricting me. Or at least, that is my aspiration. While Judaism has given me tools to create, express, mark and identify meaning in my life, so have other things, such as literature, psychology, nature, art and spirituality.

The reason I am familiar with specifically Jewish tools and not others is because of circumstances of time and place. If I had been born elsewhere and at a different time, I could have different tools that have equal potential to be useful and effective to impart meaning.

I am not naïve. People put others into boxes and even discriminate against others as a result. In the face of anti-Semitism, I defend my human rights to the end. But I do not claim I have more rights than others just because I am Jewish. What a sad reality we live in if we must be a majority here—at all costs—to feel safe.

This turning of my stomach I feel when I think about those refugees is real. It is who I am now. No one told me to feel this way. In fact, I have heard very few other Israeli Jews express the kind of deep sorrow I am feeling now over the discriminatory Israeli "Right of Return" for Jews and Jews only. This is all my own making. This is me.

I do not relate to what Jacob is feeling, and he does not relate to what I am feeling, and this scares me after nearly thirty years of life visions that were mostly in sync. And when they weren't, they managed to eventually more or less become aligned as we worked to listen to each other, respect each other's needs, and find common ground. Although I admit that it was usually I who was changing our course.

Granted, he was the one who convinced me to get married and have children. But after that, I did more convincing than he did. When I wanted to become an Orthodox rabbi, Jacob supported my unheard-of goal. When I left Orthodoxy, Jacob came along, too, and even became opposed to non-egalitarian prayer services. When I wanted to adopt a child, Jacob became a staunch supporter of adoption.

But this is different. I am stabbing Jacob right in the heart this time. His Jewish identity. I am shaking up who he is and what we share. We demonstrated together for Soviet Jewry, for Israel, against anti-Semitism. I was the editor of a national Jewish student newspaper when he was chair of the U.S. Jewish Student Union. Together, we moved far from our families to a Jewish country, to build our life here from a place of ideology. Our home centered around being Jewish.

I will not risk my relationship with Jacob, the most precious thing in my life, unless it is unavoidable. And certainly not over ideological difference. Our connection is deeper than ideology. This is not about ideology. This is about being me, which is really the only thing I can be.

But is this "me" still someone Jacob can love?

WE CELEBRATED NACHUM'S bar mitzvah on Israel Independence Day of 2016, a couple of weeks after Passover. Jacob's father was not in good health, so we were glad his parents could manage the trip. But since they were coming, they decided to come for a full month, starting with Passover and ending with the bar mitzvah. Their stay was especially challenging, because not only did we have his parents to care for, but we had a bar mitzvah to organize.

For a month, my in-laws lived with us twenty-four hours a day, seven days a week. They even slept in our bedroom (and us on the fold-out futon). Considering my father-in-law's condition, our bedroom was the only comfortable option for them. Their stay also meant hiring an aide to be with him during the day, taking the door off our bathroom so he could get in with his walker, adjusting our hectic lifestyle to their needs.

I was not proud of myself during their visit. I welcomed them into our lives. I accommodated them without a complaint. But I felt my heart clench, my compassion finding its limits.

"Are those supposed to help strengthen your muscles?" my mother-in-law asked one day while I was attaching my walking aids to my shoes. "Like weights?"

Right before we left Jerusalem for northern Israel, I discovered I could wear a contraption called a dictus on each leg to help me lift my foot while I walk. The dictuses made a huge difference in my mobility, and I had been wearing them for the past seven years, at least; yet she was asking this now.

Not only that, but I had told her many times that my muscular disorder is degenerative and has no cure, treatment or therapy. The muscles cannot be rebuilt or strengthened. In fact, trying to strengthen them exhausts them, and me, to the point where I cannot use them at all. I had explained all of this to her before.

Immediately I went to a place of self-pity and resentment. Rather than feel sorry for her, I felt sorry for myself. My in-laws had usurped my caregiver, their son, my life partner. He had been running around catering to their every need for the past three weeks (even flying to the U.S. to accompany them on their flight to Israel), while I had been asked to be the strong one, the main caregiver for our children.

I was tired. I was weak. I wanted to be taken care of. I wanted to be seen. I wanted my pain (both physical and emotional) to be recognized. I did not want to be asked to be strong. I did not want to be asked to disappear or hide my own needs once again in my life. Tears filled my eyes. I did not look up at her. "No. They help me walk." That is all I said.

Jacob flew back to New York with his parents to help on the flight and settle them back in at home. Then he flew to California on business. I was sitting at my laptop when his email arrived.

Thank you so much for hosting my parents this past month, during a time that was already stressful. I know it was far from easy — and miraculously now behind us. Not sure what the short-term future is for my father, but at least we don't have another major lifecycle event for another five years, so no pressure. He has his brief moments where he seems happy, but I am sad that so much of the time he is suffering.

Next subject for us to discuss is us. Long before my parents came, I wanted us to talk about our physical relationship — didn't push it the past month, but it's something I want us to talk through. I love you, and think you are beautiful, and I remain as attracted as ever to you. But far too often you prefer to go to sleep with a book, and even just day to day you don't seem to feel the same way toward me. Obviously, I know you might but just don't express it, but as you know I need that reassurance.

I also simply need more physical connection, even if just to come over and give me a hug (a kiss too would be appreciated).

A lot of the time I feel I am pushing myself on you.

We are nearing fifty years old, and we should be enjoying life as a couple. Time just flies by too fast to wait.

You are the most important person in my life. I hope I am to you (putting aside for a moment our kids).

Very much looking forward to being back with you on Friday. And putting the door back on our bathroom . . .

Jacob's letter was a wake-up call. I too was glad to have our space back, and I knew that if I had been especially uninterested in intimacy that past month, it was because of the altered sleeping arrangement and the stress of my in-laws' visit and the bar mitzvah. But even without those explanations, I was not sure I could give Jacob what he was requesting, what he seemed to need from me.

I could not be the wife in the sexy nightie waiting for her husband between the satin sheets with a glass of wine, when he returned home from a business trip. What I could be was the tired, emotionally-spent-and-triggered co-captain who had weathered the storm in his absence and was now waiting for him to take over at the helm so I could jump ship for a refreshing swim.

Jacob was right. I had been less physically and emotionally available to him not just for the past month, but for the past few years. As my illness progressed, I felt less sexy, less attractive. Whereas not so many years before, we would go for a monthly *mikveh* dip in nature and make love under the stars, lately I refused to even make love with the light on, worried that if Jacob saw what my body had become, he would lose his attraction toward me.

I was worn down. I was giving him as much as I could. I wanted to feel I could give him more. I was working on being able to. But how could I give to him when I was not sure what I myself needed? I felt limited, both emotionally and physically. Seeing his father suffering had triggered my own feelings of suffering, and what made it worse was I felt abandoned by Jacob, who was choosing to help alleviate his parents' suffering over mine.

Moreover, I felt trapped in a lifestyle we shared but I was not sure I owned any longer. I was still toeing the line of living a traditional Jewish life, even if we had, as a couple, left the Orthodox world. This was important to Jacob, that we maintain certain standards of religious observance in the home, such as eating kosher and not driving on the Sabbath.

Yet, *I* was taking nothing as a given. I felt torn, because on one hand, this was an unspoken agreement between us; but on the other hand, both Jacob and I knew what psychological damage feeling stifled by these religious restrictions had caused me in the past.

I did not want to restrict myself, my actions, my abilities, any more than my body and fate forced me to. Why take on man-made rules and structures (and strictures) when life was already hard enough?

These were the questions running through my head when I received Jacob's email.

I was in transition, in flux. I loved Jacob and the life we had together. But I needed him to give me space to grow, and I was scared he could not give me that space. I was not sure he could accept whatever it was I was evolving into.

So, I pulled back. I did not share with him what I was going through out of fear of losing him. He sensed this.

I had warned Jacob when we met that I was a complex person, not the kind of woman with whom he could settle down and know what his life would look like ten, twenty, thirty, fifty, seventy years (if I would even live that long) down the line. I was working on myself, but I was not sure the work was going to lead me to a place that would serve his needs. And even if it would, did he have the patience to wait and see? Was he reaching the breaking point I so feared he might?

I wrote back to him:

I am sorry for so many things. I take you for granted. I don't treat your parents with enough compassion, even if I know I should and would like to in my ideal view of how I want to be. I don't love myself perhaps as much as you say you love me. And I see myself as more broken than whole physically (although I am working really hard to see myself as whole in a more spiritual way as my body deteriorates, but it is hard work).

At least you know you have me if you want me, even if not as often as you'd like or as emotionally (or physically, which I add not because you tell me you find me less physically attractive, since you insist you don't, but because I have to assume my changing body has some effect on your sexual attraction to me, and also because I do sometimes feel like you don't completely understand or even believe just how debilitating my illness is) whole or self-confident or self-loving as you'd like.

And I do wonder if I will always be able to give you what you need.

I ended my email there. There was something blocking me, something preventing me from connecting with myself—body and soul. Something preventing me from making myself more vulnerable, letting go and taking life as it comes instead of creating protective walls to shield me from what would penetrate anyway.

Something was stopping me from letting my life flow and open into larger and larger bodies of water. Instead, I was damming the flow, making choices based on what others (including Jacob) might think rather than doing what my soul was telling me it needed.

Or perhaps I was not even sure what it needed and was afraid to find out. Not only because of what Jacob and others close to me would think, but also because that investigation would require me to go to wounded places I did not feel ready to explore.

I did not reveal to Jacob all that was going on inside me. I let fear hold me back from sharing my full self even with the person I most loved and appreciated in the world. Out of fear of losing him, and of losing myself.

THE SLIPPERY SLOPE INTO GRACE

IT IS SHABBAT. Hallel asks me to drive her to the climbing wall. I agree. Jacob throws me a judgmental look—driving on Shabbat, and with one of the kids, no less!—but I agree to take her, anyway.

Somehow, the younger kids figure out where we are going. They say they want to come too. It is not fair I am taking only Hallel. I say I will take them.

We decide to go by tandem bike instead of driving. I will ride in front, and they will ride in back. And now it is not just the four youngest kids; it is all the kids. All seven of them—even though the older ones are bigger than I am. They all jump on the back of the bike, while I am in the front. And we head out on the road for the climbing wall.

The ride is surprisingly easy for me, and fun. We ride up and down hill after hill. Although we are riding to the climbing wall, these are the roads Jacob rode me on each Shabbat to get to the indoor pool when that was our regular routine, the opposite direction of the climbing wall from our home.

I had never been the one in the front seat of the tandem bike before. Jacob was the one with the strength. I had to trust in him and let go. And now, here I am, the one in front, doing the steering and the pumping. I am the one with the strength, the power to lead. I have taken the front seat, and it feels great!

Suddenly, we reach an especially steep incline. The road is wet and slippery. It seems it has just rained. I tell everyone to hold on tight, and we speed down the hill. Zoooooom . . . I feel the wind in my hair—we are not wearing helmets—and I too hold on for dear life. We are speeding so quickly down the hill, that I no longer have control of the bike. Zoooooom . . . I must trust in the bike and the road and simply let go.

As we near the bottom of the hill, I see a piece of the metal road barrier is missing. There is water on the side of the road. It looks like a lake, or perhaps the ocean. I fear we are going to go straight off the road into the water. "Hold on!" I call to the kids. I squeeze the handlebars tighter, close my eyes, and surrender to what will happen. What else can I do?

THE FIRST TIME I drove on the Sabbath was to swim. When I was diagnosed, my doctor recommended swimming to keep my unaffected muscles strong. He said his patients who swim are the ones who seem to remain mobile the longest. So, I became a swimmer.

I began by swimming once or twice a week. Then three or four days a week. Then every day except *Shabbat*. But when the muscle weakness spread to my legs and feet, I started swimming on the Sabbath as well. I swim two kilometers every day. This is one of my top priorities, and so I extremely rarely miss a day.

I cannot lift my arms, and my back and abdominal muscles are weak, giving me bad posture, a protruding belly, and a sore neck and back. Walking is especially difficult, as my calf muscles are atrophied (which means not only weakness but also poor balance) and I have foot drop in both feet (I cannot lift my toes and constantly trip over them).

Exerting myself physically—which for me means simply going about my normal daily activities, like walking, sitting, standing, typing, cooking, cleaning and driving—leaves me in the kind of pain someone else would feel if they ran a marathon the day before. Swimming relieves that.

Swimming literally and figuratively keeps me afloat.

Swimming is the time I allot each day to go to another place. I let my mind wander to a dreamlike state. I find myself lost in the rhythm of the swimming and embraced by the comfort of the water. I emerge refreshed, renewed and with new energies to face what's ahead.

Swimming helps me deal with my condition. Gifting myself with a daily swim reassures me that I am taking care of myself, despite my disability.

When we moved from Jerusalem (where I could walk to the pool) to Hannaton, where the closest indoor pool is seventeen kilometers away from our home, swimming on *Shabbat* became challenging, since we did not drive on the Sabbath. We planned to build our own heated lap lane on our property, but it was taking longer than we had anticipated for the permits to be approved. Our interim solution was for Jacob to bike me to the pool via tandem bike on the Sabbath.

It was both terrifying and thrilling to ride on that treacherous route each week. The only way to get there was on a winding, hilly road with no bike lane or sidewalk. The views were lovely, and occasionally a shepherd would stop traffic to walk his flock across the road. But there were times I would close my eyes and just pray we made it back and forth alive.

Jacob is a biker and a runner. He sped down those hills, and I held on and tried not to scream. After all, he was doing me a favor by riding me to the pool each *Shabbat*. And it was a heart-warming ritual. I felt held and supported when we set out each week to the pool together, him in front, me in back, and the kids at home taking care of one another so I could swim.

Then I discovered I was pregnant. I was in my forties, the mother of six with a degenerative muscular disorder. This thrilling bike riding adventure was no longer a viable solution. I knew that swimming had become a kind of addiction, a coping mechanism, a replacement for my eating disorder. A way for me to try and control what I knew was, really, out of my control. I also knew that driving on *Shabbat* would upset Jacob.

Yet, I was not willing to let go of my *Shabbat* swim. It helped me feel I was keeping my head above water in this turbulent ocean threatening to swallow me. The ocean of life.

I decided to start driving to the pool on *Shabbat*.

This was a decision I knew was against tradition and would clearly place me outside the parameters of what is considered classically Sabbath-observant. It was a big step. I would be considered an outsider in the wider traditionally religious Jewish world. Driving on the Sabbath is a definite taboo in these circles.

As for my kibbutz community, I was not especially concerned what "the neighbors" would say, as a large portion of our kibbutz members drive on the Sabbath. Although I knew that if those members saw me, even they would be surprised, as we were known as one of the families who did not drive on *Shabbat*.

I was somewhat concerned about the judgment that might come from the families who do not drive on the Sabbath, as they considered me "one of them." People on the kibbutz are concerned about keeping a balance between those who are more traditionally observant and those who are not. Where would they place me now? That was their problem, however, not mine.

"It's a slippery slope," Jacob said. "You'll start driving to the pool, and the next thing you know, you'll be driving other places too."

"You know how sacred swimming is to me," I argued. Swimming was the one ritual to which I felt absolute certain commitment. It was each time, without fail, a spiritual experience. "You know I can easily distinguish between swimming and any other activity. You know I can draw the line there." I believed this was true. In fact, it was true. I could easily draw the line. But only if I wanted to.

Jacob, who knew me well after three decades of joining our lives together, sensed I might choose to use this opening to explore my relationship not only with the Sabbath, but with religious Jewish law, the religiously observant Jewish world, Judaism in general, and the notion of religion at all. He was correct.

The question of how far Jacob would be willing to stretch himself beyond his comfort zone to accommodate my spiritual seeking continued to plague me. But I would no longer let it prevent me from climbing to the top of the slippery slope and positioning myself for the ride down.

ONE *SHABBAT*, I awoke especially early and decided to head out for an early morning swim. The kibbutz was quiet as I got into my car. There was a chill in the air and the sun was just coming up, but I made sure to dress in layers, because when I left the pool, chances were the air would be warm and the sun hot.

And it was. As I drove out of the pool complex, I felt the late morning sun burning through the car window glass. It was early spring, and the wildflowers were at the peak of their bloom. We had good rains that year. Little dots of pink, white, yellow, and red peppered the abundant grasses on the sides of the road. A woman in the locker room had told me the lupines were out but would be gone within days.

If I kept driving, I would be home in time to catch the second half of the Sabbath morning prayer service on the kibbutz. But I did not want to be inside. And I did not want to be surrounded by people. I wanted to be alone with God. I wanted to hike out, even if at my slow pace, to see those lupines before it was too late. Time was short. Life was short. I wanted to do what I could while I still could.

Lupines. I was reminded of a children's book I love: *Miss Rumphius*. It is about a woman who, at the final stage of her life, decides to move to the seashore and spread lupine seeds wherever she goes. Eventually, the entire countryside near her beach house is covered with lupines. This was her parting gift to the world. This story moves me to tears each time I read it.

I was also reminded of images I had seen of lupines growing at the Westerbork transit camp (from where Jews were transported to Auschwitz) years after World War II was over. Lupines for me were a sign of hope, continuity and the spirit living on after death. I felt called to see those flowers now.

Before starting my studies at One Spirit, the following thought would never have occurred to me, but I was different now and saw wisdom in some of Jesus' teachings, even if I am not Christian. So, I let the thought come and did not push it away:

Jesus was right when he said this about performing healing miracles on the Sabbath: "My Father is working now, and I am working" (John 5:17). God had not stopped working, even on the Sabbath. The lupines are blooming, and my celebrating God's handiwork and finding peace and wonder in nature, is also a way to enjoy the Sabbath and heal my soul, even if it means traveling by car and missing Sabbath morning prayer services to see them.

The strict Sabbath rules created by the Rabbis went too far. My soul was telling me it needed more room to bloom. Unlike in college, I was going to listen to my soul this time when it asked for freedom, and trust that there would be meaning there for me. In the quiet, in the flowers, in just being. I would not let fear of emptiness stop me. I would listen to my inner voice. I was more mature now and with more life experience and tools at my disposal.

I drove to where the woman in the locker room had told me the lupines were especially abundant, recalling Jacob's words: "It is a slippery slope." But slippery slope implied a preferred place at the top of the slide, and a kind of falling out of grace. I felt myself falling into grace, not out of it.

I arrived at the hiking trail this woman had recommended. I parked the car and got out. I was not familiar with these trails. But I kept walking, one foot in front of the other, my dictuses helping me lift my toes and keep my balance. I chanted the Muslim prayer combined with my own adapted translation of the *Sh'ma* prayer I had already made a part of my morning Buddhist walking meditations in the fields and forest around the kibbutz: "*La ilaha illa Allah.*" There is no god except the One God. "*Sh'ma Yisrael, Adonai Eloheinu Adonai Echad.*" Listen, God–Wrestle/Immerserr: God is Me. God is All.

I spotted a large rock. It had a flat top, inviting me to sit. I spread my fleece jacket on the rock and looked out at the horizon. On one side was a mosque. On the other a church. Inside me, a Jew, was a sanctuary.

Suddenly I heard the *muezzin* calling Muslims to prayer.

> *Allah hu akbar!*
> God is the greatest!
> *Ashhadu an la ilaha illa Allah!*
> I bear witness that there is no god except the One God!
> *Hayya 'ala-s-Salah!*
> Rise up for prayer!
> *Hayya 'ala-l-Falah!*
> Rise up for salvation!

Allah hu akbar!
God is the greatest!
La ilaha illa Allah!
There is no god except the One God!

There is no god except the One God. *Adonai hu HaElohim.* That is what we say seven times at the end of the *Yom Kippur* fast each year, the time even Jews prostrate themselves, face down, like Muslims do five times each day.

I struggled to climb up on the rock. I heard voices from my childhood saying, "Jews only prostrate themselves on *Yom Kippur*," but I chose not to listen. I prostrated myself, face against fleece, feeling the blood rushing to my head, and spread my arms out in front of me (a position I could manage, unlike lifting my arms above my head in the air). It was not *Yom Kippur*, but that was fine with me. I was opening myself to life, in the Sabbath spirit.

I lifted my torso and looked up again at the horizon. I closed my eyes and went down again, and again, and again. Seven times to represent the Sabbath. My *Shabbat.* The one I was creating for myself between the cross and the crescent.

When I looked up, I saw a mountain goat staring at me. The lamb that was slaughtered in Isaac's stead. Or was it Ishmael's stead? It depended on which version you read, in the Q'uran or in Genesis. Or was it Jesus who went to the slaughter?

What is this need God (Life) has for suffering? What is this need God (Life) has, according to all three Abrahamic faiths, to see us surrender to our own inevitable suffering? And who is causing this suffering? God or humanity?

If we stop sinning (or, missing the mark, a closer translation of the Hebrew word חטא, *chet*), will we stop suffering? Or are both sin and suffering, human imperfection and sacrifice, morbidity and mortality, integral parts of life? Does the answer lie, as the mystics of all religions suggest, in this very posture I was assuming now? The posture of surrender.

As I sat there with the lupines, I saw how we are all asking the same questions and creating similar symbols to suggest answers. Yet, it took bringing me out to this place, alone with God, to begin to feel into these answers for myself. The stories our ancestors chose to tell us and that we choose to tell ourselves and our descendants, are significant in shaping who we are and giving us tools to express and identify meaning. But they are not the end in and of themselves.

These stories and symbols, coming from a system outside myself, were not enough for me. I would need to find the answers for myself. I would need to find my own symbols by looking around me at what presented itself naturally, and by looking inside myself at what my soul was saying. With the help of these symbols others before me had created, but not by relying on them to be or even give me answers.

Being fully present to life as I was in that moment felt like an answer.

But I knew when I got home, I would not tell Jacob what I had discovered or where I had been.

He was right. The "slippery slope" proved to be quite sleek indeed. It did not take long for me to go from driving to the pool and straight home, to driving to the pool and stopping along the way home to explore nature or visit a friend, to driving to the pool and continuing in an entirely different direction.

I AM STANDING at the border of Lebanon with my soldier son. He is based here as part of his combat army service, patrolling the border. We are standing at a lookout point where we can see the division between Lebanon and Israel. It is *Shabbat*.

"Those houses are Israeli," Adin explains, pointing off to the right. "And those houses are Lebanese," he says, pointing ahead of us. More human-constructed boundaries. *What is it with us humans that we need to create separation and distinction?* I ask myself. Seeing the border so near feels claustrophobic, restricting.

Yet, when I look out beyond and above the borders, at the spacious view, it is breathtaking. Awesome. The sky is cobalt blue and without a cloud. Verdant fields are spread out below in the valley, still and silent yet alive and growing. The hills surrounding us are covered with a myriad of colored flowers, all existing together in peace. There is a chill in the air as the sun sets and *Shabbat* draws to an end.

I drove to the pool, and when I finished swimming, instead of driving south, back to home, I continued driving north. I remembered Jacob's warning: "It's a slippery slope." But I had been driving to the pool anyway. I just kept going afterwards, that's all, I told myself. My son was calling, and I answered his call.

Adin has three-week shifts and comes home for only a few days between. He was lonely, he told me in a telephone conversation before *Shabbat*. Even a little depressed, he admitted. It felt imperative for me to visit. Why should he have to be lonely on the Sabbath if he doesn't have to be? For me, this felt like the most appropriate way to spend this *Shabbat*. I did not need the Rabbis to tell me how to spend it.

How would not visiting my son when he is in need give my life more meaning? How would it make the world a better place? How would it decrease human suffering? With my son serving in a combat army unit, life was presenting me with enough intense meaning of its own.

I had enough personal choices to make. Enough boundaries being set up in my life. Enough freedoms removed (from me and my son). I did not have to turn to religious Jewish law to create any of this for me. Especially when the Rabbis were instructing me to do something that conflicted with what my inner voice was telling me would give my life more meaning, purpose, and peace than what they were prescribing.

For some, choosing to buy into a system is comforting. For me, now, that only works when I trust that system, when I believe it can truly stand in for God. Otherwise, it means putting my trust in something other than God. If it does not help me truly put my trust in a Higher Power, in the unknown, it is helping me avoid not embrace true surrender. True surrender requires inner work. Meanwhile, I would continue testing my own boundaries, as well as Jacob's.

Adin's base was not exactly "on the way" from the pool—in fact, it was in the opposite direction—but it was still part of my pool outing, I told myself.

Jacob will not be happy when I tell him why I have been gone for so long, but he will not make a fuss. After all, we are both adults, and he knows I need my freedom now. However, if my parents knew how I am spending my *Shabbat*, they would tell me I am causing them to lose years from their lives.

Jesus would probably be proud—although the Christian mystics would wonder why I need to struggle at all with this issue rather than simply give it all over to God and be held by God's love.

The Rabbis would stone me. Although, to be fair, they do allow for breaking the Sabbath in order to save a life, so perhaps they would understand. The Kabbalists would say I am upsetting a divine cosmic order. Although they did practice fasting on the Sabbath—which was usually forbidden—when there was a spiritual imperative. So perhaps Jewish tradition is more flexible than I want to admit.

Buddha would say give it all over to life, since God was not in his repertoire. Or he would find it quaint, but not the goal, and would suggest meditating while on top of that mountain instead of hugging my son (after all, he left his own children behind to find ultimate bliss). I think a Hindu would get it, smiling patiently, thinking this was fine for this life stage, or this one of my incarnations.

The traditional Jewish God would be resting, since it is the Sabbath after all.

The Universe is doing what it does, totally out of my control. But Spirit is inside me, at peace for the moment. Even without the approval I so crave from those who brought me into this world, and even without the approval of he who chose to spend his life in partnership with me.

And here I am. As Abraham answered when called to sacrifice his son Isaac, and as Isaac said when his father called him to the altar: *Hineni*. Here I am.

# ORDINATION

I AM PREPARING to remarry Jacob in a second union renewal ceremony. It will be on the beach in Jaffa. But before the ceremony, a friend of mine who is studying to become a Conservative rabbi invites me to a women's group in preparation for the ceremony, in Jaffa's Old City.

I am resistant because I understand it will be an exclusively women's group, with no men allowed. I have moved beyond that stage in my life of women-only groups. I believe that to spread feminine energy in the world, we need to invite all humans into the circle. It is discriminatory to assume only women have and can appreciate and benefit from feminine energy. Anyone who is interested should be invited.

But I feel drawn to this group. My friend, who is a smart, empowered young woman, has organized it for me. I feel I should go. I want to go. Even if it feels a bit retro. I go.

And I am not sorry. It turns out there are men there. Even Jacob is there. But it is being led by women, or, more accurately, by feminine energy. That is what it is. Not a women's group, but a feminine energy group. And it is a group about supporting me to lead me to this marriage renewal ceremony. I do feel supported. I feel guided and supported and held to bring me forward to the ceremony.

I head down to the beach.

TWO DAYS BEFORE my interfaith ordination ceremony, our class had a separate vow-taking ceremony. My vows were based on words from the diary of Etty Hillesum, a woman who died in Auschwitz at age twenty-nine.

I had come across Etty's diary and letters one *Yom Kippur* several years before. I noticed the book sitting on my shelf and had no idea how it had gotten there. I did not recall having purchased it nor having received it as a gift. Yet, there it was: an obtrusive hardcover with a photograph of Etty herself on the book jacket, smoking a cigarette, her dark gray eyes peering at me, inviting me in.

I began reading the book that *Yom Kippur* night and finished it at the end of the fast the next day at nightfall. Her diary blew me away.

Etty began writing her diary at age twenty-seven, a young, angst-filled, self-absorbed, sexually and emotionally charged woman, grappling with the meaning of her life and of life in general. She was sleeping with her analyst as the Nazis marched into Amsterdam.

Through her writing, we see Etty rise above the worst of life circumstances. In the face of abominable human behavior, she remains filled with compassion for and faith in humanity. She does not go to a place of hatred or fear. Even when she has the opportunity to try and save herself, she chooses to stay in Westerbork and then go to Auschwitz, which she felt to be her calling at that time, and die with the other prisoners.

I could not put down Etty's diary. Since adolescence I had been obsessed with the Holocaust. Reading Etty's diary as an adult transported me back to my childhood when I read Anne Frank's diary for the first time. She too writes of her faith in humankind, that all people are good at heart. But here was Etty, a grown woman—there are accounts that she met Anne in Auschwitz—writing similar sentiments but on a more sophisticated level.

She writes of the Divine Spirit being in every human being, even the Nazis, even herself. She writes of the interconnectedness of all, perpetrators and victims. She writes of being fully present and full of hope in the most horrific of places. She never lost her faith in God and humankind. At least not before she was in Auschwitz. We don't know what her frame of mind was there, as she could no longer keep a diary or write letters at that point. We lose contact with her when she gets on the train to Auschwitz.

As I read Etty's words, I confronted my own greatest fears, and her example set the bar high but also showed me what is humanly possible. If only I could live that out in my own life. That was my constant question to myself: when forced out of my self-created comfort zone, when forced to relinquish control, would I be able to cope?

So many times, I had played the scenario over in my head: the bombs drop, the sirens wail, my health condition deteriorates, my life goes into chaos or peters out, my suffering becomes unbearable, the things that sustain me are taken from me—would I rise to the occasion?

Already I was being bombarded with this reality, living with an incurable degenerative debilitating and eventually life-threatening disease. And in Israel of all places. Horror, violence, hatred—they are all part of the fabric of life here. Many times, I thought I had reached my limit. Many times, I was ready to pack up and leave. But I didn't.

Of course, there were the mere logistics of making that happen: I had a partner and seven children; I was not a lone playing piece in my game of life. But I also asked myself, Who am I to pick up and leave while others cannot? Just because I am privileged enough to have an American passport, does that make me worthier of living in safety?

These are questions Etty asked herself, too, when she had a way out of going to Auschwitz. But she decided to accept her fate as a Jew in that time and place.

Besides, even in the U.S. life is not safe or terror-free. Nor are Americans free of guilt of oppression and displacing populations. Hate, suspicion, racism . . . they exist everywhere. There is no escaping any of this, just as there is no escaping death. It is part of life. The challenge is to rise above it all, like Etty did. And to face both death and evil, chaos and uncertainty, without fear.

I returned Etty's diary to the shelf but knew I would come back to it one day. And so, I was not surprised to hear Rev. Diane Berke, the founding director of One Spirit, quote from Etty's diary during the first months of my studies there.

Of course! That is where I had heard this universalist, interspiritual approach before. From Etty Hillesum. When I had read her diary, I felt I was reconnecting to an abandoned piece of myself I had long forgotten. And here I was, recovering that part of myself yet again.

For as far back as I could remember, I had sensed that the walls humans erect between "us" and "them" are false and destructive. If only we could break down those walls, there would be hope of breaking down the separation between myself and the Divine Flow.

That is how I had felt during the first lecture in my One Spirit ministry program. I sat in front of my computer, listening to Rev. Diane speak of many paths to the divine, and my heart broke open. As Etty herself wrote, "Time and again I have had to learn how spacious the heart can be, and time and again I have had to reclaim that space." This was the true language of my soul.

A month before flying to New York for my ordination ceremony, I encountered Etty yet again. I received an invitation to participate in an intimate ceremonial evening commemorating *Yom HaShoah*, Israeli Holocaust Memorial Day. The ceremony was to be run by three women: a German Catholic, an Israeli Jew, and a Palestinian Christian. And it was inspired by the writings of Etty Hillesum.

I knew I had to go, and I am glad I did—even if I had to drive two hours each way in one evening. This was the first time I heard the term "Etty-ist," but when I did, I knew that if I had to choose to be some kind of "ist," it was an Etty-ist, because she too was beyond all "isms" and "ists."

The message of the event was that until Germans, Jews, and Palestinians sit together and face their triangle of pain, the pain will continue to reverberate from generation to generation. We shared, we sang, we cried, and we read from Etty's diary. It was a magical evening.

If any "ism" can help dig us out of the cycles of hate and hurt we humans continue to perpetuate, it is "Etty-ism." (Although not in the sense of a personality cult. Etty was no guru and should not be treated as one, but rather as a very human and flawed inspiration.) Keep sending out love and compassion while surrendering to and being fully present in what is, Etty's diary teaches us. This was just the lesson I needed. My stretch. My learning curve in this incarnation.

And so, when I stood before my classmates and took my vows, I returned to Etty. I adapted some of my most cherished quotes from her diary into my own ministry vows. This is what I said:

Wherever I happen to find myself, I vow to do my best to be there with my whole heart; and to safeguard that little piece of You, God, in myself. And in others as well. You cannot help me, but I must help You and defend Your dwelling place inside of me, and others, to the last. Because ultimately, I have just one moral duty: to reclaim large areas of peace within me, more and more peace, and to reflect it towards others.

As I recited my vows, I remembered how moved I had been by Etty's diary but did not know what to do with her teachings back then. Although I did quote her in my second memoir, I had put the diary aside and carried on. No one in my world then had talked about this woman. Perhaps because her approach can be seen as Christian or Buddhist, Jews never claimed her as one of their own, like they did Anne Frank, Primo Levi, or Elie Wiesel.

But Etty was not a Christian or a Buddhist. Nor was she a strictly practicing Jew, although her belief in God and in the human ability to choose good over evil and make the world a better place was unshaken by the horror surrounding her. And although she did decide to die as a Jew even when she could have tried to save herself.

If I could just emulate one tiny piece of this woman, I would be on my way towards finding inner peace. She embodied what I had been looking for and found when I read her diary. Pure love. Pure compassion. Pure spirituality in the worst possible conditions. And no self-pity or resentment.

If she could face that with such faith and dignity, I could face what life had in store for me, too.

FOR THE REST of the day after our vow-taking ceremony, my seminary cohort and I were asked to remain in silence. I decided to take the silent time to walk and think.

I walked around the grounds of the retreat center. It was a hot and humid day, and the air weighed on me like my relationship with my parents. The fact that I could not tell my parents I was in New York felt both absurd and inevitable. It pained me I could not share this milestone in my life with them, could not be my full self around them—out of fear of shattering our relationship and my spirit.

My parents would not celebrate this step in my life. At best, they would ridicule it; at worst, they would tell me I had gone too far this time, throwing away everything that was important to them, everything they had tried to give me. Their parenting of me had been a failure, they would say. My inviting them to this event would cause them grief not pride. Asking them to support me in this milestone was asking too much of them, I knew. So, I had told them nothing about it.

I walked and walked, until I came upon a church with a graveyard. I recited my vows, passing gravestones, centuries old, with Christian symbols—rosaries, crosses, crucifixes, flowers. *Our love and God's light go with you.* I repeated my vows over and over in my head as I continued walking, trying to make myself worthy of reciting my adaptation of Etty Hillesum's words.

I wandered through and around the graves, reading the stones. Some went as far back as the seventeenth century. I spotted a man tending a grave.

"Hello there!" he called out to me.

I was supposed to be in silence, but he didn't know that, and I did not want to be rude. "Hello," I answered.

The man told me he tended the graves of his family who had passed. His family went back generations in this town, in this church. His words felt like a personal reprimand, although he did not mean it that way. He had no way of knowing I live in Israel, thousands of miles from my own parents. I was disconnected. I had disconnected myself.

Why? Why had I run? On one hand, I had run back to my homeland, my "true roots": Israel, the home of the Jewish people. That is the narrative I had told myself and others back when we made the big move. But I also knew there was another story to tell.

I had run to get far enough away to be myself. Part of becoming myself, I had not realized back then but knew now, meant denying the very notion that the land I lived on was any more my home than it was the home of my

Palestinian-Israeli neighbors living across the road and the valley. It meant denying that Judaism is the ultimate Truth, and that modern Orthodox Judaism is the best way of life for me and my children. These were notions my parents would never accept, even if I was living in the Jewish homeland.

I could barely hold back my tears before continuing my walk among the gravestones. When the man was out of sight, the tears came. I could run and run, and I could even be myself, but I would never get my parents' approval if I took that path. They would still love me, even if I frustrated and upset them. That I knew. But they would not celebrate me. Why did that shatter me so?

Surrounded by gravestones, I thought of my own birth. My parents brought me into this world. That is why their approval mattered so much. If they approved of my life's course, that would give my life legitimacy and purpose. Without their approval, my life would feel like a big mistake.

I stopped in my tracks. There was a huge cross on the gravestone in front of me. The inscription read: *Sarah Jones Peterson. Her spirit lives on in our hearts.* A trite saying to put on a gravestone perhaps, but still so true. What is that spirit that lives on after we pass? Did we get that from our parents, or from some other source greater than our individual finite and mortal reality?

The Talmud says there are three partners in the conception of a human being—the mother, the father and God. God. Suddenly it struck me: God loves me unconditionally. God. Is that the spirit that lives on even after we pass? Is that the me inside of me that remains truly me no matter how I evolve?

If I have the courage to be fully and genuinely me, if I have the courage to love myself enough to let that spirit inside me show, that means God celebrates me no matter what. I did not need my parents to celebrate me. This was my path, not theirs. God celebrates me. And I am God, and God is me. I celebrate me. And that *is* enough.

We all have our boundaries and needs. My parents as much as me or anyone else. I could respect their boundaries and values without having to feel guilty for not choosing the same ones for myself, even if it hurt them, and even if it hurt me to know I was disappointing them. Part of being an adult is being able to own our choices and take responsibility for their ramifications.

I didn't blame my parents for their inability to meet my need to be seen and celebrated for who I am by those who brought me into this world. I would have to find validation for my existence elsewhere. They had their own need to pass on their values to their descendants to give their own lives meaning. I respected that, as painful as it was. But I would not let the pain I was causing nor the pain I was experiencing stop me from moving forward authentically in my own life. My parents, too, would have to find validation for their existence elsewhere. That was not my responsibility.

That is when I saw her: a beautiful black butterfly, with green and white trim. She fluttered onto a flower and sat there, still as a rock. I had been in the gift shop before setting off on this walk, and I had been taken with a bookmark with the following words printed onto it: *Transformation: A caterpillar thinks it has reached the end, only to become a butterfly!*

Etty did reach the end, and she became a butterfly. What a humbling lesson to me: a lesson not to fear, to instead embrace what comes my way. Because that is the only way I can become what I am meant to become.

I remembered the memoir of Elizabeth Kubler-Ross (author of the famous *On Death and Dying*), *The Wheel of Life*, where she tells of how she visited the Majdanek concentration camp soon after the end of World War II, when she went to Poland to volunteer. She writes of how struck she was by the repeated images of butterflies she saw inmates had carved onto the barrack walls before going to their deaths, which reminded me also of the book of poems by children in Theresienstadt, *I Never Saw Another Butterfly*. She writes of how it took her twenty-five years to understand what those inmates had learned back then.

These are the final words of her memoir, as she is dying from a massive stroke. It is a prolonged death full of suffering, but also, she is convinced, lessons she still needs to learn before she can pass:

> Right now, I am learning patience and submission. As difficult as those lessons are, I know that the Highest of High has a plan. I know that He has a time that will be right for me to leave my body the way a butterfly leaves its cocoon . . .
>
> Our only purpose in life is growth . . . You should live until you die . . . And at the end of your days, you will bless your life because you have done what you came here to do. Dying is nothing to fear. It can be the most wonderful experience of your life. It all depends on how you have lived . . . Everything is bearable when there is love. My wish is that you try to give more people more love. The only thing that lives forever is love.

I had not been fooling myself back in college, when I fell in love with Jacob. Love can give life meaning. Perhaps it can be the most meaningful thing there is in life. Not as a substitute for fulfilling one's life mission, not as a substitute for truly living, but as a manifestation of it, because in order to love, one must relinquish control. And sometimes, love itself can be the mission. Spreading love. A more universal kind of love. For if we all trust in life and in one another, the world will be transformed.

When I came back to my room, I checked my email. I had two messages from Jacob.

I opened the first:

> There was a terrorist attack in Tel Aviv today. Four people were
> killed. In the Max Brenner chocolate shop.

I knew this chocolate shop was one of Jacob's hangouts. He is a chocoholic. He and our daughter Michal had just eaten lunch there together a week or so before.

My heart sank. Here I was being tested right before my ordination. The spiritual crisis that had sent me to One Spirit was right there glaring me in the eyes. The violence. The hatred. Here I was sitting in my room in this idyllic interfaith community, talking of love and interspirituality, and people were killing each other back at home in the name of God. Would I be able to fully commit to doing this work in the difficult Israeli reality once I returned?

I closed my eyes, took a deep breath and began to recite my vows. "Wherever I happen to find myself, I vow to do my best to be there with my whole heart . . ."

I opened the second email. Jacob had forwarded me an internet article about the ordination of a group of men and women by an Orthodox rabbi with whom I had studied in a similar group years before. Yet then, he had ordained only the men.

This was over ten years ago, when he did not feel the Orthodox world was ready for women rabbis. He also told me he would never ordain me, even if one day he ordained women, because he disagreed with my public campaign for women's ordination. He felt this was the wrong approach; he felt I was doing it just for the publicity.

In addition, I had had a difficult personal interaction with this man. At the time I was studying with him, I was organizing a seminar for our group of rabbis-in-training, and I invited a speaker who, unbeknownst to me, was apparently this rabbi's rival. He called me on the phone, enraged. He did not let me get a word in between his shouts. And then he hung up.

I cried. And then, when I got over it, since it was the eve of the Jewish holiday of *Purim*, I brought him the traditional *mishloach manot*, a basket of fruits and other edibles, and wrote him a long letter of apology, explaining

I did not know about his fraught relationship with this other rabbi. If I had known, I would not have invited him.

The rabbi, whom I shall call Rabbi X, never answered my letter. And I moved past it, studied with Rabbi Strikovsky and was ordained by him privately—not in a group, but I had already learned that it was often my fate in life to forge ahead alone.

A few years later, on the eve of *Yom Kippur*, the real Day of Atonement (as opposed to the "mini" Day of Atonement of *Purim*), Rabbi X's secretary invited me to his office. She did not say why. But I went. When I walked into his office, three witnesses—all friends of mine who worked for the institution where this rabbi was religious dean—were sitting waiting for me.

Rabbi X asked, in front of these witnesses, for my forgiveness. I said I would have to think about it. He asked me again. Again, I said I could not answer him on the spot. I did not sense any regret in his voice. I did not feel he had done any inner work.

He asked me again and told me I could leave. He had fulfilled his religious Jewish legal obligation of asking for forgiveness three times before *Yom Kippur*. My acceptance of his apology did not matter anymore.

I was aghast. Shocked. He was a rabbi. He was supposed to be a spiritual and moral role model. His behavior left me appalled and confused, and certainly disillusioned. And now, here was this same rabbi ordaining women, after all these years.

I closed my laptop. I felt surprisingly calm. I felt no regret or anger or resentment. I was simply not in that place anymore. I was no longer Orthodox. That fight was no longer mine. The article was calling this a historic event, calling these women the first Orthodox women rabbis to be ordained publicly. There was no mention of me or other women who had done the same or paved the way.

I did not care. I wished these new Orthodox women rabbis well. And while I could not bring myself to wish Rabbi X well, I did not wish him ill. I felt surprisingly neutral. Like a woman in my One Spirit class, who had said this the day before about her dream of women being ordained as Catholic deacons: "I am just so beyond the Catholic Church, the Pope, and his deacons!"

AFTER MY ORDINATION, I wrote an email to Rabbi X, expressing my feelings of having been emotionally abused by him and by his use of the Jewish religious legal system and ritual to absolve himself without doing the inner work.

A week or so later, I received an email from him. He said he would like to speak to me on the phone, if I was willing to talk. I agreed. When we spoke, he said he had been journaling about my email since he received it, reflecting, looking inside. Something about him had been transformed.

We spoke. He sounded genuinely remorseful now, after all these years. He had done the inner work. And I was ready to not only forgive him, but to wish him well. I was trying to integrate Elizabeth Kubler-Ross' and Etty Hillesum's words into my life: like Miss Rumphius did with her lupines, I would do my best to try and spread more love, beauty, and peace to the pieces of the world I touched.

THE DAY BEFORE our ordination, our cohort held a purification ceremony in which we wrote four letters, which we then burned: one was to our mothers, one to our fathers, one to ourselves, and one to another significant person in our lives.

> Dear Jacob,
>
> I realize I have pushed you sometimes beyond your comfort zone, testing your loyalty and love. I know that when we married at age twenty-one, we were on a more similar path. Without inflicting too much guilt, you have supported my changes and growth.
>
> I know you have changed as well over the years. But I have changed more. I have pushed you more than you have pushed me. And some of your changes were because of mine, not necessarily because you would have chosen that path if I had not pushed you.
>
> It was not unfair for me to allow myself to grow, even if it meant upsetting our relationship. I cannot be untrue to myself. I hope you understand that.
>
> What was unfair was my expectation from you to fill the role I wanted my parents to fill. That of providing unconditional celebration. It is not your job any more than it is theirs.
>
> I would love for you, and them, to celebrate me unconditionally. But I now, finally, understand, that God celebrates me when I celebrate myself. If I see the spark of the divine in myself, I should not need to know others see it in me. Me celebrating me should be enough.

Perhaps you are grateful for some of the ways in which I pushed you. Perhaps there is resentment about others. I am not apologizing or expressing regret. Just recognition. And deep, deep appreciation.

Thank you. I love you.

ME

I AM STANDING in line at the entrance to the main sanctuary of Riverside Church. It is vast and grand and has a history of social activism for human rights causes. Two rows of One Spirit graduates are about to be ordained. After two years of intense and transformative study, I will walk out of this church today Rabbi Rev. Dr. Haviva Ner-David: a post-denominational interspiritual rabbi minister. I hope to wear my new title as if my soul is my clothing for all to see.

My actual clothing is all white. Representing my pure soul. Purity, not virginity. My new *tallit*, one that I and a dear artist friend from the kibbutz designed and created for this occasion, is wrapped around me. My *atarah*, or collar-piece, is adorned with this verse from one of my favorite Jalal Ad-Din Muhammad Rumi poems: *All Religions. All Singing. One Song.*

My walking partner for the procession is a Catholic-raised lesbian massage therapist with a rainbow mantle hanging from around her neck over her plump breasts. She winks at me. We are in this together.

I look around. No friends or family from my past are here to support me, yet I feel held. Loved. My parents live half an hour's ride from Riverside Church, but it might as well be another universe.

How did a nice Jewish girl from the Orthodox New York suburbs get here today? I ask myself as I prepare for this monumental life step.

I remember a writing prompt from a workshop in which I participated: *What is the shape of your life?* I wrote how I do not think of my life in terms of shapes, rather in terms of water:

My life began as a narrow stream, feeding into a river widening slowly, until it will, one day, feed into an ocean. I don't know when that will be, nor what that ocean will look like. But I am certain there will be rapids as well as meandering currents, rocks as well as clear paths, cold as well as warm waters. All moving in one direction and opening, slowly but steadily, along the way — until one day, all flows into the one vast ocean that is the One.

I close my eyes and imagine myself an ocean pouring back into the primordial waters. I am not afraid.

The large wooden double doors swing wide open to expose an imposing church sanctuary, complete with a huge silver cross on the pulpit. The organ music starts. We walk in, two by two, like Noah's animals. Will we be able to save humanity from this flood of violence, hate and divisiveness that seems to be destroying the world? The most we can do is try and, like the Buddhist teaching says, be unattached to the outcome.

Reverend Diane Berke, who is of Jewish descent, stands at the podium, dressed in white robes. The mantel hanging over her breasts displays a Cross, a Star-and-Crescent, the Star of David, the Yin/Yang symbol, the OM icon, the Medicine Wheel, the Dharma Wheel, and the Circle of Life representing all Earth-based religions. All golden. All taking up equal space on her ministerial garb.

As she opens her arms and motions for us to sit, her wide sleeves form wings at her sides. She is an angel—one of the many angels who have brought me, humble and proud, to this moment.

An altar with symbols from many of the world's major religions stands in the front of the sanctuary. I meditate on my main revelation about religion during these past two years:

All the major world faiths are, in their essence—when one puts aside the layers of tribalism, elitism, sin, guilt, dogma, prejudice, exclusiveness, corruption, and misinterpretation—about love, compassion, surrender, interconnection, and spiritual practice. The rituals, ceremonies, prayers, and terminology may be different, and there may be different nuances to what is emphasized and how you can reach a state of peace with yourself, your fellow humans, and the divine. But for all, that is the ultimate goal. This is the mystic core of all faiths.

I meditate on the interconnectedness of all as I await my turn.

Reverend David Wallace joins Reverend Berke at the altar. I watch as each of my classmates stands, silently, to be ordained, as their turn approaches. Rev. Diane touches their foreheads. Rev. David pulls energies from the air. Rev. Diane whispers something in their ears. The Tibetan singing bowl sounds. It all looks straightforward. Yet, the faces of each of my classmates glow as they sit down blissfully after being ordained. I wonder what magic is going on up there at the altar. I will have to await my turn to find out.

My rabbinic ordination was over ten years before, and it had been a private ordination, with no ceremony and no institutional backing. All it entailed was the writing of the document, which Rabbi Strikovsky signed, and which now hangs on my office wall.

A rabbi friend of mine, who was ordained by Jewish Renewal founder Rabbi Zalman Schachter-Shalomi a few years before his death, insisted there be a public celebration. We brought together a circle of my close friends and colleagues to officially mark my ordination. But still, there was no laying-on of hands by the rabbi ordaining me, no ceremonial display of the passing on of title or status, no public recognition of the years I had spent in study and reflection with him as my teacher and mentor.

When it is my turn to go up, I take a deep breath, put my *tallit* over my head, preparing to stand between these two spiritual leaders and role models. Revs Diane and David are among some of the more brilliant, spiritually centered, socially conscious people I have met. I remember my father telling me my mind was so open my brains would fall out. Well, if my brains have fallen out, so have theirs. I am in good company.

I take a deep breath and begin my ascent. I hope I will not trip or fall. Even with my trusty dictuses attached to my shoes, I am prone to falling. What a scene that would be. Although if that is what is meant to be, then let it be, I say to myself. I will be with what is.

I make it up to the altar as if carried by angels.

Rev. Diane is seated in front of me, and Rev. Wallace behind me. Still standing, I close my eyes and bow my head. I feel Rev. Diane's finger touch my forehead. The smell of a mixture of essential oils and incense fills my nostrils: Myrtle? Sage? Palo Santo? I am not sure. But it is potent.

I feel a rush of movement next to my right ear. Energy being transferred. My body sways, yet I do not worry I will fall. I feel held. Supported. Accepted. Loved. By the Universe.

THE NEXT MORNING, after ordination, I met some of my classmates at Unity Church on the Upper West Side. Together with these friends, I had attended Friday night synagogue services at a popular Jewish Renewal synagogue the night before our ordination. As newly ordained interfaith-interspiritual ministers, we had decided to go to both church and synagogue as a group surrounding our ordination experience. We would have liked to attend the Friday morning mosque service too, but we only returned from our preparatory retreat on Friday afternoon.

A visiting preacher sang a mix of Gospel and New Age and then spoke about her journey from crack and heroin addiction to the Twelve Steps and Unity Church. She was a charismatic speaker, and her story was inspiring.

The set-up was too frontal for my taste in spiritual experience, but I did appreciate the messages of self-improvement, the divine within, and the connectedness of all.

When a man stood and announced the church community would be marching together at the Gay Pride Parade the following week, he referred to the massacre earlier that morning in Florida. This was the first I heard of the Orlando shooting in a gay bar in the middle of the previous night, leaving fifty-one people dead. I was horrified. I felt my heart pounding. Terror was everywhere, not only in the tiny country in which I chose to live.

Later that day, I joined some One Spirit friends and went downtown to an interfaith vigil at Judson Church in the East Village. It was consoling to hear priests, imams and rabbis speaking against fundamentalism and violence in the name of religion. It was uplifting to lock arms and sing songs of peace from all three Abrahamic religions, to join voices in a rendition of "We Shall Overcome" and promise ourselves to choose love over fear.

The next morning, I joined more One Spirit classmates in signing up at City Hall as wedding officiants. Huge gay pride rainbow flags adorned City Hall—a strong and important statement after the homophobic bloodbath the day before. I snapped a photo and sent it to my gay brother in Boston, my gay and lesbian friends in Israel. Then I entered City Hall and signed the huge registry of wedding officiants.

After years of carrying a rabbinic title that awarded me no official authority or privileges, it was affirming to be recognized by an official body for my years of study and work. Yet I knew that back at home, in Israel, I would still not be recognized by the government as a rabbi or a minister and could not legally officiate a religious ceremony—not just an interfaith one, but any marriage, even between two born-and-bred straight Jews.

After signing the registry and saying my last goodbyes to my One Spirit colleagues—some of whom I would probably never see again, as they lived in Australia, New Zealand, Trinidad, Texas, Canada, California—I went a few blocks over to the site of Ground Zero, where the 9/11 Twin Towers terrorist attack had taken place. The Freedom Tower had just been completed, and I had never seen the memorial pools created in the footsteps of the Towers.

The day was sunny but cool for June. I leaned over one of the square black holes and watched the water rush down the sides into a smaller inner square hole. The memorial evoked in me a mix of feelings and images—hope and despair, water and abyss, life and death. I noticed that the hole where the Tower once stood was framed with the names of those who had tragically been at the Tower and did not make it out. I wanted to know the story of every one of those names.

One name jumped out at me. Guy Bar Zvi. I assumed he was an Israeli who had moved to New York, thinking he had escaped danger and hatred. I googled his name on my smart phone. I had not been far off. His parents, Israelis, children of Holocaust survivors, had been the ones to move to the U.S., where he was born. Atheists, they did not sit *shiva* for their son. They said their son's death made them even more sure there was no God.

Guy was twenty-nine years old when he was killed. Like Etty Hillesum. Again, I recited my vows:

"Wherever I find myself, I vow to do my best to be there with my whole heart . . ."

I would head home to Israel and do my best to be there with my whole heart. I would try to cultivate a feeling of peace within myself and spread it, more and more peace, out to others. I would remember the divine in myself and in others, too. I took some water from the edge of the waterfall and spread it over Guy's name. I would choose hope over despair, love over fear. At least I would try.

On my way back to the uptown subway, I stopped in at Trinity Church, where volunteers slept, ate and prayed for nine months after 9/11. There is an exhibit in the church describing how volunteers and city employees from all faiths gathered in the church to work together to help in whatever way they could. Interfaith services were held, food was distributed, free massage and medical care were offered.

A sign in the exhibit reads: "Here there was no distinction between religion, color, race or sex. That message will live on!"

I walked over to the altar and lit a candle. Above the altar, Jesus hangs on the cross. I had never identified with the crucifix image before, but now I felt the suffering. So much suffering in the world. My own and others' suffering from illness. Suffering from crime, violence, hatred. Senseless killing. Ideological killing. Jesus died for our sins, like the biblical scapegoat. To relieve us, perhaps, Jesus suffered the consequences of humanity's imperfection in our stead.

Well, I did not feel the relief. I felt the weight of the suffering. Jesus was another victim of religious and political murder. In the face of evil and corruption, he preached love and compassion. His reaction when suffering, like that of Etty Hillesum, was inspiring. "Father, forgive them. They know not what they do," is a lofty ideal to try and emulate.

I did not relate to the notion that Jesus or Etty died for our sins. What gave me comfort were the stories of people working together to relieve whatever suffering they could, even, or especially, that caused by humans. This too is a message Jesus espouses in his teachings.

I looked up again at Jesus hanging on the cross and noticed above the crucifix the Hebrew letters: יהוה, the sacred letter combination of the Divine Name. This one of God's names has always evoked for me the name of God at the burning bush: "אהיה אשר אהיה. I Will Be What I Will Be." God, Life, the Universe, will be what it will be.

Simultaneously holding both our divinity and our humanity, our wholeness and our brokenness, our perfection and our imperfection, our soul's immortality and our body's mortality, is part of the dance we call life. As is holding the suffering inevitably part of that dance. Jesus did not suffer instead of us; he suffered like us. So much suffering, and all we can do is surrender. I saw that message in Jesus' limp body and remembered these three quotations from Etty's diary:

"Suffering is not beneath human dignity. I mean it is possible to suffer with dignity and without. I mean: Most of us in the West don't understand the art of suffering and experience a thousand fears instead. We cease to be alive, being full of fear, bitterness, hatred and despair."

"One moment it is Hitler, the next it is Ivan the Terrible; one moment it is inquisition and the next war, pestilence, earthquake, or famine. Ultimately, what matters most is to bear the pain, to cope with it, and to keep a small corner of one's soul unsullied, come what may."

"Even as we die a terrible death, we are able to feel right up to the very last moment that life has meaning and beauty, that we have realized our potential and lived a good life."

God is simply what will be. God is life as it unfolds. That is meaning enough. It is to that we must surrender. Because, really, do we have any other choice?

WHEN I RETURNED home to my kibbutz, I decided to leave my comfort zone and mark this major life transition not at the *mikveh*, my usual place for transition ceremonies, but in the kibbutz synagogue. I had been studying for two years and felt myself transformed by the experience, yet I had not shared any of this with more than a handful of people on the kibbutz—those I knew would understand and not ridicule my decision.

It felt important to go public with my new title in this tiny community of mine, rather than do an intimate transition ceremony with myself. I was not looking for their approval, but it is customary in our community for people to mark milestones in public, whether with a party, a ceremony or a sharing circle, and it was not my intention to keep this step in my journey secret.

I celebrated my ordination on *Shabbat* by reading from the Torah scroll as part of the regular Sabbath day prayer service. When I was called up to the Torah—"Arise, Rabbi Haviva the daughter of Daniel Ze'ev and Rachel Syrel!" the *gabbai* chanted—I arose from my chair and walked up to the *bimah* where the Torah scroll was laid out on a table, waiting to be read aloud to the congregation, as was being done that Sabbath in thousands of other Jewish congregations around the world.

The first time I had read from a Torah scroll was at my adult bat mitzvah, at age twenty-two, ten years after my childhood bat mitzvah. (At that childhood celebration, I had not read from the Torah scroll. Only male members of a strictly Orthodox congregation perform that public ritual.) Yet, like many other practices which were off limits to me as a female in my childhood, I had taken this upon myself despite the feeling of taboo. I had read from the Torah scroll many times in my life by now. Everything was so familiar, yet I knew I was different.

I recited the blessing. "Blessed are You Adonai our Lord, our God, Majestic Spirit of the Universe, who chose us along with the nations and gave us divine teachings; blessed are You the giver of the Torah." The words to the traditional blessing are, actually, "who chose us *from among* the nations," but I could no longer recite those words. I leaned over the ancient parchment, donning my Rumi *tallit* with pride, and read the section I had chosen to read from among the various options of the week's portion.

The text was about how, when the Israelites were to enter the Promised Land and offer sacrifices to God, they should include all the residents of the land, not just the Israelites. I had chosen this reading from the weekly Torah portion because of its interspiritual message. The sacrifices were not meant just for the Israelite nation; they were meant for anyone who wanted to partake of and participate in that religious ritual.

After receiving a public blessing from another rabbi in my community, a rabbi who was ordained in the Reform movement, I addressed the congregation. I explained why I had decided to study to become an interfaith minister, what interspirituality was about.

My hands were shaking. I wondered how this news would be received. Would I be considered too radical? Crazy? Had I gone too far? Would my interfaith ordination invalidate my rabbinic ordination in the eyes of my community? I hoped not, but I was willing to suffer the consequences of transparency and honesty. It could be no other way. Besides, I was not looking for anyone's approval. I was marking this life transition for me.

There were some quizzical looks from those seated before me. But there were also some interested eyes. And a few people came over after the service to congratulate me and to inquire more about the program and this new direction my spiritual life had taken. No one raised this new development as a reason to remove me from my post as Chair of the community's *mikveh* committee, nor to question the kosher status of the *mikveh* knowing a post-denominational interspiritual rabbi was now running it.

I had spoken my truth, opened myself to what would be, and found at least my little world ready to accept Rabbi Reverend Dr. Haviva Ner-David.

WHO LEFT THE FAUCET RUNNING?

I AM WALKING with my friend, who serves with me on the kibbutz synagogue committee; we are on our way to the synagogue for Friday night services. It was my turn to wash the synagogue floor this week, which I did earlier that day. We are going there ahead of everyone else to set up. When we get to the synagogue, we see the building is in a cage with a bicycle lock on the front door. The synagogue walls are melting, becoming water streaming out through the bars of the cage.

"I guess I forgot to turn off the faucet," I say to my friend. "My mistake."

"Mistake, huh?" my friend says, winking at me.

ONE MIGHT HAVE assumed ordination would be the end of this leg of my journey. But it was not. Those two years in interfaith seminary prepared me to minister to people interested in a broader definition of religion and spirituality. They also helped me conclude that all religious faiths—even my own Jewish faith—are at their most central mystical level trying to help us humans get through life with as much dignity, purpose and inner peace as we can manage.

Yet, after ordination, I found myself, in my own life, still resisting the label "religious." Spiritual, yes, but religious, no. I did find wisdom in the ancient faith traditions, but I found myself resisting a commitment to any set or regular religious practices. I had let go of *tefillin* as a daily practice, and I found I could no longer pray on a daily, or even weekly, basis. I could not even take on a regular meditation practice, as my seminary mentors had been encouraging me to do.

I was not only driving on the Sabbath now, but I was letting go of most traditional Sabbath restrictions. I found not only Judaism, but all religion, restricting. I wanted the wisdom without the restrictions. I wanted to learn to deal with life as it presented itself organically, without manufacturing systems of false security and protection. I wanted to learn to relinquish control.

I heard my soul telling me I had been using religion and its practices to bypass the core of my spiritual longing, to avoid addressing my deeper wounds. My soul was asking for freedom, yet I had been answering by giving it structure. Perhaps what I needed was to push myself past my comfort zone of taking on yet another rule or practice to connect to something higher, and instead look deeper *inside* myself and examine why I felt this need for the structure of a system *outside* myself.

I had been assuming the answers to my existential questions lay in religion. But perhaps there were no answers. Perhaps it was the mystery I needed to embrace. As terrifying as it seemed, I had a sense what I needed most was to enter the abyss of my own unconscious, and trust that Spirit would hold me there and safely guide me to my soul, to discovering its deepest pain and yearnings.

I decided to enroll for another two years at One Spirit, but this time in the Interspiritual Counseling (ISC) program, where I would study to become a certified spiritual counselor. Some also use the terms spiritual director or companion, and later, the program's name was changed to the Interspiritual Companioning and Counseling (ISCC) program. I personally prefer the term spiritual companion. This work is about holding space for others in non-judgment and sincere curiosity to help them find their own answers.

When we were briefly introduced to this work in the ministry program, I felt an immediate attraction. I realized how much my own wounds were about feeling judged. How healing it was to be seen as whole, just as I was, to understand deeply that I did not need to be "fixed," even if I had growing left to do.

My studies for rabbinic ordination had included only Talmud and Jewish religious law. I had not gained any pastoral skills. I had not studied anything to teach me to be with and hold space for people in a rabbinic role. Since so much of my rabbinic work includes accompanying people at sensitive times in their lives, at the *mikveh*, this training was important. Until then, I had been working on intuition. This program would help me gain that knowledge and experience.

Moreover, I could use the spiritual counseling skills to broaden my *mikveh* work to include spiritual counseling prior to immersion, to help clients create personalized immersion ceremonies and *kavanot*, sacred intentions, for their immersions. This seemed like a practical next step in my rabbinic training.

When I applied to the program and learned more about it, I understood that a big part of the experience would be doing our own inner work. In order to help others heal, we must first tend to our own sacred wounds. If we had dug deep in the ministry program, in this program we were going to hit water. This thought was frightening, but I knew it was time.

As Hillel the Sage in Ethics of the Fathers says, "If I am not for myself, who will be for me? And if I am only for myself, what am I? And if not now, when?"

Signing up for One Spirit's ISC program meant making the slope even more slippery, since it would mean being on a webinar one full Saturday and Sunday each month. The Ministry program allowed me to listen to the classes by audio book after they were held, in conjunction with the homework, study group meetings, and meetings with my advisors and mentors (which I was able to set at non-*Shabbat* times on Zoom); but since the ISC program is highly interactive, I had to commit to being "in the room," meaning participating through the computer screen, while classes were happening.

Since the classes were held in New York and began at nine a.m., that meant being on the webinar before the Sabbath ended on Saturdays. Until then, I had not used a computer on the Sabbath. I knew Jacob would not approve, but to me, being in a spiritual seminar on *Shabbat* felt right.

And so, one September Saturday afternoon, I found myself sitting in front of my laptop screen, participating in the first session of this two-year program. The speaker was leading us in a guided visualization. This time, we were working on tapping into our Higher Selves. Our teacher took us on a journey through our seven chakras, the focal energetic points in our bodies.

Chakra is Sanskrit for wheel. When our life force, or *prana*, rotates evenly and smoothly throughout our bodies, we are in physical, mental, spiritual and emotional balance. According to this ancient Hindu tradition, *prana* rotates among seven points in our bodies that mirror our emotional, mental and spiritual states.

In an emotionally and physically healthy person, the seven chakras provide the right balance of energy to every part of the body, mind, and spirit. By checking in with the state of each of your chakras and tending to those that need adjustment on all levels of your being, you can live a more harmonious life.

When I learned about the chakras in the program's Hinduism month, I was taken with how similar this ancient wisdom is to the Kabbalistic (Jewish mystic) *sefirot* and their connection to parts of the human body—just one example of the similarity among the mystical cores of all faiths.

The woman leading us in the guided visualization started with our first *chakra*, where we find grounding in our own bodies. Sitting firmly on my seat, I did feel grounded in my life, despite my seeking. It was an interesting juxtaposition of knowing I am where I need to be, yet also knowing there is more movement to come.

She then brought us to our second *chakra*, from where our emotions and passions flow. I knew I had some blockage there to explore, some emotions kept inside needing to be released. Water is my element, yet I knew there was a lack of flow in need of addressing, and I was not sure how that would play out. I was feeling open, though, to trying.

She asked us to move to our third *chakra*, where we find our power, our fire, what moves us forward in this world. From the outside, it perhaps appeared as if my life had been about doing, achieving, working to make my mark in the world. I knew my path and I followed it, even as the direction changed. But I often felt alone, misunderstood, a woman with a message people were not ready to hear. And so, I pulled back, retreated into myself. *Why push my message on others?*

When we arrived at the fourth *chakra*, the heart *chakra*, the place of compassion, openness, connection and love, I knew my heart could be so open. I did have much love to give, and I gave it. But my heart clenched, too, when triggered, and I knew that was something I needed to examine.

Next was the fifth *chakra*, located in the throat, the seat of expression. I am all about expression, telling my story. I do it in writing. And yet orally, only when called upon to do so. I will not debate. I hate to argue. I know my truth and am happy to share it with those who want it. I let them choose if they want to open the book. *Should I be pushing myself more to make my truth heard?* I asked myself.

Then we reached the sixth *chakra*, which is located between the eyes. Someone with a strong sixth *chakra* tends to see the world through the "third eye," tuning into a more spiritual realm, a plane where everything and everyone is connected. With our third eye, we recognize those connections and patterns when we are observing closely and listening carefully enough. When I moved into the sixth *chakra*, I felt I had come home.

The seventh *chakra* is at the top of the head: the crown. It is the place of divine connection. It is where we touch Spirit, God, the One—whatever name you use to name the un-nameable. Sometimes we touch this place through meditation, total immersion in water, chanting, looking up at a clear night sky, sitting at the peak of a mountain or by a quiet stream. And sometimes we can even take the plunge into this place of unknowing for short periods of time.

Those who are enlightened can stay in this seventh *chakra* place for longer than others and can even bring that consciousness into most of their lives.

For the rest of us, it is enough if we are gifted with even a few such moments of divine connection, if we can bring that consciousness into our daily living as often as we can when we work hard enough on ourselves. I was trying to do that work.

The speaker then told us to imagine an orb above our heads. That is where the eighth *chakra* lies. It is above us. It is our Higher Self. For some it lies deeper inside rather than higher above and is more of an inner witness or voice than an upper celestial presence. Or it can be a combination of both— an orb beginning at the belly and reaching up above the head. That felt right to me: both above and inside me.

The speaker invited us to inhabit this space, see how it felt for us to be there. I accepted her invitation, and after that, I do not remember a thing.

In the space of my Higher Deeper Self, I had drifted off to sleep. I was in a different state. It is where I go to meet the part of me who is wiser, truer, purer, untouched by the forces and influences of living in the waking world. It is where I relax enough to give birth to my own images, as Rilke says. I fight it, yet I know I need it.

Let go into me, sleep was saying. *No reason to fight me. I am your gateway to yourself. Your Higher Deeper Self. Your Shabbat soul.*

I might as well call it sleep.

I surrendered.

THAT IS WHEN I met Jude, a teacher in the spiritual counseling program whose specialty is dreams. Jude, a professor of psychology, clinical psychologist and therapist, and a spiritual companion, discovered and fell in love with dreamwork early in her career. Dreamwork, as offered by Fritz Perls, the founder of Gestalt therapy, became her passion and her specialty, as she began including spirituality as the larger context for all the work.

Growing up, I had never paid much attention to my dreams. Dreams were something to shake off. Mostly they felt like mere residue of the past day's experiences and therefore not worthy of attention. If they were frightening, it was best to forget them. The same with disturbing dreams and anxiety-laden dreams, like those before a standardized test about missing the bus, sleeping late, forgetting my pencils, and trying to get to the testing center but not making it. Other dreams felt shameful and also best forgotten.

The famous scene in the film *Fiddler on the Roof* is a good example of the attitude towards dreams I remember from my childhood. Tevye uses Golda's belief in the power of dreams to convince her they have received a message from a dead relative, and we, the audience, laugh at her foolishness and gullibility. Placing any weight on dreams is superstitious, and in the rational approach to Judaism in which I was raised, that was no compliment.

On the other hand, dreams in the Bible are mostly considered divine messages worthy of serious attention. God speaks to Abraham and Jacob in their dreams. God even speaks to people who are not members of the covenant, like Avimelech, warning him Sarah is Abraham's wife, not his sister, as Abraham led him to believe. And there is Joseph, of course, who not only has prophetic dreams but also interprets the dreams of others.

However, in Deuteronomy 13 and in the Prophets (Jeremiah 23 and Zachariah 10) there is a warning against people who interpret dreams or say they have had prophetic dreams. The idea behind this, I was made to understand, is that God once spoke to us in dreams (as God explicitly announces in Numbers 12:6) but no longer does. People who think they are experiencing a divine message in their dreams are either mentally unstable or have evil intentions.

This approach is mainstream in classic rabbinic literature. Rabbi Hisda (BT Brakhot 55b) is an exception, when he states how a dream unexamined is like a letter not read, suggesting the letter is from God. In other words, we are no different from our ancestors in the dream realm. Or, if we are, it is only on the level of directness of the message, but not in the notion our dreams are communication from a place that would otherwise be inaccessible to us.

While God may have spoken more clearly in visions and dreams in the Bible, today those messages are filtered through our unconscious; they are still there but require from us more work to understand their meaning. This is a radical statement that goes against the rabbinic grain, where dreams, especially "bad dreams," are treated as something to let go, not examine more carefully.

The Rabbis in the Talmud offer a few options to help dreamers turn their bad dreams into good, although these do not include delving into the deeper meaning of the dream. In fact, the intention seems to be quite the opposite. One option is a prayer recited to this day in some synagogues in a *hatavat chalomot*, or dream amelioration, ceremony. Another is a less well-known ceremony practiced in Kabbalist circles called a *ta'anit chalom*, or a dream fast, to rid the one who is fasting of a disturbing dream.

There is discussion of dream interpretation in the Talmud (see BT Brakhot 55a-b, for example), just as there is discussion of astrology, but there are mixed feelings and attitudes towards both (ranging from considering them holy to profane), and neither are part of mainstream religious Jewish ritual or praxis today. I was certainly never encouraged to try to find meaning in my dreams, especially not as part of a religious framework.

There are Kabbalistic strains that did consider dreams worthy of serious attention. Some performed a *she'elat chalom* (literally dream request) ceremony to incubate helpful dreams. The mystic Rabbi Hayyim Vital is known to have kept a *sefer chalomot*, a dream journal of his own dreams and those of others, much like Sigmund Freud and Carl Jung.

Going into the presentation on dreams in my spiritual counseling program, I had conflicting notions about dreams and their significance, but I did not feel strongly one way or the other. I felt open to what would transpire. I was not prepared for what I heard to transform my life.

Jude's approach not only places deep spiritual significance on our dreams, but even encourages us to look deeply into our unnerving dreams. Like Rabbi Hisda says, your dream is an invitation to listen to your soul, to your inner divine "still small voice." The more vivid—even disturbing—the dream, the more urgent the message.

The way to hear a dream's message is to go back into it and listen to its many voices speaking to us through the dream images, not to try and make it go away. For, as Jude explains, the dream will keep coming back in different variations until you are willing to let it have its say. The way to turn a "bad" dream into a "good" one is to let it do its healing work. That cannot happen if we ignore it.

In our dreams, feelings come to the surface that we might not allow in our waking lives—including anxieties and fears. And these feelings deserve attention. But our dreams also contain other voices that carry the buried wisdom our ego suppresses. In dreamwork, we let all those voices speak, and through working the dream, we can reach the dream's "message"—whether we see it as God's message to the dreamer, or the dreamer's message (buried in the unconscious) to themself.

Jude suggested we record our dreams in a dream journal and contact her if we have an especially interesting, vivid or significant dream to work with her throughout our time in the program. Little did she know I had started dreaming quite vividly since starting the ministry program two years before. That night, I had what I now call my "empty-to-overflowing *mikveh* dream," a dream which has become central in my spiritual journey and to which I return again and again.

I AM THE officiating rabbi at a ceremony at Mikveh Shmaya. It is the conversion of a baby, long awaited. Her two fathers are escorting her, behind me, to the mikveh with a large group of beaming, excited family and friends.

The grandmothers are carrying the baby like a precious family heirloom. This is a grandchild they thought they would never have. I sense their mix of fear and pride. They want to do what it takes to make this baby, born to a surrogate non-Jewish mother, a Jewish child. They want to support their sons in this brave effort to create a shared family life, to be a link in the chain of passing on Jewish tradition to future generations.

But they are nervous, and they have a right to be. Isn't there a better way to welcome this newborn baby into the Jewish people other than dunking her, head and all, in a cistern of rainwater?!

We approach the immersion pool, me ahead of the pack. "And this is the mikveh," I announce. "No need to worry about a thing. The water is warm and clean." I gesture towards the mikveh with an open hand, inviting them to see for themselves.

"Is there really water in there?" one grandfather asks.

"Of course, there is," I say. "It's deceptive, because we keep the water so clean with this new filter system. But it's in there."

And then I look inside the immersion pool. My stomach does a double flip. I blink my eyes and look again. I fear this man is correct. There is no water in the mikveh!

"Stop right there." I hear Jude's voice from outside my covered eyes.

I read the dream to Jude from my dream journal, and she now tells me to drop back into the dream and tell it to her again in the present tense first person from memory, as if I am back inside the dream.

"I want you to take a few breaths," she continues. "That's all it takes. Keep your eyes closed. Stay with the dream. But now I want you to move outside the role of the dreamer. I want you to become the water. Say, 'I am the water.'"

"I am the water," I repeat from the deep, dark place to where I have gone, back into this dream from the night before.

"Now describe yourself to me, water," I hear Jude say.

I imagine myself as water. I become water. "I am flowing," I say. "I am clear. I am free."

"And why did you leave us? Why did you leave the *mikveh*?" Jude asks.

I know the answer, feel it. After all, I am the water. "I did not want to be there. I did not want to be confined in that vessel. I did not want to be used in that way."

I hear the excitement in Jude's voice. She knows we are on to something big. "So where, then, are you now? Where have you gone?" she asks me.

I am elated by her question. It feels like a question I have been wanting to ask myself, to answer, to know the answer to, for quite some time.

"I have gone back to my source," I hear myself say.

"You've gone back to your source. And where is that?" Jude probes. "Where are you, exactly?"

"I am everywhere. I am in everything. Permeating everything," I answer.

Jude takes a moment, letting me be in that state of ubiquity that is the Source. "How does it feel to be back at your source?"

For a moment, I am afraid. I can't find myself. But then the fear turns into calm. I am not lost, just everywhere and nowhere at the same time. "It doesn't feel good, or bad. It just is."

"Great. It just is. Can you stay with that feeling for a few moments?"

"Yes," I say, and I sit with what is. I don't know for how long I do, but I sit with what is. I AM WHAT I AM. I WILL BE WHAT I WILL BE. I sit with that.

And then I feel a sudden rush. A nudge forward. I cannot stay there any longer.

"I am coming back," I say. I feel it urgently, this push, this need to return. "But I won't fit into the *mikveh* this way."

"No, you won't. You have been back to the Source. Now return to your dreamer role. What is the dreamer seeing?"

And then I am back in the story of the dream.

I convince the family to get something to eat and come back later, after I refill the mikveh. But when we come back to the mikveh building, water is pouring out of the windows, the door. It's flowing down the path, overflowing into the whole kibbutz. It's flooding the place. People are being lifted and carried away.

"Are they drowning? Are they alarmed?" Jude asks.

"I don't think so."

"Now I want you to be one of those people."

"I am the baby who came to be converted," I say, knowing that this baby, like all of the elements of my dreams, is part of my unconscious. "But now I am being uplifted in a different way. People thought they were making me Jewish, but it seems that is not what is happening here. Something more expansive is happening."

"How does it feel?" I hear Jude ask me.

"I'm not sure," I answer. I shift in my chair. Try to get some clarity. "I don't know where I am going. But I think I feel fine to be in that place of not knowing. I feel buoyed. I feel safe. I am floating, not drowning."

"Can you stay with that feeling of floating with destination unknown, without anxiety or fear?

"I think I can," I say, and I let myself float to wherever the water wants to take me. When an unsettled feeling starts to creep up on me, I push it away, as if it has come to the wrong place. As if it does not belong here in my dream.

I hear Jude's voice again, from far away. I am not sure how much time has passed. "And now I want you to be the water again. Say, 'I am the water.'"

"I am the water," I say.

"Water, why did you come back?" Jude asks.

I take a deep breath, drop further down into embodying the water in my dream. "I had to. I couldn't stay at my source. I needed to come back, to be felt, to be seen, to do what I was meant to do here, but not confined to the *mikveh*. I couldn't make myself fit into that container anymore. I am so much larger than that. So much vaster. So much more free flowing. I need more room."

MY EXPERIENCE WORKING my empty-to-overflowing *mikveh* dream with Jude was so profound, I was hungry for more. I joined one of her regular on-line dream groups, which was the beginning of two years of training with Jude to become a dreamworker myself. This skill proved to be extremely useful in my work as a spiritual companion once I opened my own practice. Each time I work a dream with a client, I help them open a door to their inner world.

As Jude herself explained in our training, a dream is like a knock on the door. If you have recurring themes in your dreams, or if your dreams get increasingly vivid or even startling, think of it as a louder and louder knock. Your unconscious will keep knocking until you open that door. Your soul refuses to be silenced.

But before I could use this modality on others, I had to first experience it for myself. I had to start paying attention to how my own soul was knocking at the door.

Jacob's father's condition had been deteriorating after his parents visited for Nachum's bar mitzvah. By winter, Jacob was spending almost half of his time in New York and half in Israel, so he could be with his father and help his mother and sister care for him. And since, as an entrepreneur with a winery on the kibbutz and an online wine-selling startup, he had business in New York, he was able to be in both places.

That meant I was single parenting for the time he was gone. Jacob and I had raised and were still raising our seven children in Israel, with no family to help. He had always travelled a lot for business, sometimes being away at least one week a month, or even more. But never this much.

I knew he was doing his best to be an equal parenting partner; and when he was home, he most definitely was. I did not resent his business travel, as I knew he traveled not for fun but for his work and income, which our family needed. If not for that, he would have preferred to be home with us. But this was not only for work, and the timing of his increase in travel now was especially difficult.

I was getting older, and so were the kids; their needs were becoming more complex. I was tired, and my physical condition was deteriorating, my muscles becoming increasingly weaker and my illness spreading to parts of my body not affected before. And the pain was intensifying. I wanted to feel held, supported, taken care of, when the reality of the situation was that I was the one doing the caring.

There was no room in our lives for my wounds, so I had to push them aside, or bury them deeper inside me. This was a recipe for an explosion.

The knocking of my own unconscious was getting increasingly louder, seeping into my waking life, like the melting synagogue walls in that dream were seeping through the cage I myself had erected around them. Albeit with bars, not walls, so that when the time came for the walls to melt—when my subconscious had the audacity to leave the faucet running—they could find their way out.

I AM WALKING to the *mikveh* with a group that has been on a spiritual tour of Israel, and this is their last stop. I have been emailing with the tour's guide for months to plan this meeting.

The participants have brought with them their sacred intentions for their *mikveh* immersions, what they want to leave behind from this transformative experience, and what they want to take back home. How they have grown on this trip, what they have learned about themselves and their connection to Spirit and their souls.

The spiritual intensity and anticipation are high among the members of the group. Excitement is in the air. Then I see the water flowing down the path leading out of the *mikveh*. My heart sinks. I was at the *mikveh* an hour before to set up for the group. The tour guide called to say they were running an hour late, so I went home to wait and take care of some things in the house. A memory of turning on the faucet to let a bit more water into the *mikveh* flashes in my head, but no memory of having turned it off.

I take a deep breath and close my eyes. But all is blank. I open them, and there is the group and the overflowing *mikveh*.

This is not a dream. Or if it is, it is a dream seeping into my waking life. I wonder what Jude will have to say about this.

And then comes the panic. I walk ahead as quickly as I can manage and open the door, expecting water to burst out and wash us away, like in my sleeping dream of weeks before. But that does not happen. The floor of the building, however, is flooded with water, like in my dream of the caged synagogue with its melting walls.

In my head, I bless the person who thought to put drains in the *mikveh* floors. I turn off the *mikveh* faucet, grab a squeegee and start pushing water down the drains. I push more towards the door and open it from the inside, squeegee in hand. The group is standing outside the door now, looking at me questioningly.

"We are going to have to sit outside for now, until I get the water out of here," I say. "Our *mikveh* runneth over. Your overflowing spiritual energy flooded the *mikveh*!"

I do believe that is true. But I also believe something in my own energy created this intersection between my conscious and unconscious selves. My awake world was becoming a dreamworld. Like the elements in my dream, elements in my awake world were beginning to send me messages. The Universe in all its unified energies, through emerging patterns and signs, was speaking to me. My sixth *chakra* was working overtime.

What is the *mikveh* trying to tell me? If I am the *mikveh*, am I telling myself my own cup runneth over? Or am I telling myself it is not running over enough? Or is the message something else entirely? After all, like in my dreams, I was the one who had "accidentally" left the faucet open.

I was distracted. While I was setting up for the group, Jacob and I were discussing whether he should leave for the U.S. ten days earlier than planned for his business trip, so that he could be with his parents. His father's condition had worsened, and his mother and sister requested, for the third time in two months, he come help them.

I was still feeling emotionally and physically drained from his previous few trips. The kids and their needs were overwhelming me as I tried to understand the pain and neediness his frequent traveling to help his family in the U.S. were triggering in me.

Feelings of abandonment and overwhelm were flooding me like the *mikveh* waters were flooding the room. I had been feeling on the verge of tears for a good while. It was no wonder water was overflowing its boundaries.

Jacob had committed to partnering with me in the life we had built, in raising our kids, literally building the house we were living in but still constructing. And he was still partnering with me. He was just doing his duty as a good son and brother, but I could not help the way I was feeling. I could put on a strong exterior and tell him to go without a worry, but I could not prevent these feelings from flooding me.

I had been drowning in self-pity for the past few months. Drowning in unconscious memories from the womb when my mother was unknowingly starving me because her doctor had told her not to gain weight during pregnancy. Drowning in conscious but buried memories of my first month of life in the incubator when I could not suckle from my mother's breasts. Memories of being diagnosed with a degenerative neuro-muscular disorder with no cure or treatment at the vulnerable age of sixteen.

It felt as if all of the pain of my childhood was floating to the surface, and the inner child in me was crying out—"Don't leave me! I need help too! I can't do it alone!" And as usual, just when Jacob left, things in the house started to malfunction.

The washing machine was stopping mid-cycle, leaving the clothing soaking wet, so that we had to wring it out by hand and hang it dripping on the line—something I, with my weak muscles, could not manage alone. A new motor would arrive only in a couple weeks, which meant I would have to hang the clothing sopping wet and hope for the best. The older kids could help, but they were out at school for most of the day when the sun was out.

Then the water heater for our house stopped working, too. A repairperson could only come in a week's time. Our solar heating would not suffice for us all to take hot showers whenever we wanted. An inconvenience, but nothing compared to what Jacob would have to deal with where he was going. Yet, I could not help but feel tested. Could I stoically push through this without breaking down in self-pity?

On a deeper level, these inconveniences were triggering me because of their timing, coming just when Jacob was leaving to perhaps see his father for the last time. My fear of my own morbidity and mortality was being triggered. But I did not realize that then. I just felt overwhelmed emotionally and physically.

So much water in my life was not flowing properly because of technical difficulties. Life was not flowing properly; life's challenges were preventing the flow of the current. Rocks were blocking the path, and I was trying to move them—which was an impossible task, I knew—instead of just letting the water run in a different way than I may have wanted. That is life, I knew subconsciously. But I had been resisting that reality.

Was the flooded *mikveh* telling me to just let it flow? Life would always send me technical difficulties; those rocks in the current are as much a part of the river as the flowing water is. Life is hard, unpredictable, out of our hands, and constantly in flux. I would be better off focusing on learning to surrender to this reality than on trying to control the uncontrollable. Was this the message I was meant to receive?

I had been the one to turn on the faucet and then forget to turn it off. The unconscious has a way of making itself known.

CRY OUT SO THAT MILK MIGHT COME

I AM IN the kitchen, in front of the refrigerator. There are so many different containers of milk to choose from: organic cow's milk, regular cow's milk, goat milk, almond milk, rice milk, soy milk, coconut milk. Which should I drink? I stand there, looking, for several minutes. But none is what I really want. Each belongs to another member of my family, but which one is mine? None. I close the refrigerator door.

I walk over to the closet instead. There are so many bags hanging there: a variety of knapsacks and shoulder bags. All of them belonged once to one of my kids, and each I have used at various points in my life. But not one is what I want right now. I take one with me anyway. It feels familiar, but not really what I want. I am comfortable but not satisfied.

"I want you to be the refrigerator," Jude tells me. "What is your purpose?"

"I am the dreamer's refrigerator," I say. "I preserve things. I would like to offer the dreamer what she really wants, what she really needs. But I can only offer what has been put inside me. I can only preserve. I can't create something new. And I don't seem to have what the dreamer is looking for. I have all kinds of milk, but not the one she seems to need."

"Now I want you to be milk," Jude says. "Milk in general. What are you, milk, in your essence?"

"I am milk. I am nourishing. I am nurturing. I am basic. I am what a newborn infant drinks. I am not juice. I do not give an instant rush. But I am not water either. I contain all that you need to live. One cannot live on water alone. I am what kept you alive from the very beginning of your existence."

"Thank you, milk. I'd like to talk now to the bags. What is your purpose, bags?"

"We help the dreamer in her transitions. But the dreamer never chose any of us. She used us because we were there. We did the trick. And we had our benefits. But we are not truly hers."

"So why do you think she takes you home, bags?" Jude asks.

"She takes us because we can serve the purpose of carrying things for her journeys. And we are familiar to her. We are comfortable, and we may even present some new features. But we are also not exactly what she is looking for. She is left disappointed. Not satisfied completely."

Jude asks me to open my eyes and leave the dream when I am ready so that we can process what came up. She asks me what it means to me to be looking for mother's milk.

I tell Jude that I nursed six out of my seven kids—all except Mishael, our one adopted child—and how much I loved that experience of sustaining another human being with my milk. But I myself never received mother's milk because I was born premature and was in an incubator in the hospital for a month.

"My mother never nursed me," I tell her. "I don't know what it would be like to receive mother's milk. I want that feeling of being totally sustained by a nurturing, giving, connection, but also by the miracle of being human, of being alive. I want to know what that feels like."

"And what kind of bag do you think you would need to get that milk?"

"I don't know. What I do know is it is not in the bags familiar to me. I may have to go out and find a new bag instead of just taking the ones available so readily, so easily. I may have to put in more effort to get the bag I need."

"The bag you need to get the milk you need?"

"Yes."

"Because it isn't in the refrigerator? The place of preserving?"

Preserving. Tradition. Religion. "No. It isn't. It's somewhere else."

"Do you know where?"

"I want to say it's in my mother's breasts, but it's not anymore. That opportunity passed. And it's not something available to me from another source. It's milk meant just for me. Human milk. I can find it only by looking inside of a human."

"All humans or a specific human?"

"I think that human is me."

THE NEXT DAY, in a mini elective on Rumi's poetry, I come across this poem of his:

> God created the child, that is, your wanting,
> So that it might cry out, so that milk might come.
> Cry out! Don't be stolid and silent
> With your pain. Lament! And let the milk
> Of loving, flow into you.

I am learning now to pay attention to the signs in my life. Synchronicity has become a spiritual experience. This poem has come to me now for a reason. I lean into this sign and listen for its meaning:

The milk will not flow so easily. It will require pain. It will require crying. It will involve owning my wanting, my unmet needs, my inner wounded child. First would come the lament. And only then could the milk flow.

Was I ready to let the milk of loving flow into and out of me?

WHAT MADE ME at age thirty-six, a mother of five suffering from a degenerative and debilitating muscular disorder, decide to adopt a sixth child? What hole was I trying to fill?

I look back now at that decision in my life and wonder what I was thinking. I must have known it made no sense, because I did not tell my parents what Jacob and I intended to do. And it is good I didn't tell my mother, because when I did, over the phone, when Mishael was already living in our house, her reaction was first disbelief.

"Are you joking?"

"No. He's here. In his crib. We picked him up yesterday from the children's home. He's almost six months old, with the cutest big brown eyes."

Then shock, laced with anger:

"Are you crazy? You already have too much on your plate. You can barely manage with the kids you have. And in your physical condition?"

"This is why I didn't tell you we were in the process of adopting, Mom. I knew you'd react this way."

"She's out of her mind!" I heard my father's voice in the background.

"Adoption is not a game," my mother added. "Most adopted kids are messed up. They cause their parents such pain and heartache. Some turn out okay, but not without a lot of therapy and hard work. Why do that to yourself? To your kids? Some people have no choice. You already have your own kids."

"We feel we have room for another child in our lives."

"We? How did Jacob agree to this? You're going to drive him away with all your outlandish projects. It's going to put too much stress on your marriage." How did she know to hit me right where it hurt most?

"Yes, he agreed. We're in this together. We even had to do a course with the Child Welfare Service before we could adopt him."

"Can you give him back?" my mother asked.

"I don't think so," I answered.

This was a weighty decision, a serious step. And my plate was full, especially with my physical condition. My mother was right, and her anger, I knew, came from a place of concern. Yet, something was pushing me forward despite the irrationality of it all.

Mishael Adar Binyamin—whose name was just Binyamin back then— was intended for another couple, a couple who were not able to conceive a child. As parents with biological children of our own, we could apply to adopt only a child with special needs: a baby or toddler with health issues, or a child over three.

When this couple came to pick up Mishael, he broke out in tiny red dots all over his body. The children's home staff rushed him to the hospital, and his blood count was almost down to zero. He received a blood transfusion and was diagnosed with Immune Thrombocytopenic Purpura (ITP), a blood disorder that causes dangerous drops in blood count.

When the couple came to pick him up a second time, it happened again. So, they pulled out of the process, and Mishael was transferred to the Special Needs category. That is when Leah, our social worker from the Child Welfare Service, called.

"We have a child for you," she said, and my heart missed a beat.

"Who? How old?"

"He's five months old. I can't tell you more over the phone. You should come to my office tomorrow and I can give you his medical file. But not his birth mother's name and information. That's only for him to see when he turns eighteen. You can have a few days to think it over with Jacob and give me your decision."

"When can we meet him?"

"Not until you decide if you want to take him. We don't want to keep disappointing him."

"Can we see a photograph?" I asked.

"No," Leah answered. "Only if you say yes. We don't want you to be influenced by the way he looks. Just by the facts of his case. Can you handle it or not? He's cute. He's a baby. We don't want you or him to get attached before you make a rational decision."

That seemed logical, but still, how can one decide what one can or cannot handle? No one had given us that choice with our other kids. You get what you get. But I picked up the file, and Jacob and I did as much research as we could on ITP. It seemed like a disease we could handle. And in some cases, it even passes as the child matures.

We said yes.

When we went to meet our new baby, we were worried he would react to us the way he had to the other couple who came to take him. But he did not. He took an immediate liking to both of us, but especially to Jacob.

With his big brown eyes open wide, he gave Jacob a goofy smile as he stroked his stubbly chin. Aside from the staff doctor, there were no male staff members at the children's home. And Jacob has always had a very soft spot for babies. It was love at first sight for them both.

After a couple more visits, we brought Mishael home for the weekend. The idea was we would bring him back to the children's home on Sunday and then come for him a day or two later to bring him home for good.

The kids were so excited to have their new little brother, they showered him with love and attention, and bottle-feeding meant Jacob and I could share the feedings equally, so there was less pressure on me. The weekend went so smoothly Leah said we should just keep him at home rather than confuse him with more transitions.

That is when I called my parents.

It took two years for the adoption to be final—including his conversion, which, for the adoption to go through, had to be done through the State (there is no private adoption in Israel) and therefore the Orthodox Rabbinate (although the law has changed since then, and now non-Orthodox conversions are also accepted by the Ministry of the Interior, even if not by the Orthodox Rabbinate).

The lengthy process included an interview in front of three bearded ultra-Orthodox rabbis. We almost lost our chance when one of the rabbis recognized me as the first woman to publicly receive Orthodox rabbinic ordination. Thankfully, he was willing to overlook that "blemish" on our Jewish characters for Mishael's good, since even he could see it did not make sense to take him away from us after he had been living with us for over a year.

The process also included *mikveh* immersion (not at *Shmaya*, as it is not recognized by the Israeli Orthodox Rabbinate), and a painful circumcision at age two that became infected and turned me against the circumcision ritual for good. But at the end of the two years, Mishael Adar Binyamin's name was added to our I.D. cards along with our other five children's names.

One year later, we discovered I was pregnant with Shefa Lee. But with that, I could at least plead innocent. I could call it a mistake, a surprise. After all, we had considered adoption because I had a series of miscarriages followed by not conceiving at all. We had not used contraception in many years, because we thought we could no longer conceive.

But, still, I ask myself now, what *was* I thinking? There was much wisdom in my parents' reaction. As a woman who tries to listen to where the signs are directing her, I could easily have said my body was telling me it was time to stop having children. After all, I was forty-two, had muscular dystrophy and five previous C-sections. But while my body was telling me I wasn't meant to have another child, my heart told me I was.

So, I had concluded, after all those miscarriages and then not even conceiving at all, I *was* meant to have another child—just not from my body. And that is when the idea of adoption arose. Jacob and I had never discussed the idea before. Neither of us had ever thought about adopting. Never. But suddenly the idea seemed like what we were meant to do. I was following my heart, trusting we could handle this, saying yes to life.

In retrospect, though, I wonder what wound I was trying to heal by deciding to adopt rather than adapt. On one hand, I was surrendering to the unknown, but on the other hand, child rearing was more of a known in my life at that point than not. And after adopting, we chose not to take any precautions against conceiving again. The chances of conceiving were small, but still, there was a chance, apparently, because it happened. I was more afraid to not conceive than to conceive, I now understand.

I had tried to make peace with the idea that Nachum, our fifth child, was our last. After a particularly difficult and late miscarriage, I had even done a *mikveh* immersion ritual among friends to mark my coming to peace with the fact that I would have no more children. Adoption was not on my radar screen at the time. I called the birth of the dead fetus a birth of me. I felt I was being born into myself, into a new life phase that would be about nurturing myself rather than nurturing another baby.

Yet, instead, we ended up adopting. And then, when we discovered I was pregnant with Shefa, we went ahead with the pregnancy. The question is—why? What was behind my change of heart? What was so unsettling about the idea of concentrating on birthing myself?

I believe Mishael was meant to be in our family. I have no doubt about that. I know in my heart that is where the signs were pointing. I also believe that there was something in my psyche which made that irrational thought seem rational at the time.

There was a longing. A voice inside me rebelling against the idea this was it. A force within me—like the force trying to keep my eyelids open in my three bar mitzvahs dream—avoiding the kind of quiet that might lead to the need for self-reflection. Inner work. The kind of stagnancy that might stop my chaotic whirlpool-of-a-life enough for some of my repressed fears to float to the surface.

And so, first came Mishael. And then Shefa Lee. Two huge blessings, one after the other. But eventually the water would have no choice but to settle. When Shefa was born, Jacob and I decided to ask the doctors to tie my tubes while they were already cutting me open for my sixth cesarean section. It was the rational thing to do.

It is no wonder, however, it took me three and a half years before I decided to fully wean Shefa Lee and start nursing myself.

I CRIED IN the *mikveh* when I did my weaning ritual at *Mayyim Hayyim*, the community and educational *mikveh* near Boston. It was at the beginning of my book tour that same summer I discovered One Spirit. Jacob and the kids and I were in the U.S. for my niece's bat mitzvah, which was also in the Boston area. After the bat mitzvah, Jacob returned home with the kids, and I continued to *Mayyim Hayyim* and then Manhattan for speaking engagements.

That night, I stayed in a motel near the airport. Jacob dropped me and then returned our rental car and flew home with the kids. I went through my notes for my talk, which would be the next day at *Mayyim Hayyim*. But before the talk, I would do my weaning ceremony there, at the *mikveh*.

Alone in that motel room, I compiled my book of blessings from friends and relatives I had solicited for the ceremony. They had emailed them to me, and I had printed but not read them. I wanted to receive their blessings for the first time right before immersing.

I pasted these blessings, without reading them, into the pastel flowered journal I had bought for this occasion. Although I was not reading the words, I cried as I pasted. The mere thought of Jacob and the kids flying back to Israel, leaving me alone and on my own for two weeks, was enough to bring on the tears.

My feelings were mixed: liberation, loss, fear, excitement. This time there was no escaping it. This was my last child, and this would be the end of our physical attachment. I had been winding down nursing over the summer, and I would not nurse her for two weeks, so by the time I returned home to Israel, the idea was she would be weaned.

The next day at the *mikveh*, I undressed and showered while singing to myself a tune my friend had composed to some lines from Psalm 90: "And may our encounter with the divine be pleasant for us. May the work of our hands be established in the physical realm; and may the work of our hands be established in the metaphysical realm."

My work breastfeeding my children was over. Slowly, my parental responsibilities would shift more towards emotional care and away from physical care, while nursing myself on a spiritual and physical level would only intensify. This was an exciting notion. But it was also a scary one.

At the water's edge, I read from the book I had compiled the night before. I was touched by the candor and intimacy of these personal stories and blessings. The general theme was to embrace this new stage in my life while also appreciating, even mourning the loss of what I was leaving behind.

As one psychologist friend, who also attached a photograph of a statue of Artemis, the many-breasted goddess of birth, the hunt and wilderness, wrote:

"Breastfeeding, a hugely meaningful way of nourishing, has run its course in your life, as all time-bound processes eventually do, but many others will open up for you in the future, and are probably opening up to you even as you read this. Most of them are not time-bound, and their ripple effect can last for as long as there are people to appreciate them. You are a person of many sources for nourishing; when one source has come to its natural end, others will spring up in its wake."

As my singer and peace activist friend wrote:

"May you be imbued with the deep understanding that all that you do, any project that you take on with your full heart, any *tikkun olam* you participate in, any work of art, any written word from your pen or your computer, is in its own way a birth. And as this same project, this work, this artistic endeavor is born and nursed into being, it eventually takes wings of its own. It is weaned. And in being weaned, it flowers and grows.

"May your mother's milk now be converted into a new kind of female energy. Different, yet creative and nourishing to the world. Dear God, the world is in such need of positive feminine energy. You are, in some ways, free now to enter a new phase of life. May you be blessed with long life—you have so much to give to the world!"

As I descended the circular staircase with its seven steps leading down into the black-bottomed oval *mikveh* with its underwater lights slowly changing color, I was mindful of the many steps along my journey of birthing, adopting and raising my children thus far.

During my first immersion, I closed my eyes and recalled life without children. I visualized myself back in college, always busy, but mostly with my own needs, rarely the needs of others.

After reciting a blessing "upon immersing in the living waters," I immersed a second time, this time being present in the moment, tuning into what it felt like to be me, then, in the intense period of caring for others while also trying to care for myself.

I recited a blessing a friend had composed for my ritual. "Blessed are you, Source of all Life, who sanctifies transitions." This was exactly what I was doing here in this *mikveh* at this moment—sanctifying this pivotal transition by recognizing, naming and sitting with my feelings around it.

As I immersed my entire body for a third and last time, I visualized myself with an empty nest. Despite having once been totally on my own, there was no going back to that unattached life. I had accepted Jacob's engagement ring, stood beneath the *chuppah*, and thrown myself into birthing and parenting. The "damage" had been done. As far as life might take Jacob and the kids away from me physically, they would always be in my heart.

As I recited the final blessing—"Blessed are You, Spirit of the Universe, who gives me life, sustains the rhythms of my body and brings me to this moment of renewal"—my tears mixed with the living waters of the *mikveh*. I was overcome with the emotion of having reached this moment after months of anticipation, planning, and fear. *But fear of what?* I asked myself.

There was the fear of losing all that I loved. But when I let myself feel, I noticed there were other fears as well. There was the fear of having no one to take care of but myself. Fear of entering a phase of open possibility. Fear of having my life back and not knowing what to do with it. Fear of the unknown.

By choosing to have children, I had opened myself to the vulnerability and mystery of parental love, but I had also protected myself with the busy-ness of caring for others. Now I would have to learn to love and care for myself. But in a deeper, soul-searching way that would not necessarily be pleasant.

My talk that night went well. I sold books and people appreciated what I had to say. And this is how the rest of my book tour went as well. It was exhilarating and exhausting to be heard and celebrated. I was so busy taking care of myself, promoting my book, developing my career, and spreading my truth, that I hardly remembered to call home and speak to Jacob and the children.

As I waited at passport control in Ben Gurion Airport, I noticed a woman ahead of me in line with a baby strapped to her back. Unlike in past similar scenarios, I did not feel my heartbeat quicken with pangs of jealousy and longing. I felt relief that was not me. I could not imagine lugging a baby on my back again.

I had passed over the bridge into middle age. I had managed to turn off the switch of the whirlpool and let the waters settle. Not completely out of my own choice, but there I was. Now all I had to do was wait, see what would float to the surface and try not to let fear paralyze me.

As another psychologist friend wrote in her blessing: "Every day a bit of weaning goes on. We are weaning ourselves away from life, away from the oneness of our own womb experience, into the middle oneness of mindful living, and preparing for the oneness of the return to dust."

Although for me, it would most likely be a return to the oneness of the primordial waters.

Could I manage that weaning without too much suffering? I knew it would take work. Was I up for the challenge?

LIVING IN ISRAEL, one of the groups that keeps my spirits up and my hopes alive is an Arab-Jewish narrative sharing group. We meet monthly to hear another personal story of someone living in Israel or Palestine, with a focus on where and how the Arab-Jewish conflict affects their lives.

When a new member of the group, Marcia, told her story, I was not able to attend. And when I told my story, she had not joined the group yet. But we felt drawn to each other and wanted to hear each other's stories. We decided to meet at a coffee shop one day, instead.

When Marcia told me her story, I discovered she was in her eighties and had lived in Israel for many more years than in the U.S., although she was born and raised in Minneapolis, Minnesota. When I met her, she had recently moved from the city of Safed to Kiryat Tivon, a town twenty minutes from my kibbutz, because it was more centrally located and less hilly than Safed—which became a difficult place for her to live, as she had recently had a stroke and was living alone. I was in awe of this woman's vivacity and cheer.

Marcia told me of two life-changing visions she had while listening to music.

In the first vision, she was standing on Mt. Sinai—which felt appropriate to her, as she was named after her grandfather, Moshe (Moses)—and she saw before her a burning bush. She tried to look away, to get out of the vision, to say no to God, but like her namesake Moses, she could not. A voice came from the bush, calling her name. She tried to ignore it, but she couldn't.

Finally, she answered, "*Hineni*. I am here."

The voice said, "Marcia, you must help save the soul of the Jewish people." She said, "I can't."

The voice only repeated itself. And then Marcia left the vision.

The second vision began with the urgent and sad sound of blasts from the *shofar* (the ritual ram's horn). Marcia was at the *Kotel*, the Western Wall, and it became clear to her the *shofar* blasts were calling Jews from all over the world and from all past generations to mourn the soul of the Jewish people.

Men started gathering. They put their hands on each other's shoulders with arms intertwined and then flapped their arms like wings. She heard the word "*Shekhina*" (the earth-dwelling feminine aspect of God) and she saw an energy, a light, descending into the circle. She felt herself dissolving into the energy, and she felt the energy of the *Shekhina* spreading all over Israel. She felt pink drops of love falling into the hearts of everyone in Israel. And that is when she understood that the solution is LOVE. That is the way to save the Jewish soul.

As a result of those visions, Marcia decided to become active in Palestinian-Israeli peace work, spreading feminine divine energy, *Shekhina* love, in the face of a patriarchal, violent and conflictual Middle East reality. She worked in Nablus, which is in Palestine, but during the second *intifada*, the Palestinian uprising that began in 2000, that became impossible. Disillusioned with the possibility of peace any time soon, she moved to Safed, where she lived and worked as a therapist.

In her opinion, she told me, the most effective way to work towards peace in the current political and social climate is through grassroots peace work, activities that promote mutual understanding of one another's humanity—like the group to which we both belong. That was my gut feeling, too, but it was affirming to have it reinforced by someone with so many years of peace activism behind her.

I shared my story with Marcia, and it was obvious we had points of common interest and intersection, with her spiritual and peace-work bent. When she told me about her visions, I told her about my interspiritual studies and the work I had been doing around dreams. How much I loved that work. Marcia shared with me that when she was a working therapist, dreamwork was one of her specialties, as was inner child work.

Just that weekend, we in my cohort had learned about inner child work—a modality of spiritual counseling and therapy which is about getting in touch with one's inner child to help heal old wounds that are still plaguing the adult self. We had watched one of our teachers, a Jungian and Gestalt therapist, bring one of our classmates back to infancy in a moving demonstration session.

As I watched the session on my computer screen, I felt my own infant, and even fetal, pain. I knew that I, too, needed to explore my wounded child's suffering. But I was also afraid to take that step. Afraid of what might come up for me.

I knew I had unfinished business with my sixteen-year-old self.

Apparently, the pain was still there, and so was the longing. Undoubtedly, there were other wounded children at different ages and stages with whom I needed to speak. When Marcia told me she was opening an inner child workshop, to pass on her methodology to others at this later stage in her life, I felt compelled to join.

The forces in the Universe we tend to call God were not going to let me escape this time. I was going to have to face my wounds, and hopefully in so doing get closer to healing them.

Just a few days before, I had never heard of inner child work, and within less than a week, I had already, seemingly by chance, met an inner child therapist and signed myself up for a nine-month-long workshop.

And thus began my relationship with my inner child.

"ARE YOU READY to talk now?" my adult-self asked my fetal-self.

She nodded.

"What are you feeling today?"

"I am feeling small and skinny, starved and neglected. I feel trapped and suffocated. I feel out of control. I am not getting enough nourishment in here. I need to get out and start taking care of myself. I feel curious and ripe to see what's out there. I am ready to flow out with the watery current instead of just floating around in here, waiting for the end. Just let me out of here so I can take care of myself. Let me do it my way!"

"Okay. Go ahead. Go out."

I feel myself flowing out of the womb, right into an incubator.

"You trapped me again! You tricked me. Whom can I trust? I thought I was going out into the world. Instead, I am stuck here in this incubator for a month. Still no control, and no love. No touch. No mother's milk. Unlovable. Scared. Vulnerable in a cold, cruel world."

"What can I do for you now to help you?"

"I need to feel taken care of, and at the same time, I want to be left alone to do as I please, to take care of myself and be me. Can you help me trust it will be okay?"

"What can the adult me do to help you feel taken care of?"

"I want to be welcomed into this world. Do you really think a hug will crush me? You are afraid to hold me. I need love. I can receive love. I am lovable . . .

Or maybe a hug will crush me. I don't really know what I need. I can't do it all myself!"

"What can I do for you now to make you feel loved, nourished, and taken care of?"

"Can you nurse me?"

"I can try."

I hold my arms in a nursing position and close my eyes, trying to feel what it would be like to be nursed by myself. I feel life feeding itself, rejuvenating itself. I am nourishing my own soul. That is what I need.

TEENAGE MUTANT

I AM NOT the only woman in my family who prayed with *tefillin*. My father's late sister Esther, my Aunt Essie, also prayed with *tefillin* for a period of her life. And like me, she was born and raised in New York but moved to Israel as a young adult. She married a *kibbutznik* but eventually they divorced, and she moved back to the U.S. She suffered from mental illness.

I did not know my Aunt Essie when she was young. My father was born almost twenty years after her, and she was already out of the house by the time he was growing up.

I knew her as the "crazy" aunt who would call the house and yell at me over the phone, demanding to speak to my father. I was under strict instructions not to speak to her, just to say he was not home and that I would tell him to call her. She was living in a mental institution. I was afraid of her.

I had no idea back then that later I would wish I had gotten to know my aunt. That I would feel a deep kinship to this woman who had been a source of fear and anxiety for me as a child.

I wonder if she was like me. Was she a writer and a reader? A spiritual seeker? Why did she leave Israel? Was it just to escape her marriage, find treatment for her mental illness, go back to a familiar place to raise her daughters? Or did Zion let her down? Why had she stopped praying with *tefillin*? Was it the praying she could no longer manage, or did not want, to continue, or the *tefillin*? Or was it a combination of both?

If she was a spiritual seeker, did she ever find what she was seeking? Was her life simply a tragedy? Did she die in existential pain, or did she somehow find her own version of inner peace?

I write to my cousins Daphne and Pearl, Aunt Essie's daughters, asking for more information about their mother's life. This is what my cousin Daphne answers:

> As for my mom, I feel I need to caution you not to romanticize. She gave birth to me when she was around thirty-five, so I did not know her in her younger and most

vital years. By the time I was really aware, her struggle with mental illness had pretty well consumed her. I don't know that she was ever a writer, per se, although she was always a voracious reader, a trait she has passed on to me.

From what I know, I believe my mom was passionate about justice and fairness and, before I knew her, Zionism. By the time I was aware, her feelings about Judaism were terribly conflicted (the mixed messages for women were fatal to her), and her love for Zion fairly extinguished. That is how I understood it, anyway. In the end, it was her daughters and granddaughters that meant the world to her.

"ARE YOU READY to talk now?" I ask my sixteen-year-old self, who has just been diagnosed with FSHD.

"I am here, aren't I?" she quips.

"Is that a yes?"

"I guess so."

My adult self has experience with teenagers. "I see you are a bit hesitant to talk. Should I come back another time?"

"No. We may as well talk if we're both here."

"Ok. Good. Thank you for making time for me. So, what are you feeling now?"

As if I had been waiting all these years for someone to ask me that question, my emotions pour out. "I am scared and confused. Robbed of my childhood. I suddenly feel different from everyone else. Or maybe it's more like I always felt different, but now it's confirmed. Now I know why."

"In what way are you different?"

"I look different. I feel different. And I don't know what kind of future I will have. I feel an urgency to do it all before it's too late. I have so much I want to accomplish. Will I be able to do all I wanted to do with my life? Will I fulfill my dreams?"

"Yes, you will. It might be challenging, but you will. Don't worry. I am your adult self. I can tell you that you will. What else is upsetting you?"

"I feel disappointed. Let down. I am angry."

"At whom?" my adult self asks my teenage self.

"At life, I guess. At God."

"That's only natural. You've received shocking news. Your life suddenly looks totally different than it did yesterday."

"Yes. Everything is uncertain now. I feel helpless too. Out of control."

From the place of a middle-aged woman, I suddenly feel wise. I tell my sixteen-year-old self: "At times like this we are reminded of the lack of control we always have in our lives. It is true for everyone, always. But you are feeling it now especially intensely. Or perhaps you did not even realize it until now. You are still so young."

"I am only sixteen years old," my teenage self replies. "My life is just beginning. And now it feels like I can already see the end, and the suffering I will have to experience along the way. I am scared."

"What are you afraid of?" my adult self asks.

"Of what will be and what won't be. Who will love me like this?"

I think of Jacob. My children. "Oh, you will be loved. Don't worry about that."

"I am not sure I can believe someone will love me. I am not even sure I can love myself now. Will I be deformed? Unattractive? Frightening?"

"Beauty is in the eyes of the beholder." I hear Jacob in my head when I say this.

"Don't feed me clichés. I want truth!"

I smile to myself. "That is the truth. Your beauty will be appreciated by those who will recognize it. Trust me on that one."

"I am having a hard time trusting right now."

"That's understandable. What can I do to help you now? To restore your trust."

"I am not sure what I need. I want to be taken care of. I can't do it all. I want someone to tell me I don't have to do it all. I want special treatment because I am sick. Let me be sick. But at the same time, I don't want to be different. I don't want people to treat me differently. I am not sure what I want, what I need right now."

"That's fine. You don't have to know."

"Maybe I just want to cry. Life is cruel. I want to be able to say that. Life is cruel. I am in pain. I am suffering. I want to be able to cry for myself. Why can't I cry for myself?"

"You can. You are allowed to cry. Go ahead. Cry. I am here. You can cry on me. I too have suffered. We all suffer. It's part of life. You are not alone. Just do your best. That's all you can do."

"So, I'll cry, and then what? What good will that do?"

"When you finish crying, I will take your hand and we will face this together. We will do our best with the canvas we were given to draw our unique life story. There will be challenges along the way, but it will be a beautiful life. Not without suffering, but rich and meaningful, and you will give to the world all your unique gifts, even with this illness. In some ways, even because of this illness. You can trust me. You'll see. I will take care of you."

"You will?"

"Yes, I will. But for now, just cry. Feel your pain. It is real, and it is true. And it is not shameful. I will always love you, even with your pain, and even with your

degenerating body. You are as beautiful and unique as your life promises to be. So just cry, my child, and let me hold you. Entrust yourself to me fully. Let go into my embrace."

And then the tears of thirty-two years are finally released.

WHEN I WAS a child, my parents sent me to the dentist alone. His office was not a long walk from my house, so they would make appointments for me, and I would go there. Alone. I would sit in his waiting room office, reading *Archie* comics, and wait to be called in.

I have never had good teeth. Neither has my father, so it seems I inherited that from him. I have memories from my childhood of drilling and filling cavities. But whereas most people have memories of Novocain and laughing gas, my memories are of gripping the dentist's chair in pain and praying for it to be over.

I would think about Mengele and Auschwitz and tell myself my pain was nothing compared to what I would have had to endure had I been born just two generations prior. Sometimes I would even see stars.

I don't remember if it was my dentist or my parents who did not believe in laughing gas. Or maybe it was both.

My mother had surgery on her spine when I was a child; she spent nine months in a torso cast. It was hot and itchy. I remember her scratching herself with a back scratcher, sticking it into the cast. But I do not remember her complaining.

My mother's older sister died from breast cancer in her fifties. When I told my mother about a friend who was in denial that her mother was dying of cancer, that she did not want to hear the word "hospice," not even "home hospice," my mother's reply was, "Well, tell her to get used to it. That's life."

My mother's best friend, who was like a sister to her, died in her early seventies from skin cancer. When my parents were in South Africa two years later with my mother's deceased friend's husband and his new wife (my mother's friend had told her husband she wanted him to remarry a year after her death, and he did), I asked her if it was hard for her to be there without her friend. She did not answer me.

I wonder today what it would have been like had my mother cried with me that day when I was diagnosed. I don't remember what we talked about on the way home in the car. Perhaps she did ask me how I felt. Perhaps I just did not want to be open with her then. I was a teenager, after all.

But if I did not cry, if I did not share with her my fears and sorrow, I wonder if that was because of subliminal messages I received as a child:

"That's life." Those messages are true, but they were still heavy for a teenager to bear.

It seems I inherited my mother's stoicism, on a conscious level, while on a subconscious level, the pain was still there, trying to make herself heard.

SPEAKING WITH MY inner child brought up buried memories from my childhood. Like this one:

My favorite store growing up was BIG TOP. It was a toy/candy/art supply/stationery store. What else could a kid need? I would save up my allowance and ride my bike to BIG TOP, where whatever I wanted could be found.

Hubba Bubba was the candy of choice for a while, until we heard someone found spider's eggs in a package. Then it was Pop Rocks, until we heard a kid died when they blew up in his mouth. When it was chocolate I wanted, it was Snickers chocolate peanut bars. I never heard of anyone dying of those. This was before peanut allergies became a rampant threat in the U.S.

Big Top is where we bought birthday presents, too. On the way to a birthday party, I'd stop there with my parents, pick out a present, have it wrapped, and go straight to the party.

But then my love affair with BIG TOP ended. I went in with my father to buy a present on the way to my best friend's goodbye party. She was moving to Israel, and I was distraught. I chose a diary with a lock and tiny key and a package of stationery with envelopes for her to write letters to me. I had already written her a poem, which I planned to put on the gift as the card.

We went to the front desk, and my father paid. I reminded him this was a present, which he told the cashier, who was also the owner of the store. But the man did not ask if we'd like it wrapped, as was the usual procedure there, so my father asked him to please wrap the present. He said they no longer offered that service.

I was ready to leave, but my father began to argue. He insisted that when he paid for the present, he also paid to have it wrapped. When the man began yelling at him, telling him to leave the store, my father told the store owner that he was a lawyer and that he shouldn't start up with him.

And that is when it happened. The man came out from behind the counter and slapped my father hard across the face. His glasses went flying. He was bleeding from the bridge of his nose. The glasses cracked. My father, who was born with one eye shut, needed his glasses to drive. My heart was racing. Tears welled up in my eyes.

"Let's go," my father said, picking up the glasses and taking my hand.

We left the store and never went back again.

Like God, my father could not protect me from life. They had both let me down.

I NEVER DID see my father's left eye open. The surgeries he had when he was a child, to fix his eyelid muscle, did not work enough to open his eye more than a slit.

I also never saw my father cry. But I did see letters from his six-year-old self to his own mother, begging to be brought home from sleepaway camp. Back then, all the Brooklyn kids who could afford it were sent out of the city to escape the polio epidemic. But he hated camp and just wanted to come home.

Reading those postcards, which my father kept stored in the attic, was like hearing his inner child crying.

I cried for both of us.

ONE ESPECIALLY FOGGY Sunday morning, my daughter Meira was home for *Shabbat* from her army preparation program in Jerusalem. In Israel, females, too, are drafted. She needed to catch a bus back, so I offered to drive her to the bus stop at the entrance to our kibbutz.

The air was a white mist that made it impossible to see into the distance. I was concerned; the kids were on their way to school on these roads that were covered in one big white cloud.

We talked as I drove, getting in our last pieces of conversation before she headed off for two weeks. "I have more army testing this week," she informed me, as she slipped out of the car. "For that secret artsy unit I told you about." Meira is an artist. At first, we thought that would make it hard for her to find a suitable place in the army. But it seemed the army had units for artists, too.

I watched my eighteen-year-old daughter walk to the bus stop, and waited to see the bus arrive and her board it safely. I turned the car around and headed back home. With the kids all off starting their days, I could start mine.

Another child going into the army soon, I thought as I drove. She wouldn't be in combat, at least. But still, it meant sending her off into the hands of a huge institution whose purpose was not to protect her, nurture her, or fill her needs. She would be a cog in the wheel of the national defense machine. Even if she was in an artsy unit—whatever that meant. Would she be designing weapons? Secret tunnels?

Suddenly, I saw Jacob up ahead, running along the path leading out of the kibbutz. I knew he was out running, but I didn't know he had a partner for his run. He was with a friend of mine and his. They did not notice me. They were busy talking as they ran, side-by-side, keeping pace with each other.

My friend's dark curly hair, not so unlike mine, was bouncing with her body, her bare muscular legs catapulting her forward with each stride. She was wearing running shorts. I had not worn shorts in years, as my legs were pathetically emaciated, especially my calves. When I looked in the mirror, I wondered how I managed to stand on those stick-like legs.

My friend's arms and shoulders looked muscular, too, in her tight-fitting tank top. Her stomach was flat, whereas mine stuck out like that of a woman five months pregnant, because of my abdominal and back muscle weakness. My friend was strong and healthy. And therefore, she could run with Jacob, while I was weak and sickly. I could not.

Sex with Jacob had been good the night before, although I was careful to turn the light off, lest he see too much of me and what I had become. It was nice to connect after the tension caused the day before, *Shabbat*, by the detour I took on the way home from the pool to walk on a trail halfway between the pool and our kibbutz. He said he was worried something had happened to me, but I sensed he was also upset that I did not keep my driving outing to swimming and swimming alone. The slippery slope was getting more slippery.

I had told him when I got home from that short Sabbath hike between the pool and home, if he was willing to use his cell phone on *Shabbat*, I could let him know where I was, send him a message so he wouldn't worry. Since he was not willing to use his phone, he would have to just let go. After all, isn't that what the Sabbath was about? He agreed but said if I didn't drive on *Shabbat*, that would also solve the problem. A stalemate.

Jacob did not notice it was me driving by now, on this foggy morning. Trying to retain my composure, I slipped by, as he was caught up in his running and talking.

Then the tears came. Now that my sixteen-year-old-self had released them, they just kept flowing. It was difficult enough to see with this heavy mist, but now my vision was even more blurred by my water-filled eyes.

I DECIDED TO talk directly to my disease. After thirty-two years, it was about time.

"Are you willing to talk to me, FSHD? I know you are there."

"Yes."

"Can you tell me why you showed up in me, out of the blue? A mutation. What were you trying to tell me?"

"I have always been with you. I did not happen to you. I am not an invader. You were born with me. We were born together. Pain and suffering are an inherent part of life. The moment you are born, the only certainty about life is you will die. I didn't just show up one day, out of the blue. Why do people think they are going to be spared pain and suffering? No one is. The illusion is you can avoid it somehow."

"What do you want from me?"

"I want you to let me run my course. And I want you not to blame me. I do not want to hurt you. Maybe if you stop fighting me, we can be friends. I may be different, but I am still beautiful. Maybe in my difference, I am beautiful. Why does a mutation have to be bad? Stop reinforcing that idea. Please."

"What am I doing to reinforce that idea?"

"You do not hug me. You do not embrace me. You do not love me. Laugh with me, please. Have fun with me. Be kind to me. Take care of me. But not in a condescending way. And don't fight me. I may be a mutation, but I am not your enemy. If we sprang out of nowhere, we did it together. Accept me for who I am, and you won't be sorry."

BACK WHEN I was sixteen, researchers had not yet discovered the gene for FSHD, so there was no genetic test available to formally diagnose the disease. Only a clinical diagnosis. When the gene was discovered, I felt no need to be tested. It was clear I had it. Why did I need a blood test to prove it?

A cousin of mine on my mother's side, however, asked me to do her a favor and be tested. She is a doctor. She wanted to know for sure if this disease is in our family. And so, I was tested, and, of course, the test result was positive.

If my mother was tested and did not have the gene, we would know I had inherited the gene from my father or was a spontaneous mutation, and my cousin would not have to worry about the disease showing up in any of her children. And if she did not have the gene herself, her children would not either. I don't know why she didn't do the test herself or ask my mother to do the test. Or maybe she did ask, and my mother refused.

I ask my mother to do the test. My father, too. I send them an email. I want to know once and for all if I am a spontaneous mutation.

This is my mother's reply:

Why is it important to know if you are a mutation? We always were under the impression you are. But why does it matter?

My answer:

It's not so important. I just feel it would help me close this circle. Remove the question mark. It would be interesting to know the answer. That's all.

I have always felt different—from my parents, from my community, from my environment. I have always looked a little different, too, with my mouth that cannot smile, my drooping bottom lip—a constant reminder of what sets me apart. And I have always had an aversion to groups and to communities demanding any kind of conformity. I have always felt on the outside looking in.

That feeling of being different formed alongside my mutant gene, while I was becoming me in my mother's womb. I was born with that feeling, along with my mutant gene. Or could it be that it was already in my DNA when sperm met egg?

Mutant or not, either way, I would still be me. So, as my practical mother said, why does it matter?

We are all born from a place of unity in our biological mother's womb, into a place of separation in the world we inhabit. It is possible everyone feels different. Yet, I always had the feeling I felt more different than most. Perhaps if I could discover the origin of my separate feeling, I would be able to finally feel connected, I told myself.

WHEN I WAS diagnosed, aside from recommending swimming, the doctor told me and my mother there was an organization I could join called the FSHD Society. They raise money to fund research into the disease, have support networks and regular informational and social conferences. He thought it might be good for me to meet other people with the same disease as mine. I did not agree.

My parents did join. They received the quarterly newsletter, which I tried to ignore. When I did peek at the cover articles, I saw photos of people with crooked smiles like mine, slumped shoulders like mine, but some in wheelchairs, some with walkers, some with symptoms so apparent I had to turn away. I was not ready to see my future. I was not even ready to see my present reality for what it was.

But now, with my own symptoms already impeding my lifestyle, I could no longer avoid my reality. I was going to be in the Boston area anyway for a book talk, and coincidentally or not so coincidentally, the bi-annual FSHD Society Connect Conference was going to be there, too. The forces of the Universe were leading me to my first encounter with others like me. Ready or not, I went.

Walking into that hotel in Boston was how I imagine an African child adopted by white parents into an all-white town would feel getting off the plane in Africa, or even getting off the subway in Harlem. I had never met someone with the disease before, and here I was surrounded by people who looked like me.

These people may not have had the dark curly hair, the slanted brown eyes, or the high cheekbones I had inherited from my parents, but they did have the face with little expression, the eyes that could not completely close, the almost-stagnant lips, the protruding stomach, the hunched shoulders, and the dragging feet (or contraptions to prevent the dragging).

I felt like I had come home to a hotel full of mutants like me. I cried tears of both relief and anxiety. Some of my sister and brother mutants were in wheelchairs, some with walkers, others on scooters. One young woman had a neck brace to hold her head up. Another had her mother constantly at her side, helping her with simple tasks like eating, as she could not lift her arms at all (while I can lift mine to my waist). We were all the same, yet all different.

I spoke to people older than I was and with fewer and lighter symptoms than mine, and I spoke to people much younger, children even, who were already in wheelchairs. I was glad I had come, but I also understood why it had taken me so long. This was not an easy place, even if it was where I needed to be at this point in my life.

Leaving was difficult as well. I was going back to the world of the "normal" people, where no one understood my disease and its effects. I also realized, however, even in a room full of FSHD-ers, no one could understand me completely. They may have understood what it was like not to be able to brush their hair, blow up a balloon, smile a toothy smile, run to catch their fleeing toddler, or lift their toes, but they did not know how it felt to be me.

My feeling of separation did not disappear with this conference, but the experience did help me realize the answer lay not in gatherings of like-minded or like-bodied people. They were important, and I would continue to attend them and even go on to create an FSHD Society chapter in Israel with my daughter, Hallel, who inherited the disease from me. But that was only part of the work. Only by delving into my unique causes of that acute feeling of separation, would I be able to flow from my narrow stream, slowly but surely, into the vast ocean.

MY COUSIN PEARL sends me a scan of an interview she did with her mother before she died. It turns out my "crazy" Aunt Essie was quite a remarkable, articulate and brave woman. She was an idealist who left her comfortable life in Brooklyn to learn farming in Upstate NY so she could move to Palestine (before 1948 when the State of Israel was established), live on a kibbutz and work in agriculture.

And this is what she did. She was the only woman driving a tractor on her kibbutz, and the only woman in her troop driving an ambulance in 1948.

My Aunt Essie was a strong feminist, although when she gave birth to her first child, she became much more "feminine" and began to have fears about the safety of her child and husband. Until then, she had no fear.

She lived on various *kibbutzim*, as well as in Tel Aviv and Jerusalem. She worked and studied and searched for a place where she could fulfill her potential and contribute to society, but she never found one.

In search of integrity and justice, she came to Israel with the strong belief the only way to be fully Jewish was to be an Orthodox religious Zionist. But she became disillusioned with Zionism and Orthodox Judaism and their ability to live up to her ideals.

She experimented with praying with *tefillin* for a while, trying to reconcile religious tradition with feminism. Ultimately, she realized her issues with religion went deeper than only defined gender roles. She lost faith in religion.

In the end, she began to see she was expecting too much of people and systems. She was an individualist, she came to understand, not a socialist and not a pious Jew. She was not willing to sacrifice her own self-fulfillment and individuality for the group. And besides, even socialism as it was practiced on the kibbutz was not truly egalitarian, she realized.

The interview with my Aunt Essie ends when she came to study with her husband in California. She did not talk about her life after that, perhaps because her daughter who was interviewing her already knew that part. I know my aunt and her husband, my cousins' father, ended up divorcing and she stayed in the U.S. with her two daughters. He went back to Israel, to the kibbutz.

I do not think it was only her disillusionment which kept her back in the U.S. She was not well. She was diagnosed as bipolar. Yet, when I read her words, describing how she slowly let go of her intense commitment to Judaism and the Jewish people and began to see the world in a more universalist way, I feel a soul sister speaking to me from the grave.

I did not know that like me, my aunt had a degree in English literature. And her oldest daughter, my cousin Daphne, is named Michal Daphne; she went by Daphne in the U.S. because it was easier to pronounce than Michal, but her name is the same name I chose for my oldest daughter. Michal, the wife of King David, is known in the Talmud for being rebellious and having a mind of her own—and for having worn *tefillin*.

It would be sad if my Aunt Essie never found her spiritual home, not even inside herself. It is not clear to me whether she lost her faith in humanity and God, or just in systems and religion.

My cousin Daphne shared this with me in an email:

> I do believe she moved to the States with my dad so he could get his advanced botany degree, and she supported us by teaching. When they split, she needed help as a single parent, so she returned to the East Coast. Here is one thing I remember her saying at a Passover seder one year — that the Jewish G-d is so far away and distant it was hard for her to find comfort in "him." I don't think she ended her life in existential pain, though. We saw her through those last years, and that was her comfort.

I wish I could ask my aunt these questions, speak to her, have the conversation I know I will never have. We would have much to talk about, much in common, despite our different temperaments.

I have been told I am calm, patient, and non-judgmental. Even-tempered. She was very much the opposite, it seems. I feel blessed to have been gifted with an even temperament to balance my passionate demand for integrity. A demand that has softened over the years, as I have matured into a better understanding of human complexity (even my own).

I sense part of my aunt's disillusionment stemmed from her impatience with the imperfection of humanity. I am learning to accept that imperfection, both in others and in myself, as part of what makes us human. I am also learning, slowly, to accept the brokenness of the world and the unfairness of life. Not as things to fix, but as things to examine, work with, understand, accept, and, perhaps, even embrace.

Still, I know now from where I come. I am not a spontaneous mutation, after all. At least not in all areas of my life.

ANGELS AT THE CROSSROADS

THEN ONE DAY, I fell on my face.

I was walking to pick up Shefa from pre-school, and, like usual, I was rushing. I had tried to fit in just one more thing before leaving the house and would be late if I did not take the shorter route to get her. This shorter way is not treacherous, but it is also not paved. There are rocks and holes along the dirt path, and it is not level. When it is raining, it is slippery from the wetness, and when it is hot and dry, it is slippery from the sliding rocks.

I fall often; this was not an unusual occurrence. However, in the past, I had been able to catch myself without doing much harm. I scraped knees and elbows, but most often, I was able to stand and move on. Once I did break my foot, but that was an exception. I could not help wondering, as I lay on the ground, when the exception would become the rule.

I fell flat on my face into a mound of dirt and rocks. Once I got myself standing, I had to turn around and go back home, with a mouth full of dirt, and my face pounding in pain. I could no longer pick up Shefa from preschool.

Once I cleaned my face and called a friend to pick up Shefa, I realized some of the pain was coming from inside my mouth. I touched my front teeth, top and bottom, and noticed they were tender. Some even felt a bit loose. I called the dentist and went for an emergency check-up. She said if after a week the teeth were not settled back firmly in place, she would put in a retainer.

When I checked in via email with Belinda Miller, a children's book writer and my FSHD "big sister" in Virginia, who is about twenty years older and ahead of me in the development of the disease, she said she had been fitted with her retainer years earlier, after a similar fall. She also said she had started using a cane and then a rollator (a beefed-up walker, as she explained when I asked) after that fall, and then even later, after more serious falls, a scooter.

"I knew it was time to stop walking—or trying to—after my last fall when I fractured two vertebrae. Too much pain. The walking is not worth the falling. So, that's the deal, my dear," I read in her email to me, as I fought back tears.

So, that's the deal. Had I reached a crossroads? Had that time I had pseudo-casually predicted, finally arrived? I had said it like I was okay with it, over and over again—"One day, when I am in a wheelchair"—but now that the time seemed so near I could touch it, was I okay with it? Apparently not.

One of the benefits of being in a spiritual counseling program is that you must be undergoing spiritual counseling yourself. Luckily, I had an appointment scheduled with my spiritual counselor—a Christian interfaith minister about fifteen years my senior who lives with multiple sclerosis—less than a week after my fall. As we spoke through our computer screens, she in New York and I in Israel, she hooked onto my use of the word "crossroads."

"At the mythological crossroads, one can usually look back to see from where you have come, and see more clearly to where you are going, having been where you were. How does that land for you?" she asked me.

"That feels about right," I answered. "I see all those years of insisting I could do it all. Seven kids, one adopted. Six C-sections. Always doing, always moving. Trying to accomplish it all before it was too late. Much of that, I can see now, was because of my diagnosis. And that was a kind of blessing, in a way. But now the message, the blessing, feels different."

"And now, what do you see ahead of you?" she asked.

"I see a slower and wiser me. I can't take it easy, exactly. I have too much responsibility, and I still have things I want to accomplish. But slower and wiser feels about right."

I remembered a session, as the counselor-in-training, only a couple of weeks before, with a counselee. She was a young woman who was diagnosed with a neuromuscular autoimmune disease a week before our first session.

We had discussed her overachiever non-stop parents, and how hard it was for her to accept the fact that she would have to live a slower lifestyle, giving herself permission to work only part time and sleep nine to ten hours a night.

At the time, since I was the counselor in that scenario, I had focused on her and put my own personal pain aside—as I had learned to do as part of my training. But now that I was with my counselor, I could address it. This was my time; she was holding sacred space for me. It was my turn to explore what I had learned from my own counselee.

"Another feature of the mythological crossroads," my counselor said, "is that angels tend to show up there."

She was right. I have many angels in my life. One of them was on the computer screen before me.

ONE NIGHT, AFTER coming home late from my Palestinian-Jewish narrative sharing group, I had the house all to myself. Jacob had taken the younger kids on the kibbutz's annual community camping trip, and for the first time, I did not join them.

My policy is to try and do as much nature-oriented activity as I can until I can't anymore. But it is not clear when that time will come, nor how I will know it has arrived. Will it be when I am physically no longer able to do it, or when the gain is not worth the risk? Or will it be when I am just not enjoying it because of my limitations?

This is what I was pondering before the camping trip, in addition to when to start using walking sticks more frequently and regularly when venturing outside. I had not come to a final decision about any of this, but I decided not to go camping this time. Instead, I marked this transition into making wiser choices by building an altar.

In addition to my training with Jude, I had joined a Meeting Your Soul in Nature group, facilitated by another One Spirit teacher, Rev. Ed O'Malley, after his presentation on using nature as a window to our souls. The idea of his approach is that we are all connected: people, animals, plants. Even the earth. If we pay attention, we can hear messages from the natural world.

I saw many parallels between Ed's work with nature and Jude's work with dreams. Whether we call it God, our Higher Self, our unconscious, or our inner voice, there is communication from a deeper and/or higher place when we dream, as well as when we open ourselves to the wonders of the natural world.

We dream several times a night, but we only remember some; even within those dreams, only certain images stick with us. Similarly, there is so much surrounding us, but only certain things catch our eyes at specific times. If we lean into those dream and waking elements, there are messages for us there.

The natural world is God's (or the Spirit of the Universe's) dreamscape in which we—humans, plants and animals alike—connect and play a part. If God can speak to us through our dreams, why not through creation (which, to quote Edmond Jabes, is God's dream)? As with an especially vivid or recurring dream calling out to be understood, nature can call for our attention; it is up to us to observe, listen and try to understand.

In our last meeting before Jacob took the kids on the camping trip, Ed had given us various spiritual practices to choose from while out in nature. Building an altar out of things we found was one such practice.

What a treat to sleep in an empty and quiet house for the night and wake up naturally, to an equally empty and quiet house. I pampered myself by resting before rising—getting out of bed is difficult for me, as my muscles tighten as I sleep, making them stiff when I wake up, and exerting myself the day before in any way causes soreness and muscle spasm pain in the morning—and then slowly got out of bed.

I was relieved the heat wave had broken by morning. It was still hot. It is never cool in summer in Israel. But it was not like walking into a sauna, as it had been for days. There was even a slight almost cool breeze.

I went outside and looked around my garden for a place to build my altar. I spotted an olive tree, with a sweet little flat spot underneath. The tree would represent continuity and longevity, as olive trees can live for thousands of years.

I noticed there were already small green olives growing on the tree, getting ready to ripen for the olive harvest in the fall. We would harvest them (along with other olives from trees on and around our property) after the Jewish High Holiday season and bring them to the local olive press in the Arab village across the road, to make enough olive oil to last us for the year. Then the olives would be gone, would have served their purpose.

To me, the olives represented the changing seasons, the constant flux of life, within the greater permanence of the bigger picture. I would be gone one day, like the olives, after serving my personal purpose here. But the tree would remain long after. And the earth and sky long after that. And the water even longer, as it would keep recycling itself until the end of time.

I walked around the garden looking for things to put under the tree but saw nothing I wanted to put on the altar, except flowers, buds that would remind me also of the passing of time—of the way flowers bloom, serve their purpose, and then shrivel up and die. But they do so with no angst, no resistance.

I did not want to kill one of those flowers. I did not want to pick it and put it on the altar.

I walked back to the olive tree and noticed a little pink flower hanging over into the spot where I was planning to make the altar. I did not have to kill a flower, after all. There it was, just where I wanted it.

I felt a desire to add water. I took a small ceramic bowl and filled it from the natural swimming lane we had recently completed building in our yard. This pool had been a dream of mine, and here it was. We had finally gotten all the permits and built the pool, after years of planning.

But it was more work than we had anticipated. Algae grew in this pool within hours. If I entered the pool at noon and got out at two p.m., I could visibly detect the difference. Life was never a dream come true. But the pool was worth the effort, especially because it removed the tension with Jacob around my driving to swim on *Shabbat*.

I took a piece of algae from the water and put it into the bowl as well, to remind me of the inevitable messiness and vicissitudes of life. No matter how much or often we cleaned the pool, new algae would grow back. It was amazing how rapidly things changed, and frustrating too, when I wanted to try to keep it all clean and clear. But there is no clean and clear. I put the bowl on the altar and sat.

I meditated on this new place where I had arrived in my life. The place of making wiser choices, of accepting it was no longer fun for me to go camping in the heat of an Israeli summer, even if it was by a river. Others could easily get in and out, while I needed help and would risk slipping and hurting myself. Seeing them so freely bathing in my element, water, would frustrate me, and I had come to accept that.

Not without sorrow and mourning, I made a wise decision not to go, and instead to enjoy the things I could do with more ease: sitting in the forest with my narrative sharing group; going with my oldest daughter Michal (who does not live at home anymore, so it is a treat to go out, just the two of us) to visit my cousin who was in mourning for her mother whom I loved; doing a conversion ceremony with an autistic girl and her adoptive parents; swimming in my pool; and building an altar to mark this transition in my life . . .

I intended after that morning to revisit my altar. But the temperature began to rise, and the kids came back from camping and were home from school on summer break. Life became hectic, and I did not make it out to the altar again until Friday morning. To my surprise—although why should I have been surprised by this?—the water had evaporated. All that remained in the ceramic bowl was a piece of dried algae. All that remained was the muck.

I looked over at my lovely little flower. It had shriveled and fallen from the tree. Like the algae growing on my pool walls, life came and went so quickly. But again, why should this surprise me? At least the olive tree still stood in its place, thick and low. And the olives were still on the branches, among the leaves, getting riper until they too would fall.

My surprise at this turn of events intrigued me. Of course, the water would evaporate. Of course, the flower would die. I was still fighting the inevitable, still expecting the impossible. Even if I kept telling myself that change is the only thing we can count on in life, knowing it intellectually and accepting it emotionally are two very different things.

I still had work to do. But this would be the work of a lifetime, a constant dance between moments of inner peace with what is and a more general resistance to the pain and suffering of life.

I had wanted to put these elements back into nature when I felt ready. But nature had already taken them from me. It was out of my control. And so is life.

I reminded myself the tree would still be here long after I was gone. And the water did not disappear; it merely evaporated, went back into the air and would come down again, someday, as rain, to water the plants so another flower could grow. And so on, and so on. And somehow that did give me a bit of comfort.

The next day, on *Shabbat*, I was reading the book, *God in the Wilderness*, by Rabbi Jamie Korngold. I keep a spiritual book in my *tallit* bag to read in synagogue when I am feeling disconnected from the service. The topic of the chapter I was reading was the imperfection of the Universe.

Korngold writes how God created an imperfect Universe and did not give us the tools to fix it, a notion that challenges the central Jewish value of *tikkun olam*, repairing the world. But my Buddhist studies had brought me to a place of understanding *tikkun olam* to be about doing the work of social action without being attached to the outcome. As it says in Ethics of our Fathers 2:16: "It is not upon you to complete the work, but neither are you at liberty to desist from doing it." Moreover, I had come to see *tikkun olam* to be more about healing the world than fixing it.

According to Korngold's approach, God gave us the tools not to fix the world, but rather to deal with the imperfection, the suffering, and to do with our lives what we can with what we are given. Even nature is not perfect.

When you really look at a tree, for example, you see its imperfections. But it deals with the climate and its surroundings in the best way it can. Being with a tree, and with nature in general, can remind us of this, of the fact that we are like the tree.

Korngold shares her spiritual practice of sitting with her back to a tree and breathing in and out, feeling the tree's trunk against her spine and the support of the earth beneath her. She feels how the ground accepts her and supports her as she is. Then, along with her breathing, she chants God's words to Moses when Moses asked for God's name at the burning bush: "I Will Be What I Will Be."

I was stunned she had chosen my own favorite name for God. I had even made a laminated card, to take into the *mikveh* with me, with this Divine Name on it. I had another idea. I would put this card at the end of my pool, so I could be reminded each time I completed a lap, to try and flow with what is instead of trying to fight it. I could meditate on that name for God as I swam.

I will be what I will be. God will be what God will be. Life will be what life will be. This is what is in the present right now, I told myself. This became my morning prayer: *I will be what I will be.*

And in the evenings, I began implementing Korngold's practice. I went out into my garden and sat beneath a different olive tree that sits on the opposite side to where I had built my altar. This olive tree is a young one, so the branches create a canopy directly over my head. I brought a cushion there, and a sheet for my legs and feet. I sprayed on bug repellent, and I sat. I felt embraced by the tree and supported by the earth.

I breathed in my mantra: *I will be what I will be.* I looked up at the branches, each sticking out in a different way. The tree too was what it was. Not perfect, but doing its best at being a tree with the tools it had been granted.

This tree had a story, as well as specific given circumstances, all of them so much out of its control. How much water it gets depends on us and on nature. How much sun depends on the climate and where we decided to plant it in our garden. How much strength and ability to survive in its circumstances depends on what was in its seed when it was planted.

I am like this tree, I thought to myself as I chanted and breathed. I am what I am. Not perfect. But beautiful in my own humanity, like this tree is beautiful in its own essence.

And then this traditional Jewish prayer, which is usually understood to be referring to the Torah, came to me:

She is a tree of life, for those who embrace her. Those who support her are blessed. Her ways are ways of ease, and all her paths are peace.

I am a tree of life when I embrace myself. When I feel supported (by Life), I am satisfied with what is. This is the way of ease from suffering, and thus, all paths of love and compassion, for myself and for others, will lead to inner peace.

THE TOPIC OF the day in my online webinar is grounding. I wonder how this will be for me. I think I do feel emotionally grounded, yet physically, I am challenged in that way. I love walking in nature, being around earth, smelling it, touching it, but I do not feel stable while standing on it. The ground is not where I find my grounding. It is in water I feel safe.

When we break up into pairs for a co-counseling exercise, I am meant to choose a guided visualization for my partner to practice on me. I could easily choose the one where we imagine ourselves in our safe and happy place, but I know that will be in the water. I want to see if I can feel grounded on the earth. I choose the visualization that most challenges me, the one where I am meant to be a tree, shooting her roots into the ground.

My dyad partner is skilled at guiding me. She's done this before. She tells me to imagine myself a tree, standing tall and graceful, reaching my branches skyward, but with my trunk planted firmly on the ground. She tells me to feel the floor beneath my own feet.

I am seated. If I had tried to stand for the visualization, my instability would have distracted me. I try to imagine myself standing tall and firm. I am able, but it does not feel right, as I cannot lift my arms, and I don't remember what it feels like to stand sturdily on the ground.

Suddenly, I have an urge to lie down. That feels right. I am lying on the earth, with my back to the ground and my face to the sky. I am not a fallen tree, but a horizontal tree. My grounding is horizontal, not vertical. It is a posture of surrender.

Now, when she tells me to feel my roots shooting into the earth, I feel them coming out not from my feet, but from my back, my bottom, the undersides of my legs, arms and head. My roots are growing down into the earth, soaking up minerals and other nutrients. Drinking water. Lots of water.

Now my roots are reaching the core of the earth. Suddenly, I am both Earth *and* Tree of Surrender. As my roots reach Earth's core, I am reaching my own core. In my posture of surrender, I am growing roots that go deep. And I am drinking from my own deepest place.

Moments of peace, nourishment and grounding, to strengthen me for what is to come.

I WALK INTO the house. Jacob and the kids are sitting around, looking mournful. Everyone is there, except Shefa. I ask them where Shefa is, and they hand me a dishwasher tablet—the kind that looks like candy.

I take a close look at the tablet, like a zoom-in shot in a film. The tablet becomes magnified—a powdery white and blue rectangle with a red ball in the center. I ask if she ate the tablet. They all nod their heads yes. I ask where she is. They all shake their heads. I don't believe them. She is not dead! She can't be!

I wake up and find myself in my king-sized bed underneath my comforter. Jacob is to my right, and Shefa is to my left. She comes into our bed every night without fail. Sometimes I don't even notice. Like this night. But there she is. I sigh in relief. I touch her chest. She is breathing. You see, I was right. She is not dead. She's laying here right beside me, like usual.

I am so tired. I need to get back to sleep. I reassure myself Shefa is alive and well. She is not dead at all, just sleeping. It was a dream. And it does not mean Shefa will die any time soon, either. Dreams do not have to be prescient. In fact, most are not.

The Shefa character in the dream is not even Shefa. She is me. She is a piece of my unconscious sending me a message, trying to tell me something, through the image of my youngest child. I can go back to sleep now and work the dream another time to figure it out.

I jot down my dream in my dream journal and fall back asleep.

"That was not an easy dream," Jude says when we meet a few days later, on Zoom.

"No. But I am ready to work it," I say.

"Okay. I would like to speak to the tablet. I felt a lot of energy around that tablet. Can you tell me about yourself, tablet? Describe yourself. What do you look like? What is your function?"

My eyes are already closed as much as they will shut, so I put my hands over them, take a deep breath and drop back into my dream. I can see that dishwasher tablet so clearly, so vividly, once again like a camera zooming in, enlarging it, bringing it into focus. I begin:

"I am a dishwasher tablet. I am rectangular, made of a powdery soap that dissolves in water. I have a red ball in my center, like a heart, and I am wrapped in plastic. Like a candy. I look good enough to eat. But my looks are deceiving. I am not meant for eating. Once you taste me, you know that. Anyone who takes the time to taste me knows I am not edible."

"So, what is your function? How do you work?" Jude asks.

"My function is to clean the dishes so people can eat off them. So they will feel sanitary and respectable. People put me into a dark little compartment and shut the door. And when the time is right, the door pops open, and I drop into the water. I dissolve in the water, become one with the water, and that is how I fulfill my function."

"So, you fulfill your function by dissolving?"

"Yes. But once I dissolve in the water, I am not the same anymore. I am so much less and so much more at the same time. I can't be defined or labeled.

Not like when I was wrapped in plastic in that box, along with the other tablets, with a label telling everyone what I am."

"If the label says dishwasher tablet, why would anyone think to eat you?" Jude sounds intrigued.

Good question. "Exactly. Only someone who can't read, like a child, might make that mistake. Someone innocent, someone who has not yet been shaped and influenced by society and what they say I am meant to be. Someone like that might not realize my societal function is to wash things and might try to taste me instead. Taste, but not eat. She would know right away not to eat me."

"But she ate you anyway?" Jude asks.

"No." I surprise myself with my answer. "She did not eat me. I am still here, being shown to the dreamer. Right?"

"Right. So, can you talk to the tablet she did eat? Can you ask it what happened?"

I try to close my eyes tighter, hoping something will come, hoping to be able to communicate with the tablet Shefa ate in my dream. But nothing comes. I draw a blank.

"No, I can't," I explain. "I can't speak to that tablet, because I don't even know if there is such a tablet. I don't think there is. They are showing me to the dreamer as an example of what they *think* happened to Shefa. They assume she ate a dishwasher tablet. They are showing me to the dreamer so she will assume that, too. But she doesn't. She doesn't assume things are as they appear to be."

"Looks can be deceiving," Jude agrees.

"Yes. Like me," I continue, as the dishwasher tablet. "People think I am dangerous to a child. *Keep out of the reach of children*, they say. But I am not dangerous. And my function is not to cleanse or purify. I am beyond functions. I am what dissolves in water and disappears, like everyone and everything."

"Dishwasher tablet, how did you feel when you were magnified?" Jude asks.

"I felt bigger. I felt clear. I felt seen."

"Thank you, tablet. You were very helpful. Now I would like to speak to Shefa. I know you are not in the actual dream, but can you come out and speak to us, Shefa?"

"Yes, I can," I say. "I do not make an actual appearance in the dream, because I am not being seen. But the dreamer sees me when she wakes up.

She sees that I am not dead at all. I am sleeping beside her. People assume I am dead because I look so peaceful. They mistake sleep for death. Peace for emptiness. Surrender for submission. Trust for naivete. Stillness for passivity. Contentment for boredom. They think I have to be doing something useful to have a purpose or be real."

"Why would they assume that?" Jude asks.

"Because they don't see how rich my sleeping life is. They don't see how deep and meaningful it is to be asleep. They don't understand how vital it is to trust and surrender into that state."

"Thank you, Shefa. We are glad you are still with us, sleeping and dreaming, even if other people misinterpret what it is you are doing. They think you are dead. They think you could not discern between what is dangerous, what is sweet, and what is useful. But you know you can. That is what is important."

When I open my eyes, I realize Shefa is not only the me who is just beginning to discover the depths of her soul, but she is also my soul itself—the part of me I repressed in order to fit in with and please those around me.

My resistance to religious practices and labels was my inner voice calling to me to claim this lost part of myself. From a young age I had been rebelling against rules and authority, yet I had also been thirsty for meaning. To please both those around me and my own fear of the unknown, I returned to various forms of religious observance again and again to quench that thirst. Now, I am finally embracing that inner child who has been calling out for freedom all along.

Now that I opened that wound, heard that voice, acknowledged my inner child's pain and longings, am I ready to embrace her? Will others in my life be ready to meet her? She is asking me to trust in my inner voice and in life to tell me what is best for my soul. A terrifying notion.

My inner child was not being seen, but she did not die or leave. She is still here with me. If I have the courage to shake her, we will wake up together.

BARING BODY AND SOUL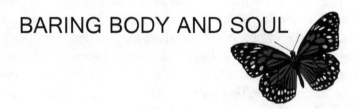

ANGELS COME IN the form of emails as well.

One morning while Jacob was away, after the kids were off to school, I sat down at my computer to work. I saw an email from a sender with a name I did not recognize. But when I opened it, I remembered her. She was a woman from the group who had come to immerse the day the *mikveh* overflowed.

Before this woman immersed, she approached me to share some of her story of childhood sexual abuse and years of therapy and inner work to feel whole and worthy. She had been meaning to email me for a while but had just now been reminded of her *mikveh* experience and decided it was time to let me know how important it had been for her.

I was thinking about how the mikveh was overflowing when we arrived. It felt dreamlike—symbolic—the mikveh generously overflowing with healing and welcome, like a living thing greeting us!

When I immersed in the mikveh, I was filled with complete amazement and joy to see that my soul had survived untouched and could not be touched. I feel I've been given an incredible gift—to discover that my glowing soul will always be available to me.

The mikveh works on such a deep unconscious level: you give yourself completely in trust to the immersion, that it will give what you need to let go—the way it feels so deeply feminine in holding you. And going down the stairs to enter it feels so sacred—entering another realm of existence, beneath normal consciousness. I had no idea it would feel so profound.

As I read this woman's words, I knew they had been sent to me now for a reason. "It felt dreamlike," she had written. She, too, had felt it.

I remembered my empty-to-overflowing *mikveh* dream of months before. The overflowing *mikveh* is my overflowing spirit, breaking through boundaries and overflowing container walls in order to lift myself and others and take them to where they need to go. But I can return to the *mikveh* and do this overflowing spiritual work only once I go back to my own source, my own sacred wounds, my own basic humanity and essence.

My empty-to-overflowing *mikveh* dream came and was continuing to come true through this deep *mikveh* and spiritual counseling work and my learning to integrate the two. And all of that amid my own emotional and spiritual tumult. In fact, that was a necessary part of being able to do the work. I could only take people to where they needed to go—carry them like the water in my dream—if I went back to the source of my own suffering.

I turned my lack of milk into a *mikveh* overflowing with water.

All humans suffer. That is part of being mortal. It is only through touching our own darkest and most wounded places we can accompany others on their journeys. Because we see and feel the wholeness of the person before us only when we truly believe we are all created in the divine image.

There can be pain and healing at the same time. It is all about touching people at their basic humanity, and touching ourselves there as well, so we can return to the vessel, the container, to our incarnation on this earth, better able to serve ourselves and others.

Organized religion is not a substitute for doing our inner healing work. It can be a companion to it, but not a replacement. It can be a means towards bringing people together in community and healing on a collective level through shared story and ritual, but community should be about supporting each member in their individual healing work and encouraging them to contribute their gifts to the community, not suppress those gifts in the name of conformity.

Until we have healthy individuals we cannot have healthy community, and until we have communities not working against or trying to destroy one another, we cannot have a healthy world.

What a beautiful blessing in my life all of this was, even if it was stirring my own inner turmoil. Or perhaps *because* it was stirring my own inner turmoil. Although I knew how important it was to deal with my own woundedness outside of my work with others, to not let my own pain seep into their sacred space, I now understood how the intersection of pain could lead to healing.

This is what I saw in Jesus' bleeding body on the cross. This is what Buddha was telling us to embrace rather than fight. This is what Lurianic Kabbalah was telling us in the story of the shattering of the vessels:

The world is broken. We are all shattered and in need not of "fixing" but healing, like the world as a whole. We all suffer. It is part of living. Trying to escape our pain will only bring more pain. Leaning into our pain and recognizing that not only do we all suffer, but when one of us suffers, even if at the hands of another human being because of their own inner suffering, we all suffer—that is what will bring salvation for humankind. Humanity is crying out to be healed from its own self-inflicted wounds.

As Etty wrote in June of 1942: "If one starts by taking one's own importance seriously, the rest follows. It is not morbid individualism to work on oneself. True peace will come only when all individuals find peace within themselves; when we have all vanquished and transformed our hatred for our fellow human beings of whatever race—even into love one day."

This work, I now realized, was more valuable to my spiritual health than another spiritual practice or religious rule could ever be. Going to the heart of the pain is the only way to heal it. We can heal the world through healing ourselves and helping others heal themselves—one soul at time. This is what I wanted to spread to the world. This would be the essence of my pulpit.

Although it is harder sometimes to do this with those closest to us.

JACOB LEFT AGAIN. He was gone for over two weeks, and he would go more. And in case the message the *mikveh* was sending me was not clear enough, I was sent a variety of messages throughout the two weeks he was gone. Messages from other living beings I had been training myself to pay attention to as a way of hearing what my own soul was trying to tell me.

First, our chickens were attacked in the night by a dog (not ours, as we were between dogs at that time, which was a relief). The coop door had not been closed well enough, and the wind had apparently blown it open. Most of the chickens survived, but a few did not. Mishael, who was very attached to the chickens, wrapped himself in his blanket and refused to go to school. We spent the day—between my work commitments—burying the chickens, eulogizing them, and marking their graves.

Then I discovered our cat had fleas. Before I could do anything about it, our house was infested. Of course, it turned out I was allergic to flea bites. I was covered with itchy red bumps. I stripped all the beds, washed all the bedding and floors, and had the entire house fumigated by an exterminator.

And as if that was not enough, once the fleas were gone, a family of birds who had built a nest in a pipe on our roof fell into our house when their nest broke. I awoke one morning to the sound of frantic birds crying and flying around our house, trying to find a way back to their non-existent nest.

Over the course of a day, I managed to get the adult birds out of the house, but then the babies were left alone, huddled in my laundry room behind the washing machine I dared not use so as not to frighten the poor birds.

In the evening, a neighbor was able to get the baby birds out, but I was helpless to reunite this family of birds. The next morning, all was quiet, except one adult bird, perhaps the mother, flying around calling out, I assumed, to her babies. For hours, she flew around my backyard, apparently searching for the rest of the family.

I could not find where the others had gone. I had assumed they would simply build a new nest, and all would be well again. But somehow, this mother bird, if that is what she was, had been left alone.

Or was it the father? Was that bird, like Jacob, separated from his family due to circumstances beyond his control, doing his best to reunite himself with us?

But then I realized my mistake. What I had thought was only one bird was two. They were speaking to each other, communicating, cooperating to rebuild the nest and bring food to the children.

Jacob had not abandoned me. He was juggling family of origin and family of making, and he just could not be in two places at once. As needy and exhausted as I was, his parents and sister needed him more than the kids and I did at that time.

That did not mean we would all make it through unscarred. It is likely a baby bird or two would not survive this ordeal. But so is life. None of us who walk or fly or crawl this earth can escape the rocks in the river.

But just in case I did not get the message loudly and clearly enough, some fairies came to make sure I had gotten it straight.

I was sitting in my study waiting for my monthly live spiritual counseling webinar to begin, when they arrived. It was four p.m. in Israel and nine a.m. in New York, where the eight-hour-long webinar was being broadcast.

The past two webinars had also taken place when Jacob was away, and I was stressed about trying to once again be present in the seminar while single parenting, as well as having to stay up until midnight for the webinar and get all the kids out for school on my own at seven a.m. the next morning.

I had wanted to participate in a calm environment where I could fully engage and get the most out of the class, but that was not to be. I was frustrated and disappointed.

I locked the study door, trying to shut out my kids on the other side. I turned on the computer and sat down at the desk. Behind one of the people in the little boxes on the screen, I saw small flashing lights. *What is that?* I wondered. And then I realized it was *my* box I was seeing. Other participants started messaging me, asking me if I knew I had fairies sparkling in the window behind me.

I turned around to see what was twinkling, but it was only sunlight shining through the leaves of our mulberry tree. The wind was blowing outside, apparently creating this sparkling effect. Filtered through the computer, what I saw was fairies. But it only looked that way on the screen. When I looked directly at the window, the fairies were gone. It was both magical and perplexing.

The presenter for that day began the session, explaining we were about to spend fifteen minutes in prayer, each on our own.

I did not know what I was going to do with myself. I was not a meditator. And I could not see myself focusing with my kids and a whole group of their friends of all ages from the kibbutz making noise on the other side of the door.

This was a waste of my precious time. The kids were quiet now, but who knew when they would interrupt me and need my assistance? I wanted to get on with the class already.

I looked up at my bookshelf, hoping to find there a book of prayers I could read to myself. I spotted a book a dear friend had given me that year for my birthday, knowing it was something I would appreciate. It was a book of Muslim, Jewish and Christian prayers titled *Lord of Peace*. I opened the book randomly (or not so randomly) to this page:

Oh God! Set a Light in my Heart
By Abu Hamid Muhammad al-Ghazali

Oh God!
Set a light in my heart
And a light in my tongue
Set a light in my ear
And a light in my eye
A light behind me; and a light in front of me
And set a light above me
Oh God!
Give me light!

I looked at the fairies behind me on the computer screen in front of me. *A light behind me and light in front of me.* They were sparks of light coming through my own darkness. I had begun the class full of resentment and self-pity. I was annoyed at my situation, and annoyed at myself for being annoyed.

The reason I had not been able to be fully present in the last few classes was Jacob's act of loving-kindness to his family of origin in their time of need. Yet, I was not able to fully overcome or set aside my own pain in this situation. Disappointed in myself for being self-centered, this only made me feel worse.

I had been challenged and triggered over the past several months, but the situation had also led to some deep inner work, and I was grateful for that. Perhaps that was the crack letting the light in, as in the lyric from Leonard Cohen's famous song—"There's a crack in everything; that's how the light gets in"—which was likely inspired by this quote attributed to Rumi:

"The wound is the place where the light enters you."

Now I was being blessed with seeing that light. *A light in my heart.*

God was speaking to me through those lights, through those fairies. God had also been speaking to me through my sleeping dreams and my waking dreams, through my inner child and my human and animal friends. And through explorations of my own soul.

And so, I prayed then and there for God to give me light. And God answered me:

Here it is! I have been giving you light. It all depends on how you look at it, how you filter the light. Just open your eyes, and your heart, and let the light in!

A FEW WEEKS later, on Israel Independence Day, Jacob returned from over two weeks in New York, divided between work and family. He had spent many hours by his father's bedside in the hospital. His father had pneumonia again; he had both a feeding tube and an oxygen mask.

I was alone with the kids over that time, which included a vacation from school for the *Shavuot* holiday. I was tired, and so relieved to have Jacob home for this next holiday, at least.

As I drove to the beach to meet a group of friends, with the kids in the back of our van and Jacob next to me working on his phone, I saw Israeli flags hanging from car windows to my right, my left, and in front of me. They were flapping with pride in the wind, declaring to everyone—Jews and non-Jews alike—this is the land of the Jews, which the Jews won fair and square.

I purposely did not put flags on our car because I did not want to broadcast that message. I find it insensitive to the Palestinians who live in Israel and have full Israeli citizenship but know they will never be treated completely equally because they lost the war that turned the country into a Jewish state. Even if it was the Arabs who attacked in 1948, that does not make Israel Independence Day any easier for those Palestinians who live here.

Suddenly, I was overcome with sorrow: for Israel, for humanity. Why can't we get beyond fighting and killing? Why can't we get beyond difference and hatred and feelings of separation? Why are we in this cycle of hatred and war, of one day "us" on top and one day "them" on top, when really, we are all in this sinking ship together? Why can't we look deeply at our own pain and realize how it is preventing us from seeing one another's pain?

I could not understand why others around me could not see what I was seeing. I felt so sad. I did not identify with the celebratory energy around me.

It was not as if I did not see anything wonderful about the establishment of the State of Israel. I did. But there had also been so many mistakes made along the way, on both "sides," due to historical circumstances and limitations.

If only instead of fighting and antagonism, the Jews and Palestinians at the time had joined together to build a joint homeland. If only more Jews who went to join the small Jewish "*yishuv*" in Palestine back then had come in partnership instead of in a colonial, nationalist spirit—even if they were a deeply wounded people.

And if only the Palestinian Muslims and Christians back then had been welcoming of their persecuted Jewish cousins in need of shelter. If only they had accepted the Partition Plan, or at least expressed a desire to negotiate a new version of it, and not attacked when Israel declared a state in its portion of the land designated Jewish back in 1948.

I wondered: Is there any hope for healing and peace in this society that is plagued with Post-Traumatic Stress Disorder on so many levels and from so many directions?

I looked over at Jacob and decided to share my feelings with him. "Are you too busy to talk?" I asked. I was usually the driver when we were both in the car. I tended to get car sick if I did not drive, and Jacob liked to take advantage of the time to get work done on his phone. Yet, as usual, he stopped what he was doing when I expressed an interest in spending time together in any way. My heart opened to him.

Jacob listened attentively, patiently, to what I was expressing; it seemed he was truly trying to understand how I felt. Yet, once again, he did not relate. I heard annoyance in his voice as he said, "I know it is all too tribal for you, but still. We are talking about the establishment of the State of Israel. Can't you muster up at least a little bit of joy, a little bit of pride in your people, on this day?"

"Honestly?"

Jacob nodded.

"I just don't feel joy right now. I feel sorrow. That is what I am truly feeling. I can't lie to you and say that I do when I don't. I know I am not the only one who feels this way. There were thousands of people at that alternative ceremony two nights ago, and hundreds at the one last night."

I was referring to an alternative Memorial Day ceremony I had attended two nights before in Tel Aviv. It was organized by bereaved Palestinian and Israeli families who had all lost parents, siblings, or children in the conflict. The message was that we are all victims and should work together to end the conflict. This ceremony had become an annual occurrence.

Then, the next night, I had gone to a more intimate and controversial ceremony that I had been attending annually. It was an Independence *Day/Nakba* (which means catastrophe in Arabic and is the term used to refer to the loss of hundreds of Palestinian-Arab villages in the 1948 war that resulted in the establishment of the Jewish State) gathering, held each year in a different spot where a destroyed Palestinian-Arab village once stood.

At this gathering, we hear Jewish and Palestinian stories of 1948. We hold both the suffering and the joy, the destruction and the building. It is precarious, maintaining that shaky position, but for us who attend the gathering, it is the only place we can imagine being on that day.

"Well, why don't you ask our friends how they feel?" Jacob said, as we pulled into the parking lot of the beach.

I was glad I had been honest with Jacob about my feelings. Perhaps this would be the beginning of an ability to expose my inner life to him more and more.

I had been afraid he would decide this was the limit, I was going too far—that he could stretch no more without breaking. After all, together, in partnership, we had moved our lives to this country over twenty years before. Now, I was not only post-denominational, but I was post-Jewish and post-Zionist too in his eyes. I couldn't blame him if he drew the line there.

But he did not draw the line. He seemed open to trying to understand me. I felt hopeful as I turned the key towards me in the ignition. I felt a load lifted from my chest as the car went into rest mode.

Jacob and the kids unloaded the car—it was hard enough for me to walk on sand without carrying anything except myself—and we headed towards the water. When we arrived at the shore, where our friends were waiting on the beach with a picnic spread out before them, one friend asked me, as is his way, "How are *you?*"

"I'm sad, actually," I said.

And then it came. "What do you have to be sad about?!" Jacob exploded. I was caught off guard. "You have a great life. Don't you think it's a slap in the face for you to be sad on this day when there is so much to celebrate and be proud of?!"

I had not seen Jacob so angry, so personally insulted by me, perhaps ever. He must have been accumulating rage and resentment as he walked from the car. I felt all his frustrations with my evolving self-coming out in that one moment.

I knew he was under pressure. He had just spent days sleeping at his father's bedside, dealing with doctors and hospitals and with his mother and sister, who have their own sets of complicated emotional issues.

I was not being a supportive and loving partner because of the stress of Jacob's frequent absences and his family of origin's neediness. I had been focusing on myself and my own angst when he had immediate and personal sorrow sitting on his chest.

Jacob had a right to be angry with me, but my heart closed, nonetheless. I told myself never to expose my full truth to him again.

A few days later, Jacob sensed I had shut down. We went out for coffee, and I explained to him why. I was trying to show up in our partnership as who I truly was and not be afraid to share that person with him. But I felt sorry I had tried.

Jacob apologized; he looked forlorn, his clear blue eyes full of concern and regret. I felt badly for burdening him with more than he was already carrying, but I could not help how I felt. He took my hands in his across the table. He said he was wrong to lash out at me that way, especially in front of our friends. He was under pressure, dealing with so much and juggling so many people's needs.

"Can you give me another chance?" he asked. "I do want to know what you're thinking and feeling. I do want you to open up to me."

"I am not sure I can," was my reply. I had tested the waters, and they did not feel safe. "I love you, but I don't know if I can trust you with all that is going on inside me. I don't want it to come between us."

And so, we left it at that.

THEN JACOB LEFT again, this time for an indefinite amount of time. He said he did not know when he would return, as it depended on his father's condition.

I was exhausted when I woke up one morning at six a.m. to get the kids out to school. The night before, Mishael had been throwing up, Nachum had been up until midnight watching a soccer final match while I was on my monthly webinar, and Shefa had insisted on staying up until midnight with me, waiting for me to read to her before bed.

Miraculously, Mishael was feeling better, and Shefa and Nachum were able to get up after so little sleep. Grateful for small miracles, I shuffled into the kitchen and saw our cat pattering out to eat as she heard me coming. The night before, she had been round around the middle, filled with kitten fetuses. But now her stomach was sagging and thin. She had given birth in the night. She looked as emptied out physically as I felt emotionally.

Working at home that day, I watched our cat coming and going. I discovered where she was hiding her kittens: in my bedroom closet. She had given birth in there, apparently, or at least brought the kittens there after she gave birth. I was so exhausted; I had not heard her make a sound.

No father was in sight. As a one-year-old new mother, our cat was a warrior, a trooper. A Buddha. She, post-partum, was caring for her kittens on her own without a complaint; she was taking it all in stride. Who would have thought my cat would be my inspiration, my teacher?

JACOB CAME AND left a couple more times that summer, as we had a feeling his father's life was nearing its end. Then, finally, his father passed; two weeks later, Jacob came home.

I was sitting in the car with Shefa in the back seat. She had only thrown up once on the way to the airport, which was good for her.

"When will *Abba* come out?" she asked. We had not seen Jacob for a whole month. He had left two weeks before his father passed—to be with him in the hospital and work in New York—and came back two weeks after the funeral. His father died the day before Jacob had been scheduled to fly back home. So, he stayed two weeks longer.

The month felt long, in the heat of a Galilean summer, and we did not speak much while he was gone. Jacob was juggling work and his family of origin in crisis in New York, and I was single parenting back home over summer break from school. Between the physical separation, the time difference, our mutual busy-ness, and the fact that he was surrounded constantly during the *shiva*, we did not manage to find time for a heart-to-heart.

And now, there he was. I spotted him walking out the terminal exit, his hair grayer than it had been when he left, but even more surprisingly, he had a full gray beard. Why had I not anticipated that? He had been in mourning for two weeks (when it is customary not to shave), and who knew if he had found time to shave while his father was dying? Jacob is a hairy guy as it is. After only a day of not shaving, he is scruffy.

The truth is I was not thinking much about the traditional mourning rituals. I personally no longer felt bound by traditional religious Jewish law, and I was not even sure how much of those traditions Jacob would take on. He had never been in mourning before, and while he was certainly attached to Jewish religious practice and custom, it was in a more personal and eclectic way. He did not consider himself a strict adherent to classical Jewish religious law, per se, even if he was traditionally minded.

So, really, I had no way of knowing what mourning traditions Jacob would adopt. Which is why I was not shocked, but somewhat surprised, to see him emerge from the airport with a full beard. I knew how much he disliked having a beard, especially in the heat of summer.

I was thrown for an emotional loop, witnessing Jacob looking so shell-shocked and like such a good Jewish son as he emerged from the terminal. But I couldn't help but smile when I saw his eyes light up at seeing me. He approached the car, and I noticed he saw Shefa hiding under a sheet in her booster in the back seat. I motioned with a finger to my lips for him to go along with the surprise.

"So, I guess you found a sitter for Shefa," he announced with a grin.

"Yes. She didn't want to drive the whole way to and from the airport. You know how car sick she gets. She inherited that from me, of course."

"So, I guess I'll just see her when I get home," he said in a stage voice, leaning into the car through my open driver's window. We kissed, and I closed my eyes. My chest relaxed, releasing some of the tension of the past month. "I missed you," I said, realizing how true that was, allowing myself only then to feel those emotions.

"I missed you too." I knew he meant it, but I also knew he had been sad to leave his childhood home with his father's body in the ground. "Can I drive home?" he asked. "I'm in a rush because I want to make an eight-thirty *minyan* so I can say *kaddish*." Jacob was the faster driver of the two of us.

I was worried I would get car sick, but I didn't mention it. He must have felt pressured to get home as quickly as possible, or he would not have asked.

"Sure, if you are not too tired," I said, trying to sound nonplussed, but I was taken aback, feeling yet another indication of our separateness. Was he planning to say *kaddish* every day, even though the only way to do so with any assured consistency would mean going to a non-egalitarian synagogue a fifteen-minute drive from our kibbutz?

All prayer services conducted on our kibbutz were egalitarian by ideological ruling, meaning women participated fully and were counted in the prayer quorum. But there were no regular weekday services at our kibbutz, only on

Shabbat. And in order to recite the mourner's *kaddish*, one needs a quorum of ten. The only way Jacob could do this would be in a nearby Orthodox synagogue with a quorum that did not count women.

Our community is small, and most members do not feel committed to praying three times a day in a quorum of ten. Being progressively minded often goes hand in hand with ambivalence and a worldview that does not put tradition and religious Jewish law first on the list of life's priorities.

Jacob knew how I felt about prayer communities who do not count women in their quorum. He knew I prioritized an ethic of equality above a commitment to religious praxis at that point in my life. He knew I did not think tradition—especially not religious tradition—worth preserving if it is not serving a higher moral and spiritual good. This was who I had become, even if that was not who I had been when he married me. He knew that. And yet, he did not acknowledge this.

I knew Jacob did not feel the way I did. He, too, had come, over the years, to oppose non-egalitarian prayer communities, but he was more traditional than I was, and he was more willing to compromise his feminist beliefs for the sake of tradition. I did not expect him to take this decision based on my personal worldview, but I did expect him to include me in his thought process, as he wanted me to include him in mine. And it made me sad to feel the chasm between us widening as our differing priorities were accentuated.

And yet I felt silenced and humbled. I was not the one who had lost a parent. Who was I to tell Jacob how to feel? Obviously, saying *kaddish*, no matter where and how, was a healing ritual for him. Whether it was because of the ritual itself, the repetitive commitment of it, the words in the prayer, knowing he was doing what his father would have expected and wanted him to do, or just knowing he was mourning in the way Jews have mourned for centuries, this was what he had chosen to do to mark his father's passing. I had to honor that decision.

I had no right to tell Jacob how to mourn, to tell him he should care more about the rights of women than his own healing process. So, I kept quiet. I scooted over and said nothing, hoping I would not throw up on the way home.

As Jacob started to pull out of the parking spot, we heard giggles from the back seat.

"Do you hear something from back there?" Jacob asked, loudly enough for Shefa to hear.

"I don't know." More laughter came from the back of the car. "Maybe the cat snuck into the car when I left?"

"It's me!" Shefa called, throwing off the sheet hiding her. "I'm here, *Abba*!"

Jacob's face lit up even more, and he waved to Shefa via the rearview mirror.

"I'm glad you're home, *Abba*. I missed you soooo much!"

"I missed you, too, Funny Face," he said. And Shefa did not even tell him not to call her Funny Face, she was so happy.

I reached out my hand for Jacob's, and he took one hand off the wheel to take mine. Yet I held back tears as I felt his *kaddish* and my evolving self like a wall between us.

As we drove, we talked. For Jacob, it was a given he would say *kaddish* for his father, as part of the natural process of coming to terms with his father's death—like going through his closets and canceling his bank account. For me, religious ritual was no longer a given. Nothing was, aside from living and dying and doing the best I could at it. I would try not to resent Jacob's decision nor take it personally. It was not about me.

I should just leave religion to the religious, I told myself. I was still a rabbi, but my own unique kind. I was no longer religious in the traditional sense and doubted whether I had ever been in my core. Religion was a tool, a means to an end, but not the end, and not even the only means. And when misused or misinterpreted, it could be counterproductive, even dangerous.

If anything, I was a spiritual humanist. But even that label felt limiting. I was beyond labels. I was not a candy. I was not poison. I was not even a dishwasher tablet. I was what pops through a passageway and eventually dissolves in water. That was all I could say I was with any certainty. A scary notion, but I was trying to inhabit that space without succumbing to fear or the expectations of others.

FOR THE FIRST few days of his return, I felt my lover, my life partner, my soul mate, at a distance, both physically and emotionally. He was home, but I did not feel he had truly landed. And while I was trying to be giving and supportive, I found myself triggered by his distraction and our lack of connection.

I was at the end of a very heavy menstrual period, which had been two weeks late, only a few days before Jacob's arrival. So, we could not physically consummate his return. Finally, three days after he came home, it was our time to go to *mikveh* and reunite physically.

As per what had become our tradition since I told Jacob if he wanted me to continue to immerse monthly in the *mikveh* after my period, he would have to do so as well, we both immersed. Although we did so separately this time, for logistical reasons.

That night, after reading Shefa to sleep, I waited with anticipation in our bed, reading. But midnight came and went, and Jacob still did not come. I fell asleep but awoke when I heard him come into the room. It was past one a.m. We had to be up at six a.m. I asked him what had taken so long.

"My mother called," he said, as he slipped, naked, underneath the cover sheet. Then he continued to check something on his cellphone and fell asleep as the phone dropped from his hand onto the mattress beside him. I tossed and turned all night, my pillow tear-soaked and my heart heavy.

The next morning, I told Jacob how disappointed I had been we had not connected the night before. He was clueless. This was not like him. He was usually the one asking me to be more attentive to his need for physical intimacy. He was usually the one asking me to tell him I love him. Again, the distance between us was palpable.

The next night, we finally had our reunion. We made love with a renewed passion and longing. I wanted to make Jacob feel good. I wanted to comfort him. I wanted us to connect. And I wanted him. In my innermost core. Inside myself. I wanted us to come as close as we could without being one.

As Jacob entered me, I was overcome with a flood of emotions. The feeling of finding my other half was so acute, and at the same time, the knowledge that one day he would be gone, or I would be gone, leaving one of us with that feeling of a missing piece, made me want to hold on to the present so tightly.

I pulled him closer and heard myself expressing things I had only that moment understood.

"I just missed you, Jake. That's all," I said, and it felt truer than any of the other things I had said to him since he had returned. "I just want to be with you, to know you. All of the other stuff doesn't matter."

"You are my favorite person in the world," he said, and I felt like the most fortunate soul to have been chosen by him.

"But with all of our differences, why do you think we found each other?"

Jacob thought for a moment. "Chemistry," he said. "Have you heard of chemistry?"

His answer felt so right, I did the best I could to smile despite my weak facial muscles.

"I'm doing the best I can," I said, soaking his freckled shoulder with my tears.

"Why are you crying?"

"It's the thought of you leaving again."

Then we talked. I told him how sad I was that I could no longer run with him or keep up with him physically in other ways. He told me he did not love or desire me less because of my deteriorating health. He had said this before, but this time I believed it.

We talked about our relationship, about how my evolving spiritual journey was hard for him but how necessary it was for me. We talked about how I now loved myself and trusted in our love enough to show up fully as myself in our relationship, even if it meant risking losing his approval.

I told him what I had written in the letter to him that I had burned before my ordination, about how I released him from the role of unconditional cheering squad. I had written it then, but now I felt it enough to tell him.

"Thanks for releasing me," he said. "But what if I don't want to retire so quickly? I like that job."

"Cute," I answered. "But it's okay for us to disagree. It's even okay for you to find me frustrating. That doesn't scare me as much as it used to."

"Good. Because I disagree with you plenty, and find you frustrating, too. But is it okay for me to love you even when you drive me crazy? Because I can't help it. I do."

I stroked his beard. "That's perfectly fine with me."

We talked about Jacob's relationship with his family, about how torn he felt between being there for his family of origin and being here for the family we had built together. I told him how his leaving so often to help them triggered my feelings of self-pity and fear of death, suffering and abandonment (by humans, but mostly by God).

I told him I felt blessed to have our children, even if my energy and time were being sapped. But that was not his fault, despite his promise of thirty years before. He was doing the best he could, which was all I could expect. Life was not fair, but it was rich and beautiful, even at its most painful.

We talked into the early morning hours, so that I heard the rooster's crow in our yard as I finally drifted off to sleep.

Although I still felt Jacob holding back his feelings about his father's life and death, I did not press him. He needed time, and I hoped we would have more of that. Besides, I was not even sure Jacob knew what he felt.

But most importantly, we reconnected like we were on a second honeymoon, discovering each other like new lovers but with the added appreciation, caring, and, yes, complexity, of thirty years.

We had more days and nights like that, of deep connection through talk and sex. We fell in love all over again. But no honeymoon is forever. I wondered how long this one would last.

BIRTHING MYSELF

A WEEK LATER, we were biking with the kids at the Tel Aviv port. Jacob had been there in meetings all day, and we had met him with our bikes (mine electric, due to my weak leg muscles).

We were having a lovely time, enjoying the ocean view and breeze, watching the sun dropping lower in a sky turning pinker by the minute—even though I had to stop to pee every fifteen minutes.

I had woken up that morning certain I had a urinary tract infection. I had peed into a sterile cup, knowing I had to stop at the doctor on our way to Tel Aviv or I would not make it through the day. By the time the kids and I reached Tel Aviv, I had taken my first dose of antibiotics.

On our way out of the kibbutz, the bikes Jacob had attached to the car with the bike carrier before he left on an early bus to Tel Aviv had fallen off. I was helpless to do anything but ask for help.

Thankfully, my kids and two passers-by were able to get all except one back on. I had made it to the doctor in time to have the nurse—a Christian Arab woman from the local town of Shefa-Amr (in Arabic; Shefaram, in Hebrew) who had been taking my blood and urine for years—check the results of the instant stick test.

She winked at me, "Have you and Jacob been playing around a lot lately?"

I laughed. This was one of those cross-cultural bonding moments I so loved. "As a matter of fact, we have," I answered, telling her about Jacob's return home after a month away.

The nurse told me what I already knew, which was that I had a full-blown UTI. She suggested we go easy on the sex for a few days, and the doctor gave me a prescription for antibiotics, which I bought on the way to Tel Aviv. By the time I met Jacob, I was emotionally agitated and physically very uncomfortable.

I informed Jacob about the UTI. "It's okay," he said. "Sex is not the only way I want to be with you." We hugged and kissed and sat down to watch the kids climbing in the oceanside park. Then he added, "My mother wants me to come for the *shloshim*. It's a week from today. I was thinking of going this Tuesday night for a week." It was Sunday.

The thought of Jacob leaving, when he had just come back after a month of being away, seemed out of the question, even though I knew rationally it was Jewish tradition to mark a month after someone's death. Jacob, being one of two children, would most likely be expected to be there, and probably even feel a desire to be there for his own emotional healing, I knew.

But still, since he had said nothing until then, I had been hoping he had decided against it, having just arrived back fewer than two weeks before. I was disappointed although not shocked. But what hurt more than the fact that he would be leaving was the way he had told me.

"I see," is all I could say. Then Shefa called Jacob to help her, and we continued riding when the kids were finished climbing.

At some point, we needed to return the one bike we had rented to replace the one we had to leave behind at the kibbutz. I volunteered to walk. The kids started arguing over who would ride my electric bike, but I could barely speak. I felt my eyes filling with tears.

"Why? If anyone should walk it should *not* be you," Jacob said.

"I just feel like walking. I want to be alone and walk on the promenade. I want to see the sunset."

"What's wrong? Why do you want to be alone? Are you angry at me?"

"Just upset. Not angry."

"Why? What did I do?"

"I can't talk about it now," I said, indicating the waiting children. "We can discuss it later. Just let me be alone now." I walked off towards the water.

I walked for about twenty minutes, alone and with tears streaming down my cheeks, watching a huge red sun dropping into the water. It was breathtaking. And then it was gone. So much beauty, gone in a moment. Our honeymoon had ended.

We drove home at eleven-thirty that night. When the kids fell asleep in the back of our van, we felt free to approach the subject.

"What's wrong?" Jacob asked.

"You're leaving again. I told you how sad I would be if you left again. I knew you'd have to, but not so soon. I am upset. But I'm more upset about the way you told me, not the fact that you're going."

"What do you mean?"

"I don't want to hear about what your mother wants. I want to hear what *you* want. Do you want to go away again now?"

Jacob was driving again. It was late, and we wanted to get home as quickly as possible. Besides, I was too upset to drive.

"It's not that I want to leave you or the kids now," he explained. "But I do want to go back to my father's grave. I think it would give me some closure. And I do want to be with my mother and sister when they mark the *shloshim*. My father just died. I've been through a lot, and I'm far from over it."

Finally, we were talking about his feelings around his father's death. I explained how different it felt to hear that *he* wanted to go, rather than that he was going because tradition mandated that he go and his mother wanted him to come. That when he framed it as him complying with his mother's wishes, he made it seem like he was choosing his mother's needs over mine, which was fine sometimes, but not all the time. Not *this* time. Not when he had just come home from such a long absence.

"But that's not even the worst part," I continued. "What hurt most was you announcing this to me after what I told you."

"What? What did you tell me? Please help me out here. I don't know what you're getting at."

I looked down into my lap. "I told you how hard it would be for me if you left again now. It was huge for me to expose my weakness, especially after trying to be so strong holding down the fort." I looked up at Jacob, who was looking at the road ahead. "When you complain I am not sad when you leave or thrilled to see you when you come home, you don't understand it's my way of dealing with your coming and going. I go into survival mode so I can get through it."

"I didn't know . . ."

"You asked me to let down my guard, and I did. I made myself vulnerable, and now I feel hurt. If you want me to give you my full self, that means me with all of my complicated emotions. You're going to have to be more sensitive to my feelings and my needs. More open to taking me as I am. The true me. You can't have it both ways."

"So, what do you want me to do? You want me not to go?"

"No. If you feel you should go—for yourself, not your mother—then go. But don't stay any longer than you must. Know I am missing you terribly at home, maybe even crying myself to sleep. And know that I am having a hard time parenting and keeping the house running alone."

Jacob took one hand off the steering wheel and reached for me. He put his hand on my leg and squeezed. "I am still going, but I'll try to be more sensitive in how and what I say, and think more about how all of this is affecting you. I do want you to express your emotions, even if they're hard for me to accept. I think I get it now."

We arrived home at one a.m. and Jacob carried the younger kids into their beds. The older ones walked themselves into their rooms and closed their doors. Jacob and I went to our room, too. We held each other beneath the sheets. Jacob fell asleep right away and I lay there in his arms, remembering that breathtaking sunset.

Jacob was the sun in my life. I was witnessing the power of the sun, the beauty of it as it was setting. It was perhaps at its most magnificent when it was setting, but also the easiest to look at. I could gaze into the sun and appreciate it in a way I could not in the middle of the day, when it was high in the sky.

My heart had opened to Jacob, in his vulnerability. And I felt his had opened to me, too, in mine.

This period in our lives was the beginning of our setting, as we were both nearing fifty and had been together for thirty years. Our reunion and its ability to be so colorful at this stage in our lives was breathtaking, like a sunset.

It took me a while to fall asleep, but I did. And I awoke calm in a way I had not been in months. I felt open and vulnerable and thoroughly spent, but a wall had come down and I—and my marriage—had survived its toppling.

Our second honeymoon may have been over, but we were still achingly in love.

I HAVE TRAVELED to New York to study art. The school is for both Jewish studies and art, but I have chosen art. I have packed a big suitcase on wheels, but when I arrive at the school, I discover Jacob has also traveled to New York and is with me somewhere. I do not see him, but I sense he is here.

When I open my suitcase, I see it is filled with three suits. Dark gray suits, with ties. Jacob does not wear suits, but, somehow, I know these are his.

I sort through the suitcase to find something to wear. Classes are starting already. I don't even know which class I am in—painting or sculpting—and I am anxious. I need to get to class.

I walk the halls trying to figure out which is my class. I see Talmud and Bible classes going on in various classrooms, but I know I am meant to be in one of the art classes. I don't know which one, however.

I am upset at Jacob for taking over my suitcase, and I cannot even figure out where all my clothing went, because it does not seem to be in the suitcase.

"Okay," says Jude. "Why don't you start with the element in the dream that draws you most now."

"I am the suitcase in the dreamer's dream," I begin. "I am large and roomy, with a zipper and wheels, to make it more user-friendly, especially for the dreamer, who is physically challenged. Travelling is hard enough for her, without having to lug a suitcase. The last three times she flew she fainted on the airplane. She is trying to make this trip more practical, trying to think of her own needs."

"That's a good idea."

"Yes, it is. She packed carefully all she needed, and went on her journey to study art. Not Jewish studies. Not Talmud or Bible. Not even *midrash* or *Hassidut* or *Kabbalah*. No, she chose art."

"How did those suits get into you, suitcase?" Jude asks.

"I don't know. When she opened my zipper, there they were. Thick suits. Dark suits. Traditional suits. The dreamer packed comfortable clothing into me, but somehow these suits got in here and are taking up most of the room; she can't even find her own clothing."

"Where did that clothing go, suitcase? Only you can know. Where is it?" Jude asks.

I, the suitcase, try to remember where the clothing went. And then it comes to me. "I have a hidden compartment. But I am not sure where it is. I see some of her clothing is in the compartment with the suits. Maybe just enough to get by for one day, but not enough to last her the whole journey. The rest is in that hidden compartment inside me."

"Great. Thank you, suitcase, for your help," Jude says. "Can I speak to the suits now?"

I take a deep breath and picture those suits I found in the suitcase of my dream. "We are three suits, for three days. One for each day of Jacob's trip." I think of Nachum's "third bar mitzvah" when I say this.

"We are all Jacob will need on this trip," I continue in the voice of the suits. "He brought us to mourn his father and do it in the way his father would have wanted. We are not Jacob's suits. We are his father's suits. Thick, gray suits, with ties. Like his father always wore. Jacob will wear us on his trip to his father's grave, and we will help him mourn his father."

"How will you help him?" Jude asks.

"When he puts us on, he will embody his father. He will feel what it's like to be in his suits, and that will be comforting for him, somehow. The dreamer cannot understand why he wants to do this, and it's not what would comfort her in his place. But she is not in his place. This is his own mourning to do, and if getting into us, his father's suits, will give him comfort, so be it."

"And what will Jacob do with you after he wears you now?"

"We don't think he knows yet. Perhaps he will leave us at his childhood home. Perhaps he will not need to lug us back home when he is finished wearing us this time. Maybe he will hang us back in his father's closet, or even give us away to someone who really needs us."

"Lovely," Jude comments. "But if you do come back in the suitcase, will there be room for the dreamer's clothing, too? If she finds that hidden compartment and her hidden clothing, that is."

"She made room for us, even if subconsciously, on the way here, so she will also make room for us if needed, on the way home. We are not concerned. It will all work out."

"And what if he does not need to bring you back home?"

"If he does not need to bring us home, there will be room for other things to bring home from this journey. Space. Breathing space. Space to be filled with other things, lighter things, things without a clear shape or form. Air. Space. Being. Just being. Space to be filled and discovered and lived now in the present."

JACOB WENT TO his father's *shloshim*. While he was away, I awoke one morning to an email from him. He was still asleep in New York, seven hours behind Israel:

Either someone has hijacked your email account, or you have changed.

The day before, I had written him a terse email asking what time to expect him home on Friday. He was accustomed to my exceptionally long emails, and suddenly I was writing one-liners.

I used the opportunity to write back another one-liner: "I *have* changed."

Jacob's answer to my email was also short and to the point: "That's why I love you. You keep changing."

I believed him.

Jacob came back late Friday afternoon, right before the sun set and *Shabbat* started. Earlier that day, Hallel and Nachum had asked if I could take them to get ear cartilage piercings. Shefa wanted to get her ear lobes pierced, too, so we decided to make an outing of it.

I took the kids to the local tattoo and piercing parlor, where I doubt many six-year-old girls get their ears pierced. But from a past experience with my kids and piercings, I knew that the seedier the place, the more professional they would be.

That time it had been Michal, my oldest, whose new nose piercing developed an infection while we were at a wedding in California, in the Bay Area. It just so happened that the bride's best friend, an executive at Google, was covered in tattoos and piercings. She sent us to the only place she trusted, deep in Haight-Ashbury, San Francisco. As I sat with Michal, then fourteen years old, we innocently flipped through the photo albums on the coffee table, only to discover places we would never have guessed one could put a tattoo or piercing.

This time, we went to Guy's tattoo and piercing parlor in Ramat Yishai, a small town near my kibbutz. Guy, of course, is covered in tattoos and sports a ponytail and an eyebrow piercing. Not as characteristically, he has horses grazing in his side yard and a photograph of his kids hanging on the wall next to an old magazine clipping outlawing tattooing.

First Hallel and Nachum got their ear cartilage pierced. Then Shefa got her ear lobes pierced. Just as Guy was about to call in the next client, I told him to wait. I was considering doing a piercing as well.

I remembered a teaching from one of my spiritual counseling seminars: *Being spiritually aligned means your outsides match your insides.*

"I think I'll do a nose ring," I announced to Guy.

"Go for it, *Ima!*" Hallel and Nachum declared in unison. Shefa clapped in delight.

I knew Jacob's reaction would be: "You were beautiful without it. You don't need jewelry or makeup." And I agreed with him one hundred percent. I was not doing this for Jacob. And I was not doing this to make myself more attractive to the world. I was doing this for me.

These past months, I had come to a place where I felt a new connection to my own body, so much so I no longer felt a need to draw as little attention to it as possible. I felt beautiful, even sexy. I got into bed sometimes without a book or pajamas and made love with the light on. I felt free. Adventuresome. Fun. Spontaneous. Alive. Ready to take risks. And anything but square.

Something in me had opened and been released. I was at peace with myself as I am. I AM WHAT I AM. And ironically—or not so ironically—I wanted to mark this on my flesh. A pact with myself.

In went the needle. There was some pain, and even some blood, but somehow that felt appropriate.

When Jacob came home from his trip, right before the Sabbath, I was already dressed for Friday night services. I was wearing a simple black dress that came to just above my knees, and I was doing some last-minute things in the kitchen. I planned to put on a pair of leggings under the dress before going out.

My calf muscles are atrophied, and the dictuses I wear to help me walk are unattractive. Plus, I can only wear specific types of shoes, none of which are fashionable or suitable to wear with a dress. To try and hide this, I had not gone out with bare legs for years.

Jacob came up behind me when he walked in and kissed me on the neck. I turned to meet his lips with mine. Then he noticed. "You pierced your nose." He laughed.

"Yes, I did. Do you like it?"

"You're beautiful without it," he said.

"I knew you'd say that."

He smiled, and I understood from that smile and the twinkle in his eyes he understood what this marked for me.

"I'm ready to go," he said. "I need to hurry to catch *minchah*"—the afternoon service—"for *kaddish*. Are you ready to go down with me now, or should I go ahead?"

"I just have to put on a pair of leggings, and I'll be ready."

"Why do you need to wear leggings? It's hot outside. You look beautiful like that."

I wondered if he was just saying his usual mantra, or did he truly mean it? "Really? With these chicken legs? Come on. Really?"

"Yes, really."

"Yes, *Ima*. You look so pretty," Shefa chimed in.

"Really?" I turned to Meira, my then-eighteen-year-old and my most honest child. She tells it like it is and is opinionated when it comes to dress.

"Really, *Ima*. It looks better without leggings."

"But look at my legs! And with my shoes? And the dictuses?"

"That is what you look like, *Ima*. Everyone knows that. And, really, it looks fine. You look nice."

I went to the mirror and looked at my reflection. I did look nice. In my little black dress and my new nose ring. I looked sexy. I looked beautiful. I looked like me. I looked like who I was and who I was meant to be. I looked like someone a person could love. Even me.

That Saturday night, Jacob and I went out to a film and dinner, which we almost never do because of the kids and our hectic, full lives. This was a rare opportunity for us to go out on a date, and it felt important and perfectly timed, considering how much apart we had been all summer.

The film started right when the Sabbath ended, so I paid for the tickets in advance, since classic religious Jewish law forbids commerce on *Shabbat* and Jacob is as strict about this as he is about not driving on the Sabbath.

I drove to the theater, and Jacob rode his bike. We were finding a way to work with our different takes on *Shabbat*. We both agreed this date felt very Sabbath-appropriate; our differences lay in how to get there. If we left after the Sabbath ended, we would miss the beginning of the film. And with *Shabbat* ending so late that time of year, I did not want to go to a later film.

It was lovely to be with Jacob at the movies again. When we were dating and then first married, before kids, we spent a lot of time in movie theaters. Since having kids, I could count the number of movies we attended together without kids, on two hands. We held hands and snuggled in the air-conditioned theater, laughing as we remembered my tendency to talk during movies and Jacob's annoyance at my questions and commentary.

After the film, we sat in an adjacent café for dinner. We shared our food, eating from each other's plates and holding hands over the table in between. When it came time to pay, the waiter mistook us for honeymooners. (Our second marriages, I assume.)

"We are," Jacob grinned, and took my hand.

When we got home, I looked at my cell phone before getting into bed. There were photos from Adin, who, after having been released from the army, was traveling in various national parks out West in the U.S. The photos were of the solar eclipse, as seen from Yellowstone National Park, where he was camping.

We could not see the eclipse from where we were, in Israel, so I had put it out of my mind. But now it became clear to me I had been experiencing its energy without realizing it.

Jacob and I had been enacting this archetypal and intense union of sun and moon in our own lives on a micro level, while it was happening in the Universe on a macro level. I was stunned by this realization. I was also humbled.

The eclipse meant union, but it also meant shadow. Shadow had brought about our reunion. I had been painfully confronted with my own limitations at compassion and altruism. I had been faced with my inability to simply release old, unhealed wounds—with my parents and in-laws, life partner, children, and even friends—some of which have been explored here, some of which have not.

This shadow of mine had been hard to accept, yet in its acceptance, I had been able to surrender to love. And in baring myself—body and soul—to my beloved, I had been able to step into myself in all my broken, imperfect wholeness and trust in him and in life, and in myself. All would be as it should.

DURING ONE OF my monthly dreamwork classes with Jude, she tells us a dream from the past can be worked and reworked over again in our lives. She asks us to recall a dream from more than a year ago and work it with her to demonstrate how it can be significant in diverse ways, depending on when we work it.

I decide to bring my dream about the feminine energy group to prepare me for remarrying Jacob on the beach in Jaffa.

"I want you to be the woman leading the group," Jude says. "What are you doing? What kind of group is this? What is happening in this group?"

I did not anticipate this question. I have no recollection of what happened in the group, except that it made me feel supported and guided and brought me down to the ceremony on the beach. I remember it was about feminine energy, although men were there; they were involved, but not in the lead.

I close my eyes, wondering where to even start with trying to conjure what happened in this group gathering. But there is no need. It all becomes so clear so quickly.

"I am leading a birthing circle. I am helping the dreamer birth herself. I am helping her to be reborn. We are all supporting her in birthing herself within this circle of support and nurturing. We are creating a sacred and safe space so she can be reborn into her truth."

"Wonderful. Now I want you to tell me, Dreamer, where you are in this circle. What are you doing? What is happening there?"

My eyes are still closed. I take a deep breath and go inward. I am remembering something so deep within me it is like rediscovering my soul. I do not feel I am remembering an image from my sleeping dream, but rather dipping into a well of dreams I carry around inside me, always, and drawing water that turns into a flow coming from that deep place.

Is it my womb? I am giving birth to myself as I sit in front of this computer screen. I feel, in my waking re-imagination of this dream, a release of water flowing from me and at the same time pulling me, carrying me in a powerful flow down to the beach to remarry my beloved. And to remarry myself, too. Haviva, whose name means "beloved."

"I am giving birth. My waters are breaking. I feel an overpowering flow of water coming forth from me. I am both giving birth and being born. And I am being carried in the flow."

"And where are you going? Where are you headed?"

"I am flowing through alleyways, descending staircases, flowing through the Old City of Jaffa, down to the shore. I am headed to the beach. To the water. To join with the other waters. We are all part of one big flow. The flow of life. There is no separation. Only love. I am ready for the ceremony of renewed marrying of souls."

"You can open your eyes now," Jude says.

I do.

THE SABBATH OF MY SOUL

IN JULY, WHEN Mishael was in soccer camp while Jacob was away, I received a call from his counselor asking if she could invite a coach from the Maccabi Haifa team to watch him play.

I agreed, of course, and then put the call out of my mind. In August, after Jacob came home from his father's *shloshim*, I received a call from the coach inviting Mishael to try out for the team.

"It is a very serious commitment," he told me. "Practices three times a week and games every *Shabbat*."

Games every *Shabbat*? Mishael would be thrilled if he made the team, but I was not so sure about Jacob. I told the coach as far as I was concerned Mishael could try out, but I would have to discuss it with Mishael's father.

When I raised the topic with Jacob, it was understood he would not be driving Mishael to games. The question was, would he mind if I did? Jacob agreed this could be a real gift to Mishael, a way for him to boost his self-confidence and learn about responsibility and commitment. Maccabi Haifa is a very serious and high-level team.

Although until then our agreement was that kids younger than bar or bat mitzvah age would not drive on *Shabbat*, except for an exceptional occasion, Jacob was willing to make this an exception. But, of course, it would depend on whether I was willing to commit to driving him every *Shabbat*.

I called the coach back that night and told him Mishael would try out for the team. What followed were weeks of anxiety and anticipation as we waited to hear if he would make the cut. And he did. Then came the reality of this decision. Every Saturday, I had to drive Mishael around to his games, sometimes as far away as Tel Aviv, which is a one-and-a-half-hour drive from our kibbutz.

This development changed the dynamic of our Sabbaths. I had already decided to drive the kids on *Shabbat*, and even myself when I felt it necessary or worthwhile. But we were still not a family who drove on *Shabbat*, and certainly not in any regular way. Now driving had officially become part of the regular family Sabbath routine. We had become a family who drives on *Shabbat*. Except Jacob.

When I agreed to be Mishael's soccer chauffeur, I had not realized that many of the soccer fields in Israel are near beaches. It became my regular *Shabbat* activity to drop Mishael at his pre-game practice and make my way to the closest seashore.

It was usually hectic and a bit stressful to get to the field on time. Sometimes we had to leave before the sun was up. But what a blessing to be on the beach on *Shabbat*. And in winter, no less. I discovered how much I love the beach in winter—even in the rain.

I adored being by the water in my fleece and then taking it off as the sun rose higher in the sky. I loved watching people in their different Sabbath morning beach activities—running, walking, playing cards and backgammon, meeting friends for coffee, dancing, roller blading, fishing, surfing, swimming. Everyone was busy with their leisure.

And the games were at various times of day. Twice there was an afternoon game, and we came down to the beach afterwards to watch the sunset. In the past, even when we had gone to the beach on a Friday, which was a popular summer activity for our family, we never saw the sunset, because sunset means the beginning of *Shabbat*. So, we always left at least an hour before the sun hit the water line.

When the game season started and I began the weekly driving, I started with the attitude I was doing this out of commitment to my son, a kind of altruism. I even harbored some resentment towards Jacob that he was not willing to pitch in. Of course, I knew there was no chance he would; that was part of the deal. But still.

Now, though, months later, I recognized the gifts I had been given by opening to the unknown, going with my instincts, and assuming everything would work out. And an added blessing I had not anticipated: Although Jacob was not willing to drive to the games, he was glad I was, as he was proud of Mishael and encouraged him to be on the team, even if it meant driving on *Shabbat*. And when the games were local enough, Jacob joined me by bike so we could watch the games together.

One *Shabbat*, when the game was in the city of Sachnin, an Arab city, I took Shefa with us, and we visited a friend of hers from her Arab-Jewish school near the soccer field. Jacob met us towards the end on his bicycle, as the city is only about twenty kilometers from our kibbutz.

This was a *Shabbat* that felt especially like grace itself. We would never have gone to visit with Shefa's friend in Sachnin on a *Shabbat* if the game had not been there. Yet once we were doing it, it felt just right. And that felt "*Shabbosdik*," the idea of opening ourselves to the unknown on the Sabbath, going outside the usual boundaries and routine of our lives.

Opening myself to the unknown meant spending hours alone with my son, talking while driving, cheering him on. It also meant spending time with my oldest daughter, Michal, who lived near the soccer fields in Haifa then. That was certainly an unexpected gift. But most of all, the hours truly alone in unknown places, mostly on beaches—walking, reading, and exploring.

ONE *SHABBAT*, WHEN I was walking along the beach in Rosh Hanikra, a spectacular grotto-lined seashore at the border between Israel and Lebanon, I saw a series of signs that made me question my path.

First was a bright green grasshopper right at the edge of the water, jumping along the shoreline. I noticed it, thinking it was a toy, its color was so bright. I did not think grasshoppers were beach creatures. But there it was.

Further up the shore, at the point where I could walk no more without hitting the border, I stopped at the rocky grotto formation separating Israel from Lebanon. On the other side of the rocks is another country, another world. Suddenly, I heard movement among the rocks.

I looked up, but I could not make out what it was. I ventured closer. And then I saw them: about twenty "rock rabbits," as they are called in Hebrew, scampering around, jumping from rock to rock.

These are furry animals that look like large gerbils. I had seen them in the desert many times. But I had never seen them up north, and certainly not by the beach. *What are they doing here?* I thought to myself. *Am I being sent a message that I, too, am in the wrong place at the wrong time? Am I being asked to rethink my recent choices?*

Later that night, exhausted from the winter day at the beach beginning that morning at five a.m., I looked up beach grasshopper on the internet. I discovered grasshoppers are not only dry land creatures; there are types who spend time by the sea. Then I looked up "rock rabbits" in Hebrew and discovered they are named Rock Hyrax in English and that they, too, are no strangers to the sea. They are found in various terrains, not just in the desert.

I had been wrong. Out of ignorance, or prejudice, I had assumed these creatures were out of place. But they were not at all. They were not in a place in which I was accustomed to seeing them, but they were just where they were meant to be. And so was I.

The next week, Mishael's game was in Haifa, near where Michal and Ahmad lived at the time. I picked them up, we dropped Mishael, and then we went to walk on the beach. It was a windy day, and the waves were choppy. It was cloudy, but there was no rain. At least not yet.

Ahmad, who grew up in Jaffa, is a surfer and a spearfisherman. We watched the surfers, and I could tell he wished he were out there with them, riding the waves. Then we all saw it: the sailboat. It had caught my eye right away, although I did not understand why. "Take a look at that!" I cried. "Doesn't it look beautiful?"

"Sure, it does," Ahmad said. "But it's way too close to shore. They're not allowed to bring their boats so close to shore."

I took another look at that boat. It may have been breaking the rules, but it sure did look magnificent. And to me, it looked happy to be exactly where it was. Even if not everyone was happy it was there, and even if it was taking a risk.

YET ANOTHER *SHABBAT*, when I was driving to a soccer game—again—the song "Dust in the Wind" came on the radio. An oldie but a goodie. From the first words, "I close my eyes," my eyes were already filling with tears. Everything would pass like dust in the wind. Nothing would last forever but the earth and sky. *And the water, too*, I thought to myself, correcting the song's lyrics. The oceans, lakes, and rivers. They would rise as vapors into the atmosphere and fall again as rain.

But all else would eventually die, disappear, never to return. This moment and the next. Tomorrow, the next day. Even my dreams. Perhaps even this song, eventually. With my writing, I would try to stay in this world past my physical body, but who knew how long even my writing would remain? All of it was dust in the wind.

What a sad, even depressing song, and yet somehow comforting. Like *Ecclesiastes*, the book of *Kohelet*, its blatant and simple truth helped me let go of my resentments, ideologies, hopes and attachments. I felt above them all. I was no longer crying. I simply was.

After dropping Mishael at his soccer game, I headed to the beach.

I closed my eyes.

I heard the waves rising and crashing around me. With my eyes open, the water felt peaceful and rhythmic, but with my eyes closed, it was not as peaceful as it seemed.

Am I being premature in seeing where I am now as peaceful? I asked myself. I was riding the waves, waiting to see where they would take me. Going with the flow. Saying yes to what life had to offer. Would that be a guarantee of inner peace?

I looked down at the sand, the many different rocks and shells brought up to shore. Some would stay, some would be brought back into the water. Everything is in flux. Always. All we can do is be like the rocks and shells and ride the waves.

In the end, we are at the mercy of the waves. A drop of water in an endless sea, as the song lyrics say. All we are is dust in the wind.

ANOTHER *SHABBAT* MORNING, I arrived at the beach at eight a.m., surprised to see scores of jellyfish spread out on the sand down the length of the shoreline. They had been washed ashore. They lay there, like beached whales, unable to move without the water to carry them.

But they did not look in distress, and they did not look like they were drying up. They were at the section of the shoreline where the water washed up every few minutes, rehydrating them. My guess was when the tide rose later in the day, they would wash back out to sea.

They had come for a visit. This was not a suicide mission or a natural disaster. They had merely come to say hello. To bring me their message. I was curious to discover what it would be.

I took off my shoes—despite my instability without my dictuses—and hobbled toward the jellyfish, walking sticks in my hands at least providing some support. I dared not touch the creatures, as they secrete a poison that has the effect of a sting. But I leaned in close, examining my morning visitors. They were translucent blobs. I saw right into their insides. These creatures had nothing to hide. What was inside was outside, too.

Jellyfish are made up 98 percent of water. They are as close to being water as a creature can be. It is hard to even see them when they are in the water. Yet, they are not completely water. They still retain something that distinguishes them from it.

Jellyfish have a muscle to help them maneuver their way, but they have no fins to push or steer. Yet, while one might think they are at the complete mercy of the waves, they do, sometimes, swim against the current.

Jellyfish also do not have a brain. They are all sense and instinct. They feel their way through life.

Trust in water, they were telling me. Trust in the wisdom of the waves and let them carry you. You too are water. Trust in water, inside and out. Trust in yourself enough to let your outsides match your insides. Trust in your own inner wisdom, even when it tells you to swim against the current. Trust in the wisdom of water. Yours and that of the Universe. They are one.

YET ANOTHER *SHABBAT*, and I was with Jacob, my kids, and fifty Arab-Israeli high school students from the village across the street from my kibbutz. I had started teaching Spoken English in the two high schools there, and today was a field trip. We were cleaning up the forest our two communities share.

This was a controversial topic. People from this Arab village picnic and barbeque in this forest, and they often leave their garbage behind. It was a sore point and a cultural difference not only dividing us but creating antagonism.

People from my kibbutz are resentful; the local forest, which could be such a beautiful place to walk and sit, has become a garbage dump. No matter how much we clean, we cannot keep up with the rate of littering that goes on daily there.

A group of young adults from the area created a clean-up-the-forests project to remedy this situation. But many people from my kibbutz do not want to go out and pick up trash they did not leave. A more long-term solution that gets to the root of the problem is needed. Educating the youth is the answer.

I decided to help recruit my high school English students for this project. So here I was, with them and with Jacob, picking up loads of trash while we helped my students practice speaking English.

I had prepared my students ahead of time to explain in English why they were here. I had taught them terms like social conscience, activism, responsibility, ecology, foresight, and sustainability. I was proud to be their teacher, and I was proud to be part of this worthwhile project.

But what gave me just as much satisfaction was that Jacob was there with me. It was *Shabbat*, and he was picking up trash. Most of the traditionally Sabbath observant people on our kibbutz had not come to help, even though I invited our whole community. In their minds, this was not in the spirit of *Shabbat* and even violated the traditional rabbinic injunctions against carrying, sorting, and fixing on the Sabbath.

In my opinion, even if repairing and healing are forbidden according to the letter of the rabbinic Sabbath laws, *tikkun olam*, repairing or healing the world, or at least not desisting from trying, is an imperative that supersedes adhering to the rabbinic interpretation of *Shabbat*. I felt confident Jacob agreed.

I thought of Jesus healing on the Sabbath and arguing that if circumcision is performed even on the Sabbath, healing should be as well. Yet, I did not mention this to Jacob. I felt no need to turn his decision to accompany me that day into a theological or philosophical argument. We were finding our way to share *Shabbat*, even with our different understandings of what that meant. That is what mattered.

ONE RARE *SHABBAT* when Mishael had no soccer game, I went to prayer services on the kibbutz. It was sweet to be in synagogue again with Jacob, wrapped in my Rumi *tallit*, singing familiar prayers in community, harmonizing and chanting, and hearing the weekly Torah portion. But I wanted some alone time with God.

With the afternoon before me and no obligation to drive to soccer, I decided to head to one of my favorite spots near my home. Few people I knew were aware of it: a silent monastery in the forest at the edge of a hilltop Jewish settlement. The combination of walking in nature and sitting alone in a sanctuary in silence was just what I needed.

In the 1960s, a Catholic monk came from Holland and settled in those woods after digging a well and building a cabin. He was joined by another Catholic monk from the U.S. They lived there together in silence and prayer.

When both men knew they were nearing the end of their lives, they called in a group of Carmelite nuns to take their place and continue praying. There are now nine nuns who live at the monastery in silence, praying for peace. I am glad. We can certainly use all the prayers we can get.

I slowed down and signaled a right turn. The silence was beckoning.

When I arrived at the edge of the forest, I parked my car and got out. The last time I had been here was for Christmas midnight mass a few months before. Then the view had been of lights from the surrounding villages. Now the view was of rectangular fields in different shades of green, the national water reservoir, and mountains and the Sea of Galilee in the distance.

A flock of birds returning from their southward migration passed overhead. Their chirping sounded so near, it was as if they were passing by my ear. The ground, the air, the sky—everything was waking up to spring.

As I walked, I repeated in a whisper a chant from a Christian mystic I had learned in seminary: "Be still and know that I am God. Be still and know that I am. Be still and know. Be still. Be." I thought about how I am God. How we all are not only created in the image of God, as I was taught in my Jewish upbringing, but that we *are* God. We are all Spirit. We, like Jesus, are both human and divine. Spirit is in each of us and in all aspects of the Universe.

As I had learned in my Buddhist studies, when we give ourselves over to What Is, to What Will Always Be, to this something that is greater than ourselves, it is not about worshipping or paying homage; it is about letting ourselves flow into this greater force without resistance. Or at least trying to.

Living in peace with oneself and the Universe is about surrendering to the mystery of simply being a mortal human in an imperfect world, surrendering to the flow of life called, in the Muslim faith tradition, by 99 names. This idea of ninety-nine, I assume, is a stand-in for the idea of endless and numberless, like the Kabbalistic concept of *"Ein Sof."* The un-nameable. The mystery.

When we remember divine love for us and all beings, when we remember the interconnectedness of ALL and what it means to truly be at peace with what is—something the Talmud teaches us we knew in utero but forgot upon birth—that is when we are truly living in spiritual alignment.

That, for me, was the challenge of *Shabbat*, I now knew. To try and touch that place, to remember it like a forgotten piece of myself—as in the Sufi tradition—at least in various moments throughout my life. In the Jewish tradition, this is a weekly practice, setting aside an entire day for this purpose, as well as three times a day throughout the week, and when we immerse ourselves fully in living waters.

The idea of *Shabbat* is to give us space to be at peace with what is and surrender to the unknown. The Sabbath is a full day of surrender. Why else would it be recommended on *Shabbat* to sleep and have sex? The two ways we come closest to dying while living. Sex with the beloved, a spiritual practice requiring complete trust and exposure with another human. And sleep with the soul, a spiritual practice requiring complete trust and exposure with God.

But the Rabbis, who were only human after all, were, perhaps, uncomfortable with this posture. With their abundance of rules for the day, they were, like I had done in my own life, filling up this scary open space with attempts at trying to know the unknowable, control the chaos, and put boundaries on the endless *"Ein Sof."*

In Islam, it is five times a day that we try to reach this place of *Shabbat*. In Sufism, this is especially stressed in the ecstatic twirling and chanting in the *zikher* (which means to remember) service. In Buddhism and Hinduism, it is through daily meditation we can touch this place in ourselves.

But as with Judaism, in all these traditions, if the end goal is forgotten, if the striving for inner peace is replaced with the easier goal of feeling a false sense of control by insisting on such rigid restrictions and regulations, religious ritual can turn into an idol. Boundaries, rules, instructions and structure can all be helpful, but they can also be harmful if abused.

This is what I came here to not only understand intellectually, but to feel inside me on this Sabbath day. The essence of *Shabbat*, the posture of surrender.

I reached a sign asking those passing by the convent to respect the nuns' silence. I started chanting instead inside my head. I reached another sign explaining how and why the convent was founded. The sign was written in three languages: English, Hebrew, and Arabic. I knew the nuns spoke many more. They were from France, England, Germany, Spain, Switzerland, Italy, Korea, and maybe more countries, too. These signs were written for visitors. The nuns knew why they were there.

As I passed the convent sanctuary, the door opened and out came a nun. She was dressed in a gray and white frock, showing only her wrinkled face and soft blue eyes.

It's not unusual for women to cover up in these parts, as there are traditional Muslim villages nearby and some Orthodox Jewish settlements as well. I'd done it, too, before I began the process of introducing more freedom into my life. I did not judge her, and I did not see judgment at my uncovered hair, jeans and tank top in this nun's eyes. We were both making our own choices, trusting our inner voices to tell us what is right for us.

"*Shalom*," the nun said. I was startled by her speaking at all, let alone in Hebrew.

"It is okay if I speak to you?" I asked in English, sensing her Hebrew was not as fluent as her English.

"Yes."

"You are allowed to speak?"

"We speak to greet visitors. That is part of our mission. It is not about being allowed. We do this out of choice. We are choosing to devote our lives to God our Father, and to Jesus, who gave His life for us. And to the Holy Spirit. Each one of us has chosen a life of devotion and contemplation. It brings us inner peace, and we hope contributes to bringing peace to the region, to the world."

This woman exuded inner peace. I wanted a piece of it. "May I go down into the sanctuary?" I asked. "Is there anyone there now? I would like to sit in silence."

"There is no one there now. I too was sitting in silence. You are welcome to go," she said. "The Holy Spirit hears all prayers." She bowed her head and hurried off, leaving the door open.

I made my way slowly down the stone steps that led into this cave of a church. It was, literally, a cave. A thick rope hung along the wall to serve as a railing. The pews were wooden benches. The pulpit was a stone altar-like structure with a dove hanging above, to represent the Holy Spirit free from the bondage of the material world. Depictions of Jesus and Mary decorated the room.

It was a simple sanctuary, basic yet beautiful. By coming here, I had seeped through the bars of my self-inflicted cage. I felt free and alive. No one knew I was here but God.

I looked up at the crucifix on the altar. This symbol, usually evoking for me the weight of humanity's suffering, felt liberating this time, especially as I contemplated the dove hanging above the altar. Perhaps that was the idea of the Resurrection, of Jesus leaving his body and rising again. Suffering is part of life, but it is not our reason for being alive. Growth is our reason for being alive—that moment of leaving our cocoon and becoming a butterfly.

I sat and closed my eyes. I chanted to myself. On this *Shabbat* day sitting in a church in the middle of a forest in Galilee, I was still, and I knew that I am God.

Shabbat is not only a day in the week for me. It is a way of being. This is *Shabbat*, the Sabbath of my soul. I was exactly where I needed to be. And that was here with me. Here with God.

FEEL YOUR WAY FORWARD

I AM BEING held captive in a house, although I am allowed to swim. There is a lap pool attached to the house, where I can swim daily. But when I swim there, I am attached to a man. He swims on top of me. We swim together. With his help, I can swim faster and stronger. He helps propel me forward. But he is on top of me. Still, I am content.

But one day, he tries to kill me. He has a set of knives in a box with a latch, and he takes out a knife and tries to stab me. I escape and run to a house next door, where I stay, waiting. I order in dehydrated fruits, and that is how I survive while I wait. Until one day, I receive a package of chocolates. I am reunited with the swimmer man, and we swim off together in total balance.

I wake up with the image of me and this male swimmer swimming along gracefully as one body, gliding along the water. The image stays in my head as I prepare the kids' sandwiches for school, and as I go about my routine. It is such a peaceful image, it gives me a sense of calm throughout my day.

I bring the dream to Jude. I call it my hermaphrodite synchronized swimmer dream. I tell her how it speaks to me on so many levels: relational, spiritual, psychological, emotional, historical. It feels like an important dream, an archetypal dream. One I will come back to many times in my life. It is both my story and that of humanity. I tell her about how calm it made me feel.

"Well, that's a lot to take in," she says. "I suggest this time, you try to just feel into the energy of the dream. Carry this energy around with you and see what happens."

I am not sure what Jude means by feeling into the energy of the dream, nor by carrying the energy of the dream around with me, but I assume that is part of the point. I am not meant to understand. Just feel.

FOR DAYS, I walked around with the energy of this dream, although I was still not sure what that meant. At the same time, slugs were showing up in my life in surprising ways.

First, I noticed them hanging around my pool when I was swimming. I would be swimming back stroke, for example, and see a slug moving along the wall, leaving a residue behind her, as slugs do. There were many. Every day, I saw more and more. But it was winter, slug season. So, I did not make much of it.

Then I stepped on one. I was walking on my patio towards the pool, barefoot, as I always do, and was startled by a gooey feeling beneath my big toe. *Yuck!* I crushed the poor thing, and it became, instantly, a puddle of water before my eyes.

I was curious, especially when I got into the pool to swim and saw what could have been three of these slug's babies moving along the edge of the pool. But once I finished swimming, I put the slugs out of my mind.

That night, I awoke to the feel of something slimy on my finger. I turned on the light, brought my hand to my eyes, and was shocked to find a slug on my hand. Now that was too much. I shook the slug off and did my best to fall back asleep, but it was no use. Besides, the slug was still slithering along my bedroom floor.

I got out of bed, picked up the slug with a tissue, and put it outside, where I felt it belonged. But there was no use trying to sleep. It was already five-thirty a.m., and the kids would have to be woken soon anyway; so, I went to my computer and did a search for "slugs" on the internet. I was amazed at the results.

What first caught my eye was that a slug, like a jellyfish, is almost all water. It is therefore always in need of water, which is why it has a protective mucus it leaves behind as it moves. The mucus is a liquid crystal, a unique and amazing substance that attracts water and therefore keeps the slug hydrated. It also helps slugs move along surfaces and find one another.

Slugs have a collective history. Slug was once a mollusk but shed her collective shell. What we are seeing is an animal that has broken free of its own boundaries. That was a description to which I could relate.

Slug has found a way to stay together, to remain whole, to not melt away, even without these boundaries. Would I be able to do the same?

Like me, like the dried fruit in my dream, a slug must be careful to remain hydrated. What is my liquid crystal that keeps me hydrated, and that I leave behind me in my wake so others can find me? My writing, my actions in the world, my meaningful interactions with others …

Slugs are also hermaphrodites. They are both male and female. Slugs have managed to do what many of us aspire to do—balance our male and female sides, our anima and animus, in a healthy way. Like my swimmer.

Slugs move slowly, like me. We have no choice. It is how we are built. And slugs move through a muscular contraction of what is called their one "foot," which moves them along. Because of my foot drop, I cannot lift my toes, so my feet also slide along the floor when I walk, which is why I trip if I am not wearing my dictuses.

My kids sometimes call me the snail, or the turtle. Maybe I should suggest they call me the slug.

When the kids were off to school, and Jacob off to work, I went out to the pool for my daily swim. I was not surprised to find Slug waiting for me. But this time, I paid attention. If Slug was me, my life, my dreams, I would do like Jude said, and feel into Slug's energy to try and discern her message to me.

I stood in the water and watched Slug moving along at her slow pace, leaving her liquid crystal mucus behind her. I put my face right up to her, so I could see her in detail, in her full Slug glory.

She was truly beautiful. Shiny and smooth. Gracefully moving forward, feeling her way with her tentacles. Yes, I had read that too on the internet. Slugs don't see, they feel. That is how they move forward.

Then I heard Slug's message: *Feel your way forward. Feel your way forward. Feel your way forward. You are my sister now, Dreamer. You are free of your shell. You are water. You are anima and animus. You have your own inner shell. Listen to your inner voice, trust your heart, and feel your way forward.*

I started to swim, with Slug's message going through my head like a mantra. *Feel your way forward. Feel your way forward.* I became the energy of my dream. A slug, a jellyfish, feeling my way forward with inner peace.

Slug is my overflowing *mikveh*. Slug is my melting synagogue walls, but self-contained in some way. Slug does not need her shell. But what prevents her from melting away? Slug does have a remnant of a shell, but it is an internal shell keeping her together. Will my internal shell—my inner voice—be enough to keep me from falling apart as I shed my own various shells?

I CHECK MY phone messages before picking up a book to read before sleep. Jacob is snoring beside me. Shefa has not yet made her nightly pilgrimage to our bed. Some precious time to myself awaits me. I have been reading a series of books of poetry to review and am looking forward to getting back to that. I have found such treasures. I have felt some of the poems speaking directly to what is in my heart.

I notice Jacob sent out a video clip in our "Tenth for the *Minyan*" Whatsapp group. He created the group when he came home from his father's *shiva*, so he could gather an egalitarian *minyan* to say *kaddish* on the kibbutz as often as possible. I am glad he is trying to pray with an egalitarian *minyan* when he can.

I click on the link. I see he has sent a clip of *"Minyan* Man," an old song by Shlock Rock, an all-men's Orthodox Jewish singing group who remake popular songs into Jewish songs.

This song is about a man who comes to stay for the Sabbath in Mobile, Alabama, where there are few Jews. The Jewish men there are so happy to see him, because he can make their *minyan*, as there are only nine Jewish men left in the town.

I know Jacob enjoys Shlock Rock, and I know he especially likes this song. It touches that place of *"Yiddishkeit"* inside him to which I just do not relate. We both grew up in the *"yeshiva* world," but whereas I have no nostalgia for it, he—despite his criticism of that same world—most definitely does.

Jacob finds it annoying I don't relate, but I cannot force myself to like something I find not only not to my taste but grating in its parochialism and offensive in its sexism. I watch the video, nevertheless. After all, Jacob, my beloved, my life partner, is the one who sent it out in the group.

The video unfolds, with a group of only men, only Jewish men, rejoicing at the arrival of their tenth Jewish man, as if all the women and non-Jewish men in their town put together could not fill his place. My stomach is turning.

I have an urge to wake Jacob and express how offensive I find this video, but he is sleeping so soundly. He does not get enough sleep. Neither of us does. It would be cruel to wake him at all, but especially to start an argument.

Besides, I am not sure I want to argue. In fact, I don't feel anger towards him at all. I feel a chasm that cannot be crossed. Can we really love each other this much and be so different? Can our love be enough of a bridge over that chasm?

I look over at him snoring. He looks so vulnerable, so sweet. As upset as this song makes me, I cannot help but be touched. Jacob has a soft spot for his fellow Jews; he is a "particular-ist," unlike me. And while he is committed to progression and equality, he is not willing to easily or quickly give up some of the things he treasures.

He prefers a *minyan* where women are counted, but if he wants to say *kaddish*, he makes that his priority and forgives the men around him their backward ways. Of course, it is easier for him to do so, since he is a man. They count him. They embrace him. They welcome his *kaddish*. Mine they would scorn. Me, they would kick out.

But the poor man lost his father less than half a year ago, I tell myself. Give him a break.

I reach out my hand and take Jacob's in mine. He stirs slightly. I can tell he feels my hand in his. His lips curl into a grin, although he is still asleep. Jacob insists he does not dream, even when I tell him everyone dreams, even if some people do not remember their dreams.

I am certain now, though, Jacob is having a pleasant dream. Perhaps he is dreaming about a strange, bearded man with a *kippah* appearing and making his *minyan*. Whatever makes him happy. This is love, and yes, it is enough of a bridge over the chasm that divides us.

I take a book of poetry from my night table, Jacob's limp hand still in mine. The book is Herbert Levine's *Words to Bless the World*. I open it to a random page.

A Song for Gratitude

What does it take to treasure each day,
To give thanks for the gifts not earned,
To savor the taste of every first fruit
And know that enough is as good as a feast?
It takes a lifetime to learn how to live,
To sort through the stuff that fills up our days,
To weigh and measure just what to claim
And know that enough is as good as a feast.
So, sit at nightfall with those you love
And light a candle to greet the dark,
Clasp hands as you bless the bread
And know that enough is as good as a feast.
Open your heart to the joy and the pain,
The bitter and sweet of the knowledge you've gained
And sweetly surrender to what you can't change
And know that enough is as good as a feast.

Yes, Herbert. Exactly.

I FELL AGAIN. This time it was while rushing to speak about *mikveh* to a group of Christian ministry students. I was, as usual, trying to fit in one last email before heading down, so when I got the text message they were at the front gate, I grabbed my bag and rushed out the door, making one last phone call as I left. I did not see the branch sticking up from the ground.

I fell on my knees. The pain was intense, but I sat for a few minutes on the ground until it abated, and I could stand again. I could tell I was bleeding, but I decided to ignore the pain and blood and continue with my day as planned.

The meeting with the ministers-in-training was extraordinary. I told my story, my journey from Orthodoxy to human-centered interspirituality, and they listened with open ears and hearts.

Then I explained to them my understanding of the deeper meaning of *mikveh*: a reconnection with our inner wholeness, with unity, with our own divinity and humanity. As we immerse fully in a gathering of the waters existing since before creation, in the divine womb, we touch our deepest most whole place.

Water rituals are a universal spiritual practice. I invited them to give this one—full body immersion—a try. And so, one by one, these Christian ministers-to-be had their first *mikveh* experience.

I returned home so excited about the day's events I forgot about my fall. But when I changed into my bathing suit to swim, I saw my bloody knees. I cleaned my wounds and eased my hurting body into the pool. While there was some pain, I could swim just fine. So, I assumed the bruises would pass on their own.

A month later, my right knee still hurt. I went to an orthopedist and told him about the fall. He diagnosed me with bursitis—a collection of fluid caused by trauma to the joint—and prescribed pills but was not sure they would help. Perhaps he could drain the fluid, he said. But I may have to simply live with this pain, like I do with my illness.

That evening I had one of my group dreamwork training sessions with Jude. The topic of that lesson was body parts. Jude told us how our bodies can be treated like a dreamscape, how our body parts and sensations can be treated like elements in a dream.

She asked each of us to choose a body part, perhaps one in which we had been feeling a certain sensation lately. I chose my right knee.

"Haviva's right knee, how are you feeling today?" Jude asked me.

I closed my eyes and became my right knee. "I am in pain. Fluids have collected inside me due to trauma, and now I hurt. I am not in constant pain, though. Only when pressure is put on me, when something rubs up against me, when I must lean on something or someone, or when someone has to lean on me."

"Do you want to say anything to Haviva? What is your message to her?"

"I want to tell her to be careful with me. The fluids in here may never dissolve, but she can at least try to minimize the pain by not putting too much pressure on me. She may just have to live with the pain. With me. But being gentle with me will make it easier. Make it hurt less."

"Is there anything else she can do to ease the pain?" Jude asked.

"Yes. Sometimes she will have no choice but to touch the spot where it hurts most. It is unavoidable. At times like those, she should not fight the pain. Instead, she should let go into it, and remember she is not the only one feeling pain at this time. That will not end the pain, but it will make it easier to take."

Some pain does not go away. It collects in our most vulnerable yet also most flexible parts. Like the waters of the *mikveh* that collect where there is an opening, an indentation, a place open to receive, the source of the pain can also be the cure.

When we immerse, the *mikveh* absorbs all the baggage we choose to leave behind in those waters in order to become renewed and reborn. Yet, the *mikveh* waters themselves are unchanged. They absorb our pain but are not affected by it. Rather, they turn the pain into a vessel of healing.

As I had learned that day when the *mikveh* waters had overflowed and the abuse survivor had written to me about her profound healing experience in the *mikveh*: our collective pain can be the instrument of personal renewal and divine connection. Being enveloped and embraced by the collective pain of humanity, I now understood from my own experience, can help us see deeper into that place where we are all before and after and beyond that pain.

It is that untouched place we call our God-given soul.

I WAS NOT able to attend my graduation ceremony from the ISC program at One Spirit, but I watched it live with Jacob by my side in front of the computer screen. The program participants graduate in the same ceremony with the ministry students at Riverside Church, so although Jacob had not attended that ceremony when I was ordained, I was glad he would get a taste of what it was like when he watched with me now.

As I watched the ministry students on this transformative day in their lives, I remembered my own ordination vows:

Wherever I happen to find myself, I vow to do my best to be there with my whole heart; and to safeguard that little piece of You, God, in myself. And in others as well. You cannot help me, but I must help You and defend Your dwelling place inside of me, and others, to the last. Because ultimately, I have just one moral duty: to reclaim large areas of peace within me, more and more peace, and to reflect it towards others.

Suddenly, it all made sense. That is who I truly am. That is the ME I have been looking for. This is the ministry into which I am being ordained. To serve. To be there for other humans, on a human level. It is not about the religion itself, or even its practices. It is not even about God, if God is outside us.

It is about being present for people, being present for myself, letting life unfold and believing God is within every human being, even those who do not believe God is within anyone but those like them. And even those who do not believe there is a greater power that connects all.

Our job is to defend the notion that we are all divine and human, and that we are all connected. Our job is to cultivate peace inside ourselves and project it out to the world.

I watched my classmate, Christopher, stand to deliver the speech he had prepared to represent our graduating class. He spoke about sacred listening and feeling called to heal others and create more peace in our troubled world; I felt filled with purpose and peace. Then I heard him say my name. In the excitement of the moment, I had forgotten he was going to read the words I had been asked to compose to bless my class:

He announced he was about to read my blessing:

May Life grant us:
Ears tuned for sacred listening.
Eyes focused to the divinity in every soul, the wholeness in every human.
Hearts open to hold the pain of others while tending to our own pain in our own time.
A mind fresh and clear to approach each human life with genuine curiosity and wonder.
A balanced body that recognizes its own holiness.
Courage to continue to dig deep into the depths of our souls, so we can unearth both wounds and treasures. For the depths are endless, as is the work.

Time to tend to ourselves so we can better tend to others.

Presence and grounding to hold space for others.

Strength to hold our own ground while holding space for others in non-judgment.

Tools to crack open our hearts and let the pain of the world come in.

Space to hold suffering without closing our hearts and giving up in despair.

Discernment to know what is of service to ourselves and others rather than the ego.

A channel to let Spirit flow through us.

Integrity to have our outsides match our insides.

Wisdom to read our inner compass and let it guide us.

Humility to follow the wisdom of others.

Grace to let Life's blessings reach our wounded places.

Please, Oh Flow of Life, help us to reach our own Higher Selves,

Help us to help others reach their Higher Selves,

Help us to help humanity reach its Higher Self.

Then, Christopher—a born-and-raised-Catholic gay man who was now an interfaith minister and spiritual companion in addition to his practice as a human rights lawyer—raised his hands above his head (which I had instructed him to do but myself cannot do) in the Priestly posture that is said to date back to the High Priests in the Holy Jewish Temple (the hand gesture used as the Vulcan salute in Star Trek), and said:

"Now, I would like to invite us all to raise our arms as I am and bless one another with Rabbi Reverend Haviva's adaptation of the Priestly Blessing found in Numbers 6:22-27."

I watched as an entire sanctuary of people raised their hands in the Priestly posture and together recited:

May Divine Presence bless you and keep you.

May Divine Light shine upon you and guide you.

May Divine Flow grant you peace.

And let us say, Amen!

My heart was full.

IT IS THE Sabbath. I am climbing over a wall. It is a wall surrounding a Reform synagogue in Jerusalem. I am climbing over it with Jacob and Shefa. We are going to Mishael's soccer game, which is meant to be after the prayer service. With a puppet show, as well. But as we climb over the wall, it starts to crumble. The whole synagogue begins falling to pieces. The Holy Ark, which is standing tall and grand, comes down last. Crumbles down to the ground. Everything is falling apart.

The synagogue's rabbi is doing a Buddhist ritual, a meditation of sorts. He is sitting in lotus position at the foot of the crumbled Ark. I ask him if the ritual will still work with the Ark no longer standing. He says, "Yes, it will." And the soccer game goes on as planned. The puppet show, too.

"I would like to speak with the wall," Jude says. "What do you look like? What is your purpose?"

"I am a stone wall. A retaining wall. A protective wall. A wall built to keep people out."

"And yet, Haviva climbs over you."

"Yes. She and Jacob and Shefa climb over me. And I come falling down."

"How does that feel?"

"I don't mind. I didn't want to keep people out, anyway. I was built for that purpose. But it feels good to come down."

"Thank you, wall. Can I speak to the Holy Ark now?" Jude asks me.

"Yes. I am here. I am the Holy Ark. I hold the sacred Torah scrolls. I am usually closed, keeping them from sight. From access. But sometimes I am open, and when I am, people stand out of respect for the scrolls. That's what it's about: ritualizing reverence for and containing access to the sacred."

"And how do you feel falling apart?"

"I don't mind. It feels freeing. I didn't really want to have to stand so tall, to act so high and mighty, so holy. To keep the sacred hidden, with only short peeks and designated times of access."

"Thank you, Holy Ark, now in pieces. I'd like to speak to the rabbi now. Rabbi, who are you? What is your purpose in this dream?"

I enter the persona of this rabbi, who is a friend. "I am the founder of this synagogue. I spent my career building it up and serving its community. I just retired. I have time to travel the world, do some spiritual seeking of my own. I went to India once for a year. It was wonderful. I am also a water person. I swim regularly. And a cancer survivor. Yet, I approach life with joy and a sense of adventure."

"What is that meditation ritual you are performing, Rabbi?" Jude asks.

"I am just sitting here, Buddha-like. That is what I am doing. I'm letting everything crumble to pieces around me, while I sit here and do this meditation ritual. I am letting it all flow over me while I sit here in peace with what is."

"How lucky you are. To create that when all of the formal structures have crumbled."

I feel a shift from this rabbi himself speaking, to me speaking from his body. "Yes. It is something I created for myself. Worked on. Creating a space of peace within the chaos, and without the formal structures people think you need in order to access it. That is why it works even when the Holy Ark no longer stands, when the synagogue no longer stands, when the walls protecting it all no longer stand."

"Thank you, Rabbi," Jude says. "Can I speak to the soccer game and the puppet show now?"

"Sure. We're here. We go on without the synagogue. We don't need it, either. Never did. Sometimes we happen in conjunction with the synagogue prayer services, or on the same premises. But not always. We can also happen on our own. We are play and simple pleasure. We are a different kind of ritual. Ritual just about living life with joy. Feeling the ground beneath your feet, the wind on your face. And laughing. Even getting to play different roles sometimes. Trying out different things. All in the name of feeling emotions— sorrow, joy, pleasure. Just living life."

JACOB, THE KIDS and I are camping, as we do every year the *Shabbat* before *Rosh Hashanah*, for the annual national Sea of Galilee Swim. People come from around the country. It is at a narrow point, so the swim is not too long. There are different lengths one can swim. I do the longer option with the older kids, almost four kilometers. Jacob takes the younger kids on the one-and-a-half-kilometer swim.

It is customary to immerse in a *mikveh* during the High Holiday season as a rebirth and renewal ritual for *Rosh Hashanah*, as well as a spiritual cleansing for *Yom Kippur*. Swimming in this annual event is like joining in one huge collective *mikveh* immersion. What a wonderful way to start the Jewish new year.

The Sea of Galilee has been receding over the years, so the walk down to the water is even more challenging for me this year than last. Especially since the first twenty or so meters of the Sea bottom is a clay-like mud that feels like quicksand and is impossible for me to maneuver, especially without my dictuses. My two oldest daughters hold my hands on both sides, and we manage to get to where we can start swimming.

"See you at the other side!" they say, and, being faster swimmers than I am, they swim ahead. I am left to myself.

I imagine the biblical story of the birth of the world:

Before the world as we know it, there was only water and Spirit. All was whole and eternal. God's womb. Then Spirit made room for the world, for mortality, by making space for duality and imperfection. The waters collected into seas and dry land appeared. Duality was born. The imperfect, mortal world was born from God's eternal womb. As humans, we are destined to live out our lives in this world, doing a dance between wholeness and imperfection, eternity and mortality, divinity and humanity.

But we can return to God's womb at moments in our lives, whether it be through connection to others, to our own souls, to nature, to Spirit. One way to do this is to return to the sea, to the primordial waters that still exist and will forever exist, as part of our dual reality but also as part of divine reality. We can feel the eternal embrace of the divine and enter the flow of life. We can be born and reborn onto dry land, into our own human condition.

As I swim, for the three hours it takes me to get across the Sea, I tell myself this story over and over again. My story. The collective story of humanity. At some point, the story becomes a full-body experience. I feel held by the water. Like I am swimming in God's womb.

I am part of life's flow, part of the eternal story, part of God's dreamscape. I feel calm, wonderful, and at peace. I feel connected to myself and to all the thousands of other people swimming around me who have come to swim the Sea today, and to the lifeguards who are watching us from their boats. I feel connected to the Universe.

As I near the shore, I see a man coming towards me with a small, inflated raft. As he draws closer, I realize it is Jacob. He has come to escort me over the mulch.

"How was your swim?" he asks, as he kisses me and lifts me into his arms. Once again I feel held, supported, as he places me on the raft, carrying me back to our mortal, imperfect, human joint sojourn on dry land.

I AM IN an institution of some sort, a mix between a hospital and boarding school. There are many open fields with small buildings, like dormitories or bunks.

Suddenly, bombs are falling from the sky all around me. I run for cover. I don't know where to run, but I start running, looking for a safe place, even though I know really no place is safe. I go to various classrooms and buildings, trying to take cover, but the bombs keep coming, and I keep running, moving, trying to escape what feels inevitable.

I reach a sort of infirmary. A doctor calls out to me, tells me to come take cover there. He tells me to hide in a stall, but I don't feel safe. I feel like he is offering me shelter when we both know it is hopeless; the bombs will reach here, too.

Then, suddenly, Jacob is with me. We are in bed, making love. I feel so grateful, so content here. Happy in the moment. Even though I know it is fleeting, that it will all disappear momentarily when the bombs reach us.

I wake up in Jacob's arms and remember I fell asleep last night with that same feeling. We had made love after a week of no sex. I had gotten my period the week before, and although we are not especially strict about how many days of separation we keep around my bleeding these days, my bleeding time is still considered separate time.

That morning, we had gone skinny dipping in our natural pool together. Our private *mikveh*. When I was getting out, I asked Jacob to hold out my robe so I could get right into it, lest the neighbors catch a glimpse of my naked body. Jacob asked why it mattered so much. I answered I am not exactly a sight to behold.

"This is you," he said. "And I think you're a sight to behold. Besides, so what if people see what you look like, even with all your imperfections? I never expected, or even wanted, perfect. I think you're beautiful."

When he said that, I did not object. It even resonated on some level. Progress. The mere fact I was skinny dipping in my side yard in total daylight was progress.

That night, we had made love and snuggled into sleep. Like usual, Jacob fell asleep before me, and I lay in his arms thinking about how grateful I was for my life—for him; for my seven children; for my beautiful home we designed together; for my naturally filtered swimming lane; for my fulfilling work and creative outlets; for the agent I had just found for my debut novel; for my growing spiritual counseling practice; for this new sense of freedom I was allowing into my life.

For everything.

I felt so blessed I even tried to wake Jacob to tell him.

"Are you sleeping?" I asked, knowing he was in fact asleep. I reached for his hand.

"I was," he mumbled with a smirk, closing his fingers around mine.

"I just wanted to tell you how grateful I am feeling."

"Good. That's nice," he said, giving my hand a little squeeze and stroking my other arm with his other hand. "Now go to sleep." His hands became instantly limp again, and I was left to myself. I lay there feeling content with our naked bodies fitting together so perfectly. I did not want the moment to end.

And then I felt sad. Because I knew it would end. It would not last. It could not last. Nothing does. I would lose Jacob. Or he would lose me. One day. But even before that, this honeymoon would peter out, like most intense periods do.

Even if this was the beginning of a newly revived passion as our kids were getting older, our youngest child just starting first grade, could we really keep this up? Could we manage to sustain intense feelings of being "in love" until the end of our sojourns here on this earth? Was that possible?

Still, I couldn't shake that feeling of contentment, of feeling happy in the moment. Of feeling so much love and appreciation for my partner, for our relationship, and for the life we built together. No matter how much my thoughts tried to bring me to a place of fear or worry about the future, I could not stop myself from feeling at peace.

And then I must have fallen asleep, because I dreamt what I dreamt. Even in my dreamworld, my ego tried to lead me to a place of fear. God was dropping bomb after bomb, and eventually one would bring my life as I knew it to an end.

But when I awoke and worked the dream, when I became the bombs and let them speak to me, I realized they were not trying to hurt me. God was not trying to hurt me. Life's challenges were not there to hurt me; they were part of life and would help me grow if I let them.

The eventual bombs of life would not detract from the feeling of contentment I was having in the present moment lying in Jacob's arms. That feeling of peace was my soul's message to me.

MY CELL PHONE rings. It is the day after *Rosh Hashanah*, and it is my mother calling.

We just had a nice visit over the summer. We even talked about Michal and Ahmad's plans to marry when he graduates from engineering school in a year's time.

They have been living together for years and already signed a "couplehood certificate" that gives them legal rights as a couple in Israel, even if there is no such thing as civil marriage, per se, here. All legal marriages in Israel happen only through the State-run religious established institutions (of all recognized religions here), so there is no legal intermarriage, and even non-

Orthodox Jewish weddings are not legal. But they want to have a ceremony and celebration, with family and friends around them.

I explained to her Ahmad is a wonderful human being and he and Michal make a good pair. It was not an easy discussion, and it was not as if I felt my mother was coming around to accepting the situation, but she did not blow up at me or threaten me. I thought we had made progress.

"Was Michal with you for *Rosh Hashanah*?" my mother asks. I tell her no, Michal and Ahmad were away on a much-needed, well-earned vacation in Spain over the holiday.

There is silence on the other end, and then, in an agitated and upset voice, my mother says, "That is what she did on *Rosh Hashanah*? Your children know nothing. This is what you need to atone for this *Yom Kippur*! You've raised a bunch of ignorant children."

By that, of course, my mother means ignorant about Judaism. But I know this is not true. They are not ignorant. They may not know as much about Judaism as I did growing up, but they are not ignorant. They are simply choosing their own paths. Like I did. Like I am.

I take a deep breath and explain to my mother I trust my children and respect their life choices, that if this is how Michal chose to spend her *Rosh Hashanah* this year, that is her decision.

"I don't know what's happened to you. You don't care about anything. I'm beside myself."

I am about to start defending myself, and then I see the image from my dream. The Holy Ark is crumbling while the rabbi sits like a Buddha, letting the walls of the synagogue fall apart around him as he meditates in peace.

I am this rabbi. I am the Buddha. This is not something for which I must atone. It is something I must embrace. Celebrate. This is me.

A MUSEUM GUARD is on duty. She is at the front door of the museum, guarding the precious art and artifacts. She hears her boyfriend outside. He is talking to a group of his buddies. He is talking about her! She takes out her pistol, goes outside and shoots him. Then she shoots a row of statues standing in the museum entrance. She shoots each one. One at a time. In the heart. A hole in the chest of each statue. But they do not fall, break or crumble to pieces. They stand tall, even with holes in their hearts.

This is the first dream I can remember since starting my dreamwork in which I do not appear. The ego figure does not appear.

I wonder what this could mean. Could it be a sign I am making spiritual headway? Perhaps my ego is learning to take a back seat, rest, and leave the driving up to my soul.

I close my eyes and re-enter the dream. I become the woman. I ask her to tell me about herself.

"I am a museum guard. I protect precious things."

I ask her why she got so angry at her boyfriend, why she shot him.

"He was judging me," she answers. "I couldn't stand that he was judging me. So, I shot him. I wanted him to be gone from my life once and for all."

Because I am now a certified dreamworker, I know I am not only the woman guard, but I am also the boyfriend. I am the one judging and I am the one being judged. I am judging myself. And I want to put an end to that once and for all. But in order to do so, I must step outside and leave something precious unguarded. I must leave my post and let my defenses down. They served me well until now, and I am grateful. But I do not need them anymore. At least not all the time.

I embody the statues. Who am I? I am a precious and unique piece of art. I am both ancient and current. I am from the past, yet I am standing here, in the present. I am standing here, watching, like a Buddha. I am passive, yet graceful and peaceful. Bearing witness. I am standing tall and proud.

Then I am shot. In the heart. But I do not fall. I remain standing tall and proud and Buddha-like. I am my soul unguarded, vulnerable, showing the world who she is. I have left myself without my defense mechanisms and protective armor. That has opened me to criticism, judgment and pain. Sometimes even from those most close to me. Unprotected, I will inevitably be hurt. Yet, I remain standing. Even with this hole in my heart.

I AM IN my natural swimming lane in my yard, swimming laps. Back and forth, back and forth. The air is still and clear. The colors of the plants— red, purple, yellow, and many shades of green—look especially bright to me as I swim.

When I finish swimming, I get out of the pool and dry off in the sun, looking out from my backyard at the view of brown hills, olive orchards and Palestinian-Israeli villages. It is fall, the holiday of *Sukkot*, so the rains have not yet come this year. Yet, the sauna-like summer heat has passed, and the blue sky is spotted with cottony clouds. I am overcome with gratitude for my life, for love, for being part of the mystery.

I walk over to the *sukkah* which Jacob built with the kids the week before. It is a temporary dwelling place, a kind of hut with leaves and branches for a roof, outside of one's home. The custom is to spend as much time in there as possible over the holiday. People eat in their *sukkah*, spend time with guests, read, and even sleep in their *sukkah*. Even when the weather is cold, stormy or sweltering hot.

This is one of a few nature-oriented Jewish holidays, and this one is specifically designed to send us out into the elements, to experience the tension between the vulnerability and awesome security of being out in the wild.

God's protective presence is often referred to as *"sukkat shlomekha,"* God's hut of peace. That is the constant tension during this holiday, in the readings and the prayers: the tension between the transience of life and the peace of surrendering to what we have no control over anyway. That feeling of being under God's wings. The *sukkah* is a dwelling place, but a fragile, temporary one. Like life itself.

I take the "four species": a *lulav* (a palm frond in the center with a myrtle branch on one side and a willow branch on the other) and *etrog* (a citron fruit like a bumpy large lemon which smells delightful) from the table and bring it with me outside the *sukkah*, where I can see the view as I shake these plants-turned-ritual-objects in the six directions, as per the traditional Jewish practice—like the Native American ritual of calling in the directions.

"Hodu l'Adonai ki tov, ki l'olam chasdo. Thank Spirit because all is grace, because all is compassion," I say as I look out at the view. Then I say just the word, *"hodu,"* as I slowly shake the species northward, at the beautiful view of the fields and orchards. I meditate on the word *"hodu,"* thank, and I feel overcome with gratitude at living in a place with this view of nature in my backyard.

Before moving to the kibbutz, we lived in various cities: New York, Washington, D.C., Jerusalem; moving to the country was a move for my soul.

When I say the word, *"l'Adonai,"* to Spirit, I place the *lulav* and *etrog* on my heart, and meditate on Spirit within me.

"Ki," because, I say, as I shake the *lulav* behind me and meditate on my "because," my past, on what built me, what brought me to this moment and to who I am today. I focus on being grateful, not resentful, for all that complicated stuff.

I call out the word, *"tov,"* grace, to the sky and shake the *lulav* upwards. I focus on grace, the grace of God, the love of God and the wonder of Spirit, of mystery, all around me.

When I say the word, *"ki,"* because, I shake the *lulav* again, this time to the ground, to the earth, and meditate on my own mortality, on the fact that

I will one day return to the earth. Death is the "because," the "why" of life in some ways.

As I call out the word "*l'olam*," to all (literally the world, but here it connotes all of humanity and all of time), I shake the *lulav* to my right, to the East, to one of our neighboring Palestinian-Israeli villages, and meditate on the idea that God's grace is upon all, even those some may consider "other," even those with whom we may have a national history of revenge and hate, and even those with whom we may disagree ideologically or religiously. All means all. Humanity includes all. We are all in this together. When I say the word "*l'olam*," I meditate on the unity of all.

I say the word, "*chasdo*," God's loving-kindness, in a quieter voice, as I shake the *lulav* to the West, in the direction of my neighbor, the Educational Center (which houses many sleep-in programs for children and young adults who cause much noise at all hours of the day and night), and I meditate on what feels at times like the limits of my own capacity for compassion.

I hold the four species to my heart again. I close my eyes and inhale the lemony scent of the *etrog*. I take a deep breath.

I HAVE DROPPED five fourteen-year-old boys off at soccer practice and have twenty minutes to myself while I drive back home. Jacob is away again. He had two conferences to attend in Boston and Washington. But he will stop in New York to see his mother for *Shabbat*. He said this was something *he* wanted to do. Which is fine with me. I am at peace with what is, feeling no resentment.

"I will miss you," I told him when he announced his trip. "But I'll be fine. It will be fine. Do what you must. I trust your judgment. I'll be here when you get back."

And I meant it. I do miss him. I am counting the days until his return. But I am also fine. Not the survival kind of fine, with all my defense mechanisms up. Rather, the kind of fine open to feeling the full range of emotions caused by his absence and by life in general, while managing to hold my spiritual center, that sense of inner peace that will not be shaken even as the bombs are falling.

Just as I start to drive, a song plays on the radio. It is Ehud Banai singing Yonatan Gefen's lyrics. A song from my childhood, from the seventies, written after the Camp David Accords. *Yehiyeh Tov*. It will all be fine.

It is a song about war, terror, military occupation and political corruption. Not much has changed in my lifetime. He sings that one day the wolf will live with the sheep and the leopard sit with the lamb. Yet he makes it sound so far off that I am not left with a sense of hope for the future of this country or humanity. The final lines, though, are so sweet, I smile to myself as I clutch the steering wheel and look at the road ahead:

> But in the meantime
> Please don't take your hand out of mine
> And it will be fine . . .
> I look out the window
> Maybe a new day will come.

I don't see peace on the horizon, but maybe, just maybe, a new and better day will come. Meanwhile, I continue to do my spiritual practices (even if erratically), my inner work, my sacred activism.

But most importantly, I cherish the love in my life in the present moment. Jacob is thousands of miles away, but I hold him inside me. Even driving a carpool is holy work, because it is an act of love.

WHAT ARE YOU WAITING FOR? JUMP IN!

I AM IN a cave-like basement. The place feels like a loft, only I know it is underground. I wonder who lives here, and then I realize it is Bohemian Woman.

Suddenly, I am at a rally in Berlin. Bohemian Woman is standing in front of a crowd of people. Everyone is wearing comrade-clothing—khaki canvas army-communist uniforms. Bohemian woman is wearing both this clothing and bohemian clothing. She is wearing both at the same time, somehow.

She is leading a chant. "I once had a head. I once had a head. I once had a head." I understand she means she once had a head, or we all once had heads, but now we don't need them anymore. Our heads were chopped off in punishment, but somehow that ended up liberating us.

Bohemian Woman walks off. She has long gray hair and piercings (I know this although I cannot see her face, only her back), and she is wearing bohemian clothing, like I used to wear in high school, and a big trekking backpack. She is walking off into the sunset.

"This is a significant dream," Jude tells me. "There are some powerful images and details here. Where do you feel most drawn in the dream?"

I drop back into my dream. I feel pulled to the cave, but also to the chant. And then I feel pulled towards the final image of this woman walking off into the sunset. "I guess I am pulled towards the woman. I feel like I am following her, almost like I am trailing her."

"Okay. Where are you from, Bohemian Woman?"

"I am from nowhere. I am simply who I am. Belonging to no one and no group. I do go back from time to time to my cave-like room, but it is just a place to rest and renew myself. It is home, and it is not home. It is nice to know I have a place I can be safe and warm, but I don't feel attached to it. I could call another place my home. It is good to have a home, but I don't feel possessive of it. It does not define me."

"Thank you, Bohemian Woman. I am interested in that chant you led at the rally. Can you say it to me again and then continue talking? I would like to understand what it means."

"Sure. I once had a head. I once had a head. I once had a head. I once had a head. But I did not conform. They wanted us to all be the same and to follow their rules. And I did for a long time. But then I had enough. So, I refused, and they chopped off my head."

"Oh my. So, what head are you wearing now?"

"I grew a new head. But it's a different kind of head. I didn't need that head anymore. They thought they were punishing me. But really, it was a blessing in disguise. When they chopped off my head, I realized I was still alive. I realized I didn't need a head to live. I could live from my heart."

As I say this, I think of all those years I spent studying the intricacies of Jewish religious law, trying to find a way to reconcile it with my moral conscience. It felt important to me then to find a loophole, a text to prove what I was doing was still within the rules of the game. That does not matter to me anymore.

"Beautiful. You learned you could live from your heart."

"Yes, and that was when I grew this new head. My head is bigger now. It is more expansive. There is room in there for much more, and much less at the same time. It's emptier of stuff—of all of those details and arguments that get in the way of the bigger picture, and of the heart—and therefore more spacious."

"Where are you going, Bohemian Woman?"

"I don't know. I'm from nowhere and going nowhere in particular. I am free to go wherever my heart takes me. I am heading off into the sunset. The beautiful sunset. That is all I need to know now."

"Thank you. I would like to speak to the cave now. Cave, are you there?"

"Yes. I'm here. I am underground. There is light in here, but I am underground. Deep. Down. Beneath the surface."

"So, Bohemian Woman lives deep down, beneath the surface?"

"Yes. That is where she lives. But she comes up and out, too, when it is time for her to move on or spread her message."

Jude says she would like to speak to the dreamer. "What does the energy of the dream feel like to you?" she asks me.

"It feels like it is in two states at once. There is the comrade clothing and the bohemian clothing. The comrade energy and the bohemian energy. They co-exist in the dream."

"At the end, too?"

I am not sure. I drop back into the dream. I picture that last image of Bohemian Woman walking off into the sunset. "No. At the end it is just the bohemian energy."

"This is a dream of transformation," Jude states, matter-of-factly. By now I know to trust her judgment.

THAT NIGHT, AFTER I work this dream with Jude, is the beginning of the twenty-four-hour holiday of Purim, the Jewish carnival holiday, when people dress in costume, trying on different identities. One could even say they are tapping into different aspects of themselves, like when we dream.

I am dressed as a Greek goddess. I come to synagogue and find one friend who has undergone her own transformation, dressed as a butterfly, another as an overwhelmed mother who did not have time to get dressed after her shower (she is wearing a bathrobe), another as a nymph, another as Super Girl. A male friend of mine is dressed in women's clothing, another as Minnie Mouse.

And then I see Bohemian Woman. She has her back to me. Her hair is whiter than it is gray, and her backpack is smaller than the one in my dream, but the resemblance is uncanny.

Like in my dream, her back is to me. I cannot see her face. I approach her and tap her on the shoulder. When she turns to face me, I am not surprised to discover she is my dear friend, a woman in her sixties, an artist and an art therapist. And a Buddhist. While her life has not allowed her to be quite as physically free as she may desire, she is a free spirit. And she is wise. And I know it is not by accident that Bohemian Woman has appeared to me in my waking life in her body.

When I return from synagogue, I send a photo of my friend in her Bohemian Woman costume to Jude. She tells me Bohemian Woman's appearance in my waking life is a sign, an affirmation of the dream's message, a confirmation of Jude's intuition this dream is a significant one in my life.

"Bohemian Woman has appeared to you because you have done so much inner work," she tells me. "She is the result of all of your work. That does not mean you have no more work to do. But she has come to tell you something. To guide you. She is a wisdom guide, coming from inside you. Bringing you inner wisdom. Now the invitation is to listen."

The next day is Purim day. Jacob and I take the kids on a long bike ride along the ocean further north of our kibbutz. The shoreline here is rugged, just how I like it. And there is no one in sight except a few people fishing out on the rocks.

When we sit on the beach to rest, I find a rock by the water and begin to write. I have brought along my journal and my water bottle—my two sources of nourishment, my magical crystal mucus—and it is clear to me what I need to do. I am ready to start creating my Wisdom Council. Bohemian Woman appeared to me to tell me it is time. I am ready.

Bohemian Woman sits at the head of the Council. But Slug is there too, as well as Spider, Jellyfish, Butterfly, Overflowing *Mikveh*, Sleep, Mother's Milk, Dishwasher Tablet, Hermaphrodite Swimmer, Buddha-Rabbi-Statue, the "Let Me Go" song, and other characters and images who have appeared to me over these past years in my dream and waking worlds.

My Wisdom Council is the gift I have given myself by embarking on this dream journey. Its members are here for me whenever I need them. Because they are all me.

I AM AT my own wedding, only there are two brides, and both are me. I watch Haviva #1 walk down the aisle.

Everyone stands and starts singing the Hebrew version of the Happy Birthday song: "Hayom yom huledet, hayom yom huledet, hayom yom huledet shel Haviva. Chag lah sameach v'zer la poreach. Hayom yom huledet shel Haviva." (Today is the day of the birth of Haviva! May she have a joyous celebration, with a blooming flower wreath. Today is the day of the birth of Haviva!).

They do a kind of flash mob dance down the aisle after her. I watch this and wonder if what I had planned for my walk down the aisle will be interesting, performative and spectacular enough.

"That is quite a dream," Jude says. "There is so much rich material in this short dream. Two brides, and both are you. A wedding that is also a birthday, perhaps. Are you, the dreamer, one of the brides or both?"

"I am watching from the point of view of the second bride, Haviva #2."

"Okay. Let's start with the song. I feel a lot of energy there."

I am glad she did not start with the brides. I am not sure I can inhabit the first bride yet. "Okay. The words in the Hebrew version are different than those in the English one."

"In what way? Embody the song. Tell me who you are."

I drop back into the dream. "I am the Hebrew birthday song. I am a declaration of the dreamer's birth, a celebration of it. I am not a song about being happy on the anniversary of the dreamer's birth. I am about celebrating the birth itself. I am a declaration of a special and unique birthing into the world, like when Jesus was born. It's that grand. And thus, the flash mob. It's a big deal.

Haviva was born into this world! Joy to the world! She will flower and bloom and continue to grow and contribute what only she can contribute to the world. What a joyous moment to mark and celebrate!"

"Beautiful," Jude says. "It sounds like quite a celebration. Thank you, birthday song. We may come back to you later. But now I would like to speak to Haviva #1. How do you feel about all of this?"

"I am Haviva #1. I am dressed like a bride. I look like Haviva did at her own wedding. Dressed in her vintage cream-colored lace wedding dress, a lace band around her head with her curly dark hair spilling out and down her shoulders."

"And ... ?"

"Well, I walk down the aisle, and everyone starts singing and dancing. I am not sure I like all this attention and fanfare. It's not my way. But I go along with it because I know it is what everyone is expecting of me. But I feel pulled and pushed by the crowd. I am swept away by their energy and enthusiasm. I am not sure this is how I want this all to be."

"And yet you go along?"

"Yes. I am being swept up by it. And it does not feel wrong, exactly. I go along willingly, as if I know this is what I am meant to be doing. Yet, I do not feel a hundred percent right with it. It is my only choice now, but it's not the final word on the matter. That's it. It's just a step along the way."

"Thank you, Haviva #1. Can I speak to the wedding now? Who are you, wedding? What is your purpose?"

"I am a celebration of a joining. And a public declaration of love and commitment."

"Commitment to what?"

"To sticking by each other and supporting each other in mutual growth."

"So, who is joining together here in this wedding? Who is committing to this support of mutual growth?"

I think. I feel. I know the answer but hesitate to say it. "I think it is the two brides. They are marrying each other. This is both a wedding and a birth. A joining and a new beginning. Haviva #1 was born into the world a divine mortal, like Jesus, like all human beings. She was born to bloom and grow, like a flower. It was a moment to rejoice. But it was not the end of the story."

"How so?"

"Now it is Haviva #2's turn to walk down the aisle as part of that growth process. But for that to happen, there must be a joining. A marriage of Haviva #1 to Haviva #2. Haviva #2 needs to realize with her step forward now, she is continuing the process set in motion on that joyous miraculous day she was born. She needs to acknowledge, own, embody even, that it was, indeed, a joyous day to celebrate, and it was all part of the continual journey. All parts of a whole."

"And now?"

"Now it is time for Haviva #2 to decide how she is going to walk down to join hands with Haviva #1 and embrace her birthright."

"Dreamer, did you hear that? Haviva #2, did you hear that? You were hesitating, wondering if your way would be spectacular enough, interesting enough. How do you feel now?"

I speak from the second bride's voice. "I don't know. I feel like the crowd wants to dance me down the aisle. But I don't want to give in this time. I don't want to do it their way to please them this time. I want to do it my way."

"And what is that?"

"Well, it is not clear from the dream. The dream ends with me standing at the aisle. But I feel I want it to be quieter. More authentically me. I don't need them to announce and celebrate my birth. I can walk down without all of that. At least I think I can."

"Why don't you try?"

I close my eyes and get inside Haviva #2 in my dream. Can I take a step and start walking down the aisle? If I do, what will it look like? What will happen?

I am holding a bouquet of flowers. I put my face into the flowers and take in their scent. The fragrance of the flowers fills me like air in a balloon and I feel myself rising into the sky. I lift my arms like I can only do in a dream, or in water, and my bouquet turns into a bunch of colorful balloons. This time, I will not walk down the aisle. I will do it my way.

I send a telepathic message to Haviva #1. Come join me. Come float with me. And she does. We are joined and reborn as one. And then the heavens burst out in song: "This is the day of the birth of Haviva! A day of celebration! Flowers will bloom for her and lift her up. Joy to the world!"

MY MOTHER HAD a dream. She called to tell me.

"I dreamt you had performed in some kind of show," she said. "It was not clear what kind, but it was clear you had done a really good job."

Interesting, because I do not like to perform. I have stage fright. Even more interesting, because my overly critical mother is not one to tell me I am doing a good job. At least not in her conscious waking state.

My mother continued, "The woman who was the choreographer or director or something came up to give you a gift. I am not sure what the gift was. Maybe flowers. She gave you the gift, and you asked who it was from. She said it was from Jacob. A present for having done such a good job."

"And?" I was clutching the phone, not daring to blink, lest this be a dream, too.

"That's it."

"That's a nice dream," I said. "And you know, I've been learning dreamwork. I'm in a dream group, actually." I had not told my parents about anything related to my interspiritual studies or ordination, not even the dreamwork.

"A dream group? What's that?"

"Well, we work our dreams together, with a teacher. The idea is every element of the dream is an aspect of the dreamer. In this case, you would be me, and you would be the gift, and the director, and even Jacob. If I were working this dream with you, I would tell you to start by becoming—by speaking from—an element in the dream."

"What do you mean, speaking from?"

"You'd say something like, *I am the director of the show. I am not in the show itself, but without me it could not have happened. I feel just as invested in the show as those acting in it do, if not more . . .*"

"Well, that seems silly. Why can't it just be a dream about you receiving a gift from Jacob after a wonderful performance? After all, you deserve it. You've been through a lot these past years."

Now this was getting even more interesting. "How so?" I asked.

My mother answered my question with a question. "Why couldn't I just be dreaming Jacob was saying thank you for all of the hard work you've been doing keeping things going there while he's been away so much? It can't have been easy. But you managed."

No, it was not easy. But it was rewarding. I had been stretched. I had grown. She did not know the least of it. I had not even told her about my ordination. I had gone to New York and back and she knew nothing about it. But somehow, she sensed this had been a transformative time for me.

"It can be about that," I said. "There is such a thing as a prophetic dream, actually. But it can also be about much more. It's your dream, so it can also tell you something about yourself, about your soul, something deep in your unconscious that would not come out in your awake time."

There was quiet on the other end. My mother was clearly thinking this over. "Well, I think it's just about you receiving the appreciation you deserve. That's all."

A sip of mother's milk in the form of a bouquet of flowers. This bouquet would lift me up too, but in a different way, because I knew finally I could be lifted without it.

I AM A tour guide for a large synagogue group visiting Israel, getting on and off buses. I leave my shoes somewhere and can't find them. I keep looking—under all the seats in the bus, on the seats, but I still can't find them. I am panicked. I cannot walk without them, as they have my dictuses attached. A woman starts coughing. She is choking on something. She can't breathe. I try to help her, but I can't.

I wake up from this dream short of breath. Jacob is away. I can't breathe. I am coughing, hyperventilating. I gasp for air, but I can't get enough. I try to calm myself, and after a few minutes, I can breathe more easily again. But this incident worries me. I have never had trouble breathing, but I know that as my disease progresses, it can spread to the respiratory system.

I make an appointment to check my breathing, and, alas, my diaphragm is showing signs of weakness. It is only a matter of time before I will need to use a BPap ventilator. Until even that won't help anymore. The bombs are starting to fall.

I work my dream with a dreamwork partner who studied with Jude when I did. "Be the synagogue group," she says.

"We are a group touring Israel. This is not the way we really want to see this place, getting on and off buses. We would prefer a slower pace, where we could really experience life here, not like onlookers, but from the inside." Me, experiencing life fully, with my guard down.

"Thank you, tourists. I'd like to speak to the dictuses now."

"We are the dreamer's dictuses. We help her walk. We help her get around. Without us she would trip and fall. Without us she needs to be more sedentary, slow down, take her time, and be at peace with what she can do without help. Without us she needs to surrender to what is."

"The dreamer feels helpless without you. Is there something you would like to tell her?"

"Yes. She is not helpless without us. She just can't do more than is humanly possible for her. And that is okay. She needs to learn to live with that. In fact, if she does that now, it will help her ease into death, when that comes. After all, even aids like us are only a temporary solution. Eventually, even we won't be enough."

"Is that why you disappeared? To teach her that?"

"Yes."

"That's pretty harsh."

"Perhaps. But that's the way it is. Life is harsh, but it would feel less so if the dreamer stopped trying to fight it. She can stop looking now. She can just rest."

"Thank you, dictuses. I would like to speak to the air now. Air, describe yourself."

"I am air," I say. "I am needed here on earth so that humans can breathe. But before they are born, they don't need me. They live without me in the womb. It is only when they come out into the world of me, of air, of dry land, that they need me. When they stop breathing, it is because they do not need me anymore."

"What did you come here to tell the dreamer?"

"She already knows what I am telling her. I just came to remind her. She swims every day. She knows she cannot live without air, but she can *be* without it. If she does not panic, she can be without breathing, as she did before she was born into this world. It is the panic that is preventing her from remembering that. If she can relax and trust in the process, in what is instead of worrying about what isn't, she won't need me or the dictuses anymore. Her body is slowly letting go, and now her soul must follow. Her body needs air, but her soul doesn't."

I AM OFFICIATING an immersion ceremony for three biological siblings who were adopted abroad by different Israeli families. When the families returned to Israel, they discovered their adopted children had biological siblings in Israel. They reached out to one another and have since been one extended family.

The parents decided to truly celebrate the event, so they invited friends and family from all sides to join in the party. They brought balloons, music, a cake, and an abundance of food. Even with all the pre-wedding immersions we host here, *Shmaya* has never seen such a large and lively crowd.

As I emerge with the children and their parents from the *mikveh* building, joyful guests throw candies and form a dance circle around them. The children's faces are beaming, like the face of the man whose conversion ceremony I officiated earlier this morning.

This man had waited forty years to convert. He came to Israel from Germany to volunteer on a kibbutz, which is where he fell in love with the woman, a Jewish Israeli *kibbutznik*, who later became his wife. Since then, he has lived in Israel and thrown his lot in with the Jewish people.

He had studied for conversion back then and had wanted to convert and get married in Israel, but the Israeli Rabbinate did not let him. He was living a Jewish life with his wife-to-be. Not a strict Orthodox life, but a life that suited them both.

The Rabbinate said if he wanted to convert, the couple would have to live separately for a year and both would have to live and study in ultra-Orthodox *yeshiva* programs, she with the women, and he with the men. Like me back in high school, they knew this was not the right path for them.

Instead, they married outside of Israel in a civil ceremony and came back to Israel to register as married. (This was before the option existed to sign a couplehood certificate like Michal and Ahmad did.) He continued to live a Jewish life, celebrate the Jewish holidays, eat only kosher food, not travel or work on *Shabbat*. He felt Jewish but knew he was not considered Jewish by those around him.

This was a deep wound for many years, until he discovered he could convert through the Reform movement. The conversion would not be accepted by the Rabbinate, but it would be accepted by the Interior Ministry. The law changed since he had originally investigated his options so many years before. So, this morning, forty years later, he finally closed that circle. He cried as he shook my hand and thanked me.

After him, but before the three adopted children, was another conversion. A grandmother with her adopted granddaughter, both from Ukraine. The grandmother is married to a Jewish man, so she was allowed to immigrate with him to Israel and obtain citizenship. The couple had officially adopted their granddaughter when she was just a baby—as her parents were not able to take care of her—and brought her with them to Israel, to start a new life.

But it took years for this woman to convert. Her husband had a stroke, and she was supporting the family by cleaning houses. She did not speak Hebrew, so even if she could find some time to study for conversion, she could not understand the classes. She lived a Jewish life but had given up on the dream of becoming Jewish.

She discovered through her Reform synagogue in Haifa that there was a new track for Russian speakers. She did not know if she could learn the material, though. She was ashamed. She did not even have a high school diploma. But she managed. Her connection with Judaism was a heart connection. Like Bohemian Woman, she did not need a head to know she was on the right spiritual path. After each immersion, she repeated the blessing after me and her ten-year-old granddaughter, who read it from a laminated card in the *mikveh*.

After her third immersion, I asked if she knew to recite the first line of the *Sh'ma* by heart. She said she did and proceeded to sing, with a voice like a cantor, these six words. She bellowed them out from a place so deep inside herself, it was inspiring to behold.

Later this afternoon, I will be meeting on Zoom with a client, a rabbinical school student, who is one of many rabbinical students I companion on their spiritual journeys. My practice is thriving, and I am grateful for the opportunity to provide this service to others, especially rabbinical students, as it was something from which I would have benefited when I was studying to become a rabbi.

After that, I will meet with another client, a seventy-seven-year-old woman with whom I have been meeting monthly as her spiritual companion. This woman decided, at this final stage of her life, to delve into her Jewish roots and connect to this heritage.

She is the only elder left in her family who will pass this on to her descendants. But she needs help finding a way in. She is not one to accept tradition without critique. She is finding her own interpretations and applications. Companioning her on this path has been my role, and it is a privilege.

Not long ago, she and her husband decided to come to Israel for the first— and perhaps last—time. We are planning a *mikveh* immersion ceremony at *Shmaya*, for her visit, marking this decision in her life to "get off the fence," as she calls it, and commit to exploring and passing on her connection to Judaism.

As much as I love officiating conversion and pre-wedding ceremonies, it is creating these individualized ceremonies that I love most about my *mikveh* work. The time I spend with clients before these ceremonies ranges from hours to months to years. It is an amazing process that requires deep listening, an ability to see each person's unique soul and its specific spiritual needs, and the creative vision to turn what they share in our sessions into a ceremony uniquely for them.

My clients' stories are different from mine, and their journeys are theirs alone. Jacob asks me how I feel about converting people to Judaism when I am an interspiritual rabbi, and about helping others draw closer to Judaism when I have come closer to finding my own inner peace by allowing myself, on some level, to move further away. For me there is no contradiction, and this work comes naturally. I will support, companion and carry all humans on their individual spiritual journeys, like the water in my empty-to-overflowing *mikveh* dream. Doing so is an honor.

While most of my clients are Jewish, not all are. I recently created a sixtieth birthday immersion ceremony for a Catholic client who is also an interspiritual minister and lives in California. We created the ceremony together online over the course of several sessions, and she went to the ocean at sunrise to do it.

And while some clients come to the *mikveh* to mark a religious transition or transformation, others come to mark other events in their lives. I recently helped a woman create a ceremony before having an elective double mastectomy after discovering she has the gene for breast cancer. We called it her "Choosing Life" ceremony. I have helped others create ceremonies to mark divorces, birthdays, healing from illness or abuse, gender transition, starting the army, deaths of relatives, even preparation ceremonies for their own deaths. The list is as long as the imagination can stretch.

Later this evening, I will be teaching an online dreamwork course. The course combines Jewish and other texts on dreams with actual dreamwork in pairs and as a group. I use dreamwork often with clients, to help them go deeper and hear their souls speak. I want to share with others what I have learned and what has served me so well on my own spiritual journey.

This is no dream. This is my work, my life. I am fully present here, savoring each breath while I can, doing the work I am meant to do in this body here and now. Giving my soul the nourishment it needs, and helping others do the same. Until it is time for me to become water and overflow my vessel.

I AM STANDING at the top of a long tunnel. Or is it a chute? Or a canal? It is a tunnel or a deep narrow hole, leading downwards. I cannot see where it is leading. There is no end in sight. I feel I am meant to jump in, but I am afraid. I fear I will suffocate in there. I won't be able to breathe. I hesitate.

Then along comes Alona. I know her from various contexts, but mostly from counseling her at a time of major transition in her life. She takes out a thermometer and checks the temperature in the tunnel. She says it is a good temperature, safe to go in, but that we should sell the thermometer anyway, since it is expensive and not necessary.

"Are you ready to start?" Jude asks from inside my computer screen. My eyes are closed, but I hear the smile in her voice. "I feel a lot of energy around that tunnel, or chute, or whatever it is. What are you? Speak to me."

I focus my attention on that tunnel, that chute, that passageway leading downwards. I can picture it so clearly, but I am not sure what it is, what I am. "I am long and narrow, with smooth edges. I am not muddy, or rocky. I am smooth and clear and not hard to maneuver."

"But what are you? What is your purpose?"

"I am a canal of some sort. I am not even sure what I am, but I know I am not a hole dug into the ground. I am more organ-like. Maybe a canal or passageway. Maybe a birth canal?"

"Do you know where you are leading?"

"No. I don't see my end. But I am headed somewhere. I am long. The end is not clear from here. You will need to just get in and follow where I lead you. Give up control, because you won't have any once you get in. I may be long and with an unknown destination, and I may not be as spacious as you might want me to be. But I am not uninteresting, and I am leading somewhere. That's for sure."

"Is there anything inside you?"

"No. I am hollow. I guess there is air inside of me, though. Maybe water at the bottom, but I don't see any from here. But yes, there is air, even if the dreamer is worried there isn't enough. Or maybe there isn't air. Maybe air is not needed in here. But there is what is needed. That much I know."

"Thank you, tunnel heading downward into the mystery. Can we speak to the temperature now?"

"I am the temperature in this tunnel. Just right, so you don't even feel me. Like the temperature of water when it's just perfect for swimming. That's when you know it's right to jump in, when it's so easy and smooth you don't even feel me. When everything feels like it just is. So you can get in and stay in with ease."

"Great. Let's talk to the dreamer now. Dreamer, why are you hesitating to get into this canal? Should we call it a birth canal? If the temperature is just right, why are you hesitating?"

"I am the dreamer, and I am sitting at the edge of this canal, at its top. I know I am supposed to get in and go down through the canal, but I am hesitating. I am scared. It looks so narrow and long. I am not even sure there is enough air in there. I feel like I might get stuck or suffocate. Yet it is long.

That I can see. In that way it is spacious, I guess. Just not wide. Long and narrow."

"What do you look like, Dreamer, in this dream?"

"I don't see me, since I am inside of me. But I know I am not wearing anything. I am naked, sitting at the edge of this tunnel, this canal, this passageway of some sort, leading down, down, into the unknown."

"Let's talk to Alona now. Who are you, Alona? And what are you doing here in this dream?"

"I am Alona. My name was once Bilhah, a biblical concubine. But I changed it to Alona, which is an oak tree, when I needed to feel more grounded in my life while reaching for greater heights. When I needed to step into my own power. It was not easy, but it was necessary, and the time was right."

"What are you doing in this dream, Standing Tall Oak Tree? What message are you trying to give to the dreamer?"

"Isn't it obvious? I said it straight. Loud and clear. The temperature is just right. In fact, you didn't even need me or this thermometer to tell you that. You knew it already. You are making excuses about why you can't get in. That's the ego in you speaking. Not your soul. Your soul is ready. So, what are you waiting for? Get in already!"

IT IS A pleasant evening for September. Not too hot, not too cold. The pomegranates are ripe on their trees in our backyard, which has been turned into a wedding venue today. Michal and Ahmad stand beneath our canopy of grapevines, a fruit falling every few minutes among the petals strewn out on the terra cotta beneath their feet.

They are reciting their wedding vows among their immediate families and closest friends. Telling the story of their love, their relationship, the hard work they've done to reach this day, and of their certainty, after that work, that they want to spend their lives together.

Ahmad is already part of our family and Michal part of his. But they did not yet express their love and commitment in a public ceremonial way. Today is a chance for them to celebrate and be celebrated by those who love them.

We all laugh and cry, and hug. And then we dance until midnight. Jacob and the kids pull me into the circle, making sure I am supported and won't fall. But it does not take much coaxing. I never dance. But today, my joy lifts and energizes me. Even if I will be in pain tomorrow.

I am not dreaming. This is waking magic.

My parents are not here. My mother made it clear she would not attend if Ahmad did not convert to Judaism. My father feels torn, but he will not cross my mother. Michal asked my father to pay for them to spend the weekend after the wedding at a spa in the Carmel mountains. My daughter is not afraid to be her full true self in front of her grandparents, and she is not afraid to say what she needs from them.

I am proud of Michal's courage, inspired by her ability to be her unapologetic self in front of my parents. Something it has taken me until now to come close to accomplishing, and I am still doing that work. I cannot take credit for her strength, but I can take heart in the knowledge that my shortcoming helped build her character.

My father said he would subsidize their spa honeymoon weekend if my mother agreed. And, apparently, she did, because Michal and Ahmad are heading to the spa after the wedding.

Am I dreaming? If I were, wouldn't my parents be here in person rather than sending their money? Still, I am thankful for how far they have come to meeting her, at least, part of the way. They, too, are doing their work, even if not at the pace I wish they would.

I am sad for my daughter that her grandparents have chosen not to come to her wedding. But I respect their decision, since, at least for my mother, attending would mean compromising her values. She, too, has boundaries, which, fate has it, her daughter, I, cannot fit myself into. I wish she were able to let love break them down. But she, too, has a need to feel in control. She, too, has her own sacred wounds.

The love she has shown through her attempts to control, to be the "director" of our lives, and her anger when we do not comply, she is now learning to show in more positive ways. Even if she cannot condone her granddaughter marrying out of the faith, by agreeing to pay for her honeymoon, my mother is telling Michal—like she told me with a bouquet of flowers in her dreamscape—that she loves her and wishes her well.

And I do celebrate my daughter without having to compromise anything. I thank the Universe for that.

IT IS *YOM Kippur*, the Sabbath of all Sabbaths, when traditionally Jews do not eat or drink, do not bathe or have sexual relations, and spend the day in prayer and contemplation.

I appreciate the prayer and contemplation part, but fasting will not change the fact that I too shall feel pain and die—a lesson I learned long ago while pulling myself out of anorexia. But it has taken me this long to have the courage to apply this lesson in all aspects of my life.

Nor do I need a reminder that I live in a mortal body; my illness has taught me that lesson already. My body suffers enough on its own. Because of my condition, my mouth is constantly dry, and I can barely make it through the day in hot weather even when I am drinking. Like Slug, I must keep myself hydrated. No one else can or will do that for me. Fasting is not a practical option for me. I will not deprive myself of water to try to reach a more spiritual state. Living in my body reminds me constantly of my own mortality.

Life itself takes care of sending the suffering. I do not need to manufacture it. Life itself sends its own boundaries and limitations. Life provides its own joy and sorrow, purpose and challenges. That is my work, to trust in that, let go into that, rather than fight it by imposing it from outside. Especially when the meaning life provides on its own conflicts with the meaning I or others try to impose. That has been my source of suffering.

There is no need to create suffering and boundaries to give life meaning or structure. That only creates its own kind of suffering. Life provides everything on its own and in its proper time. There is a season for everything, as the author of *Ecclesiastes* discovered in his wise old age. I trust in that and in my inner voice and rhythms to gage what I need: around desire, nourishment, modesty, pleasure and everything else that shapes my life.

There is no need to create restrictions before life provides them on its own. I want to enjoy life in the present, in this moment, while I can, and I am confident in my ability to create a healthy balance between my responsibilities to myself and my responsibilities to others and the world around me.

I wake up with the sun. Since I am not fasting, I do not need to sleep in for as long as possible this *Yom Kippur* to make the fast feel shorter and easier. I will go to synagogue to pray in community. But I will also read and contemplate at home, sit in my garden. But first, I will swim.

Everyone is still asleep in the house as I put on my robe and let myself out to the backyard. The air has a morning chill, but it is still warm here in October. I can swim outdoors with no discomfort.

I put my foot into the water, which feels almost warm compared to the air. I hang my robe over the pool's railing, and I ease my naked body into the water. I want to feel as fetus-like as possible on this day of new beginnings, ten days after *Rosh Hashanah*, the day Jewish tradition calls "the birth of the world."

The world is so quiet, I can feel it resting. I relax into the calm, feeling at one with myself, with the Universe. This is exactly what I want to be doing at this moment in time: the Sabbath of all Sabbaths. No need to beat myself up about wanting to swim, no need to feel guilty about feeling pleasure, and no need to apologize for giving myself what I need.

After high school, when I stopped depriving myself of nourishment and got myself back to a healthy weight, I found healthier, more socially acceptable and even beneficial addictions—like swimming—to give me that false sense of control. I did not let go of my need to feel control. Instead, I channeled it. I could not bring myself to completely put myself in God's hands.

For years, I was ashamed I did not feel able to let go of my swim on even this one day a year. I would search for places I could swim after the fast was over, although the public pools in Israel I know of are closed on *Yom Kippur*. Even if I could find one that was open, in a Palestinian-Israeli village or city perhaps, I could not drive there on *Yom Kippur*, as the main roads are closed to cars on this day. Even those pools that might be open during the day would surely be closed at night, given that it is a national holiday.

Yet, I always found places to swim after dark when the fast ended, at the homes of friends with private pools, in natural lakes, or even just a dip in a natural spring. And swimming after the fast was its own kind of renewal ritual. But I still felt inadequate for not being able to let go of my swim entirely on one day of the year.

I was able to let go of swimming after giving birth or when I broke my foot, I remind myself.

The difference, I now know, is that in the case of *Yom Kippur*, the restriction is artificial, man-made, and exterior to my body. Imposed from the outside. I feel ready now to put my trust in my own instincts and in the natural flow— call it God, Spirit, Life, the Universe, the Flow, or I Will Be What I Will Be.

That does not mean I have to also put my trust into man-made systems, even if they were designed to help me reach higher levels of spirituality. For some people, that works just fine. For me, I finally can admit, it does not.

I remember what one of my spiritual counselors had suggested about renaming my daily swim: "How would it feel if you stopped calling it an addiction?" he asked. "Can you call it, instead, a ritual? A spiritual practice? If it does you good, why punish yourself for your commitment to self-care?"

I closed my eyes that day and tried it out: "my self-care swimming ritual." No reason to feel guilty about that.

"Has this ritual ever caused you or anyone else you love any harm?" he asked.

"No. They may find it annoying, but I try my best to swim on my own time, when they are all at school or work."

"Addictions usually take precedence over everything. And they cause pain and conflict. They are harmful and destructive. Does your ritual swim cause you any pain?"

"No, it gives me strength. It is good for my body and soul. It is my daily meditation and my daily exercise all at once." Could my daily swim be the regular spiritual practice I thought I was resisting? Could it be it was here all along, in a different container, yet still a sacred ritual helping me inhabit the space between divine and mortal? Was I resisting embracing it because it came from me, from trusting my inner voice instead of looking to others to tell me what will do me good?

"So . . . ?"

"So, I guess I worry that one day, if I have to choose between swimming and something else very important to me, it will become the source of anxiety."

"But you don't know it will until you are faced with that choice. Right?"

"Right."

"So why worry about it now? All you have is the present. The most you can do now is the inner work to prepare yourself for the rocks in the river. That is all any of us can ever do."

Perhaps another message of the crucifix. If Jesus died for our sins, we are absolved of guilt. We do not have to beat ourselves for not being perfect. We are what we are. This is not a license to err, to "miss the mark" (a more accurate translation of the Hebrew word *chet*, חטא, than the word sin), but it does make it okay to be human, recognizing even if we are all divine, we are all also human. And that is as it should be. God loves us as we are. Even as we continue to miss the mark.

I remember my mother telling me I should atone on *Yom Kippur* because Michal chose to spend her Rosh Hashanah vacationing in Spain. I know I am not perfect, but I do not agree that I need atone for letting my children be who they are.

My spiritual counselor suggested I meditate on renaming my swim while I am in the act of swimming. He said:

"You have no reason to let go of your daily swim. It is doing you good. What you want to let go is the story you are telling yourself—that it is an addiction. Meditate on saying goodbye to this label you have given your gift to yourself. Say goodbye to the title of addiction. Welcome home the title of self-care ritual. Say goodbye to the notion this is something you 'need.'

Welcome home the idea it is something you rightfully want and deserve and choose for yourself each time you do it."

As I swim, I recall this conversation. This is all I can do—be in the present, relish this moment, let myself feel good and accept life's gifts. *Goodbye addiction, hello self-care. Goodbye needs, hello desires. Goodbye guilt, hello joy. Goodbye worry, hello presence. Goodbye contraction, hello expansion. Goodbye fear, hello love. Goodbye control, hello flow* . . .

I do not know for how long I swim, feeling myself immersed in abundance, but suddenly I find myself on my death bed—sick, weak, my body no longer of use to me.

I am alone. But I feel a powerful sense of connection to everything, like I am melting into the air—no, it is water—around me. And it feels surprisingly okay. Blissful, even. I am calm, at peace, knowing I have done what I was meant to do in this world while in this body. Now my body can no longer serve me, so I will leave it behind.

It is this body that made me feel separate and in need of defense and coping mechanisms. Now my body is no longer of use, I do not feel separate anymore. Death is not a tragedy; it is part of life. No more fear of death. No more frustrations and disappointments. No more sorrow and angst. They are all part of this body I am now letting go. There is meaning in freedom, after all.

When this body stops working, I will join with everything, with ALL. *There is no need to be separate.* No more separation, no more pain, no more suffering. All physical and emotional barriers will fall away. I will melt into the water of eternal life and death and join the eternal flow. I will reach that ocean. I will become one with the One.

I am ready now to trust in life to provide its own meaning for me, hold me, support me, and lead me to where I am meant to be. I am ready to embrace what is, let go into the flow, and live fully until I die. *Hineni.* Here I am.

EPILOGUE

I AM WALKING through an amazing art exhibit. Yedid-Yah, Friend-of-God, is the artist, the creator of all this incredible work: sculpture, glass figures, hand-sewn clothing, machines, paintings, contraptions with all kinds of uses and surprises . . . So many media. Everything is so intricate and carefully planned, to the last detail. Exquisite. Unique. Expressive. It is the work of a lifetime, about a lifetime. It is a mirror to his soul. I am in awe.

I am awake now. My third bar mitzvah speech has been found.

Ethics of the Fathers 2:9:

Rabban Yochanan the son of Zakkai had five disciples: Rabbi Eliezer the son of Hurkenus, Rabbi Joshua the son of Chananya, Rabbi Yossi the Kohen, Rabbi Shimon the son of Nethanel, and Rabbi Elazar the son of Arakh. He would recount their praises: Rabbi Eliezer the son of Hurkenus is a cemented cistern that loses not a drop; Rabbi Joshua the son of Chananya—fortunate is she who gave birth to him; Rabbi Yossei the Kohen—a chassid (pious one); Rabbi Shimon the son of Nethanel fears sin; Rabbi Elazar the son of Arakh is as an ever-increasing wellspring.

To this I now dare to add:

Rabbi Reverend Dr. Haviva the daughter of Ruth and Daniel was a precisely measured kosher mikveh whose water returned to its source, only to come back and overflow beyond the mikveh's walls, but without fear and without losing herself in the process.

POSTSCRIPT

IT IS *ROSH Hashana* Eve, 2020. A new Jewish year in the midst of a global pandemic, in which I have tried to isolate myself as much as one possibly can with a partner and seven children. I am at high risk of contracting a bad case of COVID-19 due to my compromised breathing.

I am swimming, keeping an eye out for Pigeon while I swim. A lone pigeon has been visiting me daily at my pool since Jacob was hospitalized almost a month ago.

For the past several months, even before COVID-19 reached Israel, Jacob has been suffering from severe skin issues: lesions on his body, massive scales on his scalp, sores in his mucus membranes. He has been in terrible pain, but nothing any doctors prescribed helped. It only got worse. Finally, when the doctors realized they could not help him and his situation became unbearable, they referred him to the skin unit at Rambam Hospital in Haifa, where he is now.

I dropped Jacob off at the hospital, thinking he would be there just for a few days. That is what they originally told us. I did not even go inside with him, due to COVID-19. I was still the sick one then, ironically, even while dropping *him* at the hospital.

And that is when Pigeon started visiting me at the pool. Always alone. She would come to the side of the pool and watch me swim. Pigeons have historically been used for delivering messages. I would look at her and wonder what message she was trying to bring me, and from whom.

The first few days Jacob was gone the doctors were doing tests, and I was feeling sorry for myself, alone with the kids at home with school just starting amid a pandemic. As numbers of daily positive COVID tests rose to shocking numbers, the kids went back to school. I was scared to visit Jacob in the hospital, scared to be at home with my kids who were coming and going from school. And I was single parenting again.

Then the diagnosis came: Pemphigus Vulgaris, a rare life-threatening autoimmune skin disease. Jacob is now being given aggressive corticosteroid drugs themselves so dangerous he must stay at the hospital during the duration of the treatment. Before these meds existed, people with this condition died within a year. But still there is no cure, only treatments to try and keep it under control. But what if the treatments do not work? The meds themselves can be fatal in some cases. And the side effects range from unpleasant to debilitating.

Over the years, I had been doing the inner work to come to peace with my own morbidity and mortality, only to discover they paled in comparison to this. I could handle my own suffering and death, but I was not prepared to watch Jacob suffer and die. I was the sick one. *This* was not the way it was supposed to be.

Pigeon continued to visit. Pigeons, cousins of the dove, are known for their mournful song that stirs the internal waters. I would hear her mourning call—Woo-oo ... Hoo, hoo, hoo ... Woo-oo ... Hoo, hoo, hoo—echoing the feelings in my heart, stirring up all my emotions; and that is when the tears would start to flow: saltwater mixing with fresh water as I swam back and forth, back and forth.

Jacob was out of my reach, alone in a hospital, being pumped with chemicals making him sicker but hopefully also getting this attack under control so we could start thinking about long-term treatment—which itself was no guarantee and could mean serious lifestyle changes for my rock who thought himself so invincible he had convinced me of that illusion as well.

My beloved was suffering, and there was nothing I could do to relieve that except tell him I love him, that his love is the most precious thing I have in my life, that our love is something we alone created and only we share, a joining of two unique souls, the most spiritual thing I have experienced in my life. Those were the most authentic and deeply felt words I had ever uttered. I felt so achingly vulnerable yet so completely alive.

I knew I loved Jacob, but not this much, even after all we had been through together. I walked around for days, unable to stop weeping unless I forced myself not to think about him there alone in the hospital, or the possibility of me alone without him.

I imagined his funeral. I would not go. I would have my own private ceremony with his body. I would not share him with anyone else. Our love was intimate, just between the two of us. I would refuse to be with anyone but my beloved as they put his body in the ground.

I drove to visit him outside the hospital, as I was afraid to go inside because of COVID, crying the whole way there with Carole King ("You're so far away") and Celine Dion ("Near, far, wherever you are!") expressing over the radio what was in my heart. We held each other, crying in each other's arms, expressing all the things that mattered. Every moment with him was so precious, I refused to waste it on talking about unimportant things. I only wanted to speak of our love.

I cried when I had to leave, but I could not stay. The kids needed me at home. I felt ripped apart inside. I only wanted to be with *him*. I did not even want to be with my own children, *our* children. I told the older ones to visit him on their own time, when I was not there. I did not want to share him even with them. I tolerated sharing him with the younger ones, though, as they had no other way to see him but to come with me. But that felt like a huge sacrifice.

I had never felt so bereft in my life. Not when I was myself diagnosed with muscular dystrophy at age sixteen, not when I was a teenager suffering from anorexia nervosa, not when my son stopped breathing at age two weeks and nearly died, and not since my teenage son had been struggling with mental illness. I had no idea what the word "grief" really meant until now.

Yet, I never knew what the word "alive" really meant until now, either. I was feeling life so intensely, all defense mechanisms down. Nothing was hidden, all was on the outside. I was hurting so much, but on a deeper level it felt so good to be letting myself feel.

All my inner work led me to this moment. This was the bomb of all bombs I knew was coming. But rather than put up my old defense mechanisms again—going into self-pity or survival mode—I let all barriers fall, allowing the feelings to flow in and out with no limitations or regulations.

I cried and cried and could not stop telling Jacob how much I loved him, how I just did not want him to die. I did not want to be here in this life without him. I did not care if he could not take care of me. We would just be sick and suffer and die together. Our love was deeper than any characteristics, circumstances, or conditions. All I wanted to do was hold him—once we found the few spots where I could touch him without hurting him—and be with him and share our deepest selves.

I could even imagine having to miss my swim to stay by his side at the hospital, I knew. And then it hit me: I am not addicted to swimming. It is a spiritual practice, a lovely, wonderful, important part of my life that helps keep me going. But it is not life. This is life. Love is life. That was Pigeon's message in her mournful love song.

During these weeks, I tried to keep up my commitments and responsibilities as much as possible, dealing with this emotional and logistical upheaval in our lives. I found that continuing to meet with spiritual counseling clients helped me get some perspective and focus on other people's challenges—

at least for the duration of a session. In some cases, the sessions even held messages for me personally.

One client—I'll call her Sarah—told me she had been dreaming about looking for and finding hummingbirds but then losing them, not being able to hold on to them. And then, in her waking life, her son brought home a wounded hummingbird he had found on the sidewalk. Sarah kept the hummingbird, which she named "Quincy," for a few days, nursing her back to health and becoming quite attached to the bird while looking for a place that could give her professional care. Sarah found a wild bird shelter that took Quincy in and promised to be in touch. But then the people at the shelter did not answer Sarah's emails. She was concerned.

Sarah shared what she was learning from the experience, lessons about the beauty and fragility of life, about attachment and letting go, about trust in the mystery and in the cycle of life and nature. In her sharing, I found wisdom for my own situation. Jacob was my fragile and beautiful bird to whom I had become so attached the thought of having to separate from him was wrenchingly painful. I was not willing to let him go. But if I were given no choice, I would not have traded our thirty-three years together for anything. He was the biggest gift of my life, even if I had to return the gift back to its sender.

When the treatments were not working quickly enough, I became even more worried. I wrote to his doctor, the head of the skin clinic at the hospital, to ask if we could speak. I said I did not want to risk going into the hospital building—Jacob and I had been continuing to meet outside—since I am at high-risk for COVID-19, so could she please speak with me on the phone. The doctor did not answer. I called the clinic and left messages, but still no answer. So, finally, I gathered up my mask and my courage and decided to risk it. I went inside the hospital. My beloved needed me.

It felt good to speak face to face with the doctor. But she too was concerned. The treatments were working, but not as fast as she had hoped, and Jacob could not stay on such a high dosage of corticosteroids for much longer. I cried all the way home and tried to collect myself to go into the house where the kids were waiting. I went to the bathroom, checked my emails, and found Sarah had forwarded me this letter from the wild bird shelter:

Dear Sarah,

Thank you for reaching out to us. I am happy to inform you that the Ruby-Throated Hummingbird, nicknamed "Quincy," is still in our care and doing well. He is still unable to fly, so he is getting flight practice in order to strengthen his muscles. He is also receiving pain medication. Once he is fully recovered, he will be released in a safe location with plenty of his favorite kinds of flowers. We are unable to provide ongoing status updates on all of our patients due to our current volume of them, but rest assured we will do our best for this little one. Thank you for rescuing this little bird and bringing him in to us. He was in great need of help and would not have survived without your intervention.

Sincerely,

The Wild Bird Fund Animal Care Team

I closed my eyes, took a deep breath, and knew this letter was sent to me for a reason. Jacob would come home. If he survived his treatments and their side-effects, he would still need to heal, and he would never be as healthy as he was before this ordeal. And his life would always be in danger from this brutal chronic disease. But the doctors were doing their best, and so was I. Life is just very, very hard. And also fragile and beautiful. But better to have taken in the bird than not to have had that precious time together at all. It is all part of the package we call life.

After three weeks of treatments, Jacob finally came home. Today, the eve of *Rosh Hashanah*, the Jewish new year. Next week, he will receive an infusion of a drug that will suppress his immune system completely, which is a terrifying thought as the country is full-on into a second wave of the pandemic. Today we head into a second lockdown, which is somewhat comforting. But we live with our seven children who cannot be kept under lock and key once this lockdown ends.

Now Jacob and I are both high-risk—he is even higher risk than I am—but we are high-risk together. We will enter this new year with everything feeling on the edge of extinction, even us. I remember my dream from a few years ago, where Jacob and I cling to each other as we shelter from bombs falling all around us. When I worked the dream, the bombs told me they were not trying to hurt us but were just part of life, intensifying the moment so we would appreciate our love in the present.

Jacob and I will cling to each other until the end, as the bombs fall, truly feeling what it means to be alive. My worst nightmare and best dream have both come true.

As I complete my final lap, I wonder what has happened to Pigeon. This is the first day I have not seen her since Jacob was hospitalized. Pigeons are known for their homing sense; they know how to find their way back no matter how far they go.

And then I see her. Pigeon has returned to visit. But this time she is not alone. She has brought her mate. Her beloved has finally come home.

ACKNOWLEDGMENTS

Thank you to my readers for your thoughtful feedback: Sarah Bowen, Sara Brandes, Chava Megan Evans, Margalit Jakob, Debbie Jacobson-Maisels, Diane Kaplan; Rebecca Krasner, Ilana Kurshan, Jen Maidenberg, Julie Landau, Nechama Langer, Shoshana Lavan, Ruth Mason, Hila Ratzabi, Dorothy Richman, Bryan Schwartzman, and Elana Sztokman.

Thank you to the team at Bedazzled Ink Publishers (Claudia, Casey, and Liz) for your professionalism and support.

Thank you to my teachers and spiritual companions for all you have given me, and to my dream group and dreamworkers who helped and continue to help me speak to my soul.

Thank you to my family and friends for being part of the journey.

Thank you to my beloved Jacob for everything. No words of gratitude could be enough.

Haviva Ner-David is an ordained rabbi and interfaith-interspiritual minister, with a doctorate in philosophy and an M.F.A. in Creative Writing. She runs *Shmaya: A Mikveh for Mind, Body and Soul*, where she officiates ritual immersion ceremonies and offers group workshops. A certified spiritual companion with a specialty in dreamwork, she works with individuals and couples. Rabbi Ner-David is the author of two previous spiritual journey memoirs (*Life on the Fringes: A Feminist Journey Towards Traditional Rabbinic Ordination*; and *Chanah's Voice: A Rabbi Wrestles with Gender, Commandment and the Women's Rituals of Baking, Bathing and Brightening*). *Dreaming Against the Current: A Rabbi's Soul Journey* is her third. She is also the author of a novel, *Hope Valley*, and a guidebook for engaged couples, *Getting (and Staying) Married Jewishly: Preparing for your Life Together with Ancient and Modern Wisdom* (due to be published in 2022). Rabbi Ner-David is involved in peace work, promoting a shared society for Jews, Christians and Muslims in Galilee, where she lives with Jacob, her life partner of thirty-two years, their seven children, and their dog and cat. She also lives with a genetic muscular disease called FSHD, which has been one of her greatest teachers.

Visit Haviva's website at http://www.rabbihaviva.com.

Just aim your phone's camera at the qr code.